THE BOOK BROWSER'S GUIDE
TO SECONDHAND AND ANTIQUARIAN
BOOKSHOPS

The Book Browser's Guide To

SECONDHAND AND ANTIQUARIAN BOOKSHOPS

ROY HARLEY LEWIS

DAVID & CHARLES
Newton Abbot   London

British Library Cataloguing in Publication Data

Lewis, Roy Harley
  The book browser's guide — 2nd ed.
  1. Antiquarian booksellers — Great Britain —
  Directories
  I. Title
  381'.450705'73   Z286.A55

ISBN 0-7153-8095-8

Typeset by Typesetters (Birmingham) Limited
and printed in Great Britain
by Redwood Burn Limited, Trowbridge, Wilts
for David & Charles (Publishers) Limited
Brunel House Newton Abbot Devon

CONTENTS

PREFACE TO THE SECOND EDITION

My incentive for compiling the original guide was an assumption, based on certain economic factors aggravated by persistent inflation, that with more and more booksellers operating from home, the number of shops was diminishing. One could still buy books but there were fewer opportunities for browsing, which has always provided the greatest element of satisfaction to bibliophiles.

Seven years later I find that assumption was only partially valid. There is still abundant evidence that the odds are stacked against running a secondhand bookshop as a proper commercial venture — especially with a general stock — yet from the ruins of each business that goes into liquidation or cannot afford to renew its lease, emerges another determined to try. Bookselling is one of those trades run *in the main* by men and women to whom the aesthetic reward is more important than profit; and often for that reason they are ill-equipped to cope with the cold reality of business today. There are successful booksellers, of course, particularly in the purely antiquarian sector, but far too many come into the business because the life-style seems appealing, not because a carefully devised three-year plan and their projected cash-flow charts look healthy. On the other hand, if the entrepreneur waited for the 'sure thing', he could wait for ever, and it is to some of these people that browsers owe a debt of gratitude. Perhaps we can convey our appreciation by buying a little more spontaneously. Turnover of books is the lifeblood of the trade from *everyone's* point of view.

Coincidentally, the dramatic increase in parcel post rates in recent years has taken some of the gilt off the gingerbread for the postal bookseller, sometimes making him nostalgic for having a shop where browsers could pick some of the books from his shelves, between catalogue issues. Many have compromised by opening a bookroom or two where they see potential customers by appointment and I have included a significantly larger number in this category.

Spiralling costs have had some other unexpected results. Seven years ago, for example, many shops were getting rid of cheap fiction because the margins did not justify the cost of shelf space. No one then could have forecast that the price of paperbacks would shoot up so much that they would become a viable proposition for the busy shop that has a quick turnover. It begins to make sense to buy at the rate of (say) five to one (ie five for 25p, and sell at 25p each) when the shop can sell several hundred a week with little effort, and they occupy next-to-no space. At some shops second-hand (s/h) paperbacks can be bought for the cost of an evening newspaper. This is particularly noticeable in areas where the stock is general, and there is a shortage of 'quality' hardback material.

Because of the continuing shortage of antiquarian and older modern books, with too many buyers (in the main institutional libraries) chasing too few books, the more affluent booksellers skim the cream from sales — which means that others may have to rely on 'local' material, and the chances are that this may be very run-of-the-mill (a generalisation, of course, because some well-established suburban or country shops can often buy before outsiders even hear about the material for sale). The fewer 'better' books which can justify higher profit margins are essential to keep these shops viable; ordinary material in competition with new paperbacks and remainders is only profitable in high-turnover shops where prices can be kept low. This is good for everyone, you might think, but an undercapitalised bookshop has the same problems as an undercapitalised motor-car manufacturer.

Another trend in London and some of the larger cities, where retailers in general depend on commuters from the suburbs, is a decline of Saturday trade. In the capital more shops are closing on Saturday because of the drop in the number of visitors caused by continually rising transport costs.

There was a period in the past seven years when I was concerned that most of the very large operations would decide to concentrate on new books, which have a faster turnover, and exclude second-hand — following the policy Foyles adopted in the late 1960s. Heffers of Cambridge eventually did the same, as did the very beautiful Ancient House at Ipswich, Bredon's at Brighton and Walker's at Headingley (although they did keep a few antiquarian books). However, other first-division 'giants' decided to take a careful look at *all* aspects of their business, and took a calculated decision to invest in their secondhand or antiquarian activities. Blackwell's of Oxford is one which separated secondhand from antiquarian and supported them both independently. Dillon's University Bookshop, which few realise is one of the largest general, as opposed to academic, bookshops in the country, was another.

8

Other healthy developments in the period have included a change of ownership in one of the world's great bookshops, Francis Edwards (see 'Rich Pastures' and 'Central London') and the 'arrival' of a rather surprising presence in 1976 — the Society for Promoting Christian Knowledge (SPCK), formed in 1698 but virtually ignored by bibliophiles except those interested in theology. But with the purchase of the enormous stock of Charles Higham at that time, SPCK (the oldest Anglican missionary society) decided to open secondhand departments — not confined to theology — in many of their bookshops in the provinces (see 'Rich Pastures'), which must make them the largest chain of secondhand outlets in the country.

WHAT MOTIVATES
THE BROWSER?

If all the books in the world were laid end-to-end, they would reach all the way to . . . well, you name it; precisely where is scarcely important, although speculation with mind-boggling statistics is always a fascination. Consider that, in the United Kingdom alone, an average of 38,000 new titles are published every year. Unlike the population explosion, the constant compound accumulation of books cannot be interrupted, short of a *Fahrenheit 451* situation. The number of volumes completing new-antiquarian 'evolutionary' cycles since the days of the first printing presses obviously runs into many billion. But where have they all gone?

Most of this output has been, and continues to be, of superficial interest or, as some would say too indiscriminately, rubbish. But whatever label we give to books of little importance — even if we ignore them — there are still a staggering number left, mostly produced in the past 100 years, which must be somewhere. University libraries absorb an enormous amount, and often now compete with dealers for collections. The rest should be found within the trade but, for reasons I shall define, the number of secondhand and antiquarian bookshops is dwindling all the time and already too many people are chasing too few books. There are booksellers who are genuinely reluctant to sell, because they know items in demand are never likely to be replaced.

This guide is concerned with secondhand books, which range through modern first editions, specialist books for collectors, inexpensive reprints for the person who just buys for a good read, and the antiquarian sector. The word 'antiquarian' is used loosely these days to encompass the vague area of 'old books', whereas the definition of antiquity should remind us that we might be dealing with a period before the Middle Ages. In practice, bookshops may classify as antiquarian even late 19th-century volumes, especially if they are attractively bound, while some authoritative antiquarian booksellers will dismiss 17th-century works as merely secondhand and show relatively little interest in material published after 1650. There have been half-hearted efforts to suggest that the classification should refer to books published before 1830, but no agreement is likely. The reader should interpret my use of the word in its more general bastardised sense.

To have got as far as here — if you are reading this in a bookshop — identifies you as a serious browser; yet the outsider does not understand the philosophy of browsing — or care. What is it then that distinguishes the browser from the rest? A definition of the word might help, but the *Oxford Dictionary* refers not to books but to feeding on leaves and young shoots! Nor can we be much more explicit about the type of people who browse, except possibly in one respect — their sex. The significance escapes me, but nine browsers out of ten are men. It would be monstrous to suggest that women do not buy and read as many books as men, but undoubtedly they have a different approach to buying. A woman tends to know what title she wants, and it is unusual to see her browsing. Why? A less traditional trade would commission a market-research survey in which motivation was carefully analysed. Women might claim they do not have the time to spare but this hardly rings true, and many women actually check the browsing habits of their male companions. One is more likely to see women going for bestsellers, which are read immediately and later possibly discarded, than in a second-hand shop where books are generally bought to keep. Mind you, just as some husbands believe it is their God-given right to spend the bulk of their earnings in the pub or betting shop, one can appreciate the anxiety of the woman whose partner is a bibliomaniac, even housekeeping money being turned to feed his passion.

Apart from the difference in their approach, women are of course equally enthusiastic about books and I know a number of very knowledgeable collectors. Virginia Woolf, in *Death of a Moth*, expressed her feelings somewhat romantically: 'Secondhand books are wild books, homeless books; they have come together in vast flocks of variegated feather, and have a charm which the domesticated volumes of the library lack . . . in this random miscellaneous company we may rub against some complete stranger who will, with luck, turn into the best friend we have in the world.'

But if we classify book addicts broadly as people sharing a common interest, we must still enquire why browsing is so compelling. The reasons are many, and vary according to the individual — although a love of the end-product (the book) is the common denominator. However, browsing — like seduction — is often enjoyed more for the pursuit of one's objective than its fulfilment. Part of the charm of the book-shop is the atmosphere which allows us to wander un-chaperoned, to browse and — too frequently, perhaps — not to buy. Fortunately for all concerned, the browser does put his hand in his pocket too. R. M. Williamson's summing-up of browsers in his interesting book *Bits from an Old Bookshop*, written more than 75 years ago, is just as apt today. 'Of all kinds of human weaknesses, the craze for collecting old books is the most excusable. During the early phases of the disease, the book-lover is content to purchase only books which he reads. Next he buys books which he means to read; and as his store accumulates, he hopes to read his purchases; but by-and-by he takes home books in beautiful bindings and of early date, but printed in extinct languages he cannot read.'

The book world is remarkably free from class barriers, because respect is afforded the book and not the establish-ment. It is probably this very respect that makes browsing synonymous with antiquarian/secondhand books. Admit-tedly one looks at, and does not idly handle, a masterpiece of 15th-century printing; reverence putting a rein on temptation. But there is something toffee-nosed about new books with their peculiar smell and immaculate dust jackets that rejects the sense of intimacy enjoyed in handling an older volume.

The pastime of browsing is not only spiritually satisfying, but rewarding from time to time because of the bargains every enthusiast has found — and occasionally resold. One of the delights of most old books is that they have no uniform value, so that something we find for 10p in one shop can be worth £10 to the specialist. Many booksellers genuinely do not know the extent of their stock, which accounts for some cases of mislaid titles being underpriced; others do not have the knowledge to value certain items, and this is not a criticism, because no individual can keep abreast of prices in such a diversified field; others may carelessly miss features such as signatures or inscriptions of some importance. A Czech writer friend found several books by Dr Beneš, signed and inscribed by the author, selling for a few pence in the back room of a country shop. The writing had been dismissed as 'foreign scribble', although the name was clearly decipherable. Similarly, I was once pleased to find for my own Pepys collection a book which had obviously been the property of Hugh Walpole and contained his signature. Admittedly Walpole is no longer 'fashionable' and therefore added nothing to the money value of my copy, but the bookseller had not noticed the signature.

In good browsing territory, the average addict spends 60% of his time just *looking*; less than 35% actually reading. But the second figure is important — the time spent being equivalent to the tasting and sampling session of the food and wine connoisseur, because serious reading should be prompted, as Samuel Johnson said, by inclination. 'What we read with inclination makes a much stronger impression. If we read without inclination, half the mind is employed in fixing the attention.' Even during World War II when a few million books were pulped for salvage, people found time to read and to look selectively for their material. The threat against which the booklover is helpless is simply the economic pattern of the 1970s and 80s, which is steadily rolling up the once-fertile plains of browsing territory, in much the same way as 'progress' dealt with the Red Indian and buffalo of 19th-century America. With the exception of a few coastal or university towns which have attracted more bookshops in recent years, the trade is shrinking. In another 100 years or so, the word 'browsing' may have been interred in the dusts of time.

The cost of shop-floor space has rocketed to such an extent that, in cold business terms, it makes sense — if one chooses to stay in bookselling at all — to replace bulky volumes with paperbacks. One of the first portents was the decision of Foyles, probably the world's largest bookshop 'on one site', to close down its secondhand department. Rents and overheads (which of course include the cost of staff) have pressurised other leisure industries also. Some years ago, theatre owners on New York's Broadway discovered that they were sitting on some of the most expensive real estate in the world. They cut their losses and sold up. But drama cannot survive without an auditorium; new off-Broadway theatres arrived and became fashionable. However, booksellers discovered they do not need a shop, and more and more dealers are selling from their homes, and operating a postal service, mainly to the trade.

Using *A Directory of Booksellers* for 1893 as a guideline, we can see that although the number of booksellers has risen from just over 500 (including those selling new books) to 1,500 (not counting exclusively new booksellers), today two-thirds are dealers working from home, and many part-time — which means that one can still buy, but how does one look first? The booklover can only be more active, put his money where his mouth is, and give the shopkeeper something more than moral encouragement. Another serious headache he can try to help combat is the theft of books. *No* shop can afford to lose stock; the small for obvious reasons, and the large because the value of 'target' volumes is usually considerable. Undoubtedly book stealing is more of an economic hazard than is generally realised. Some book addicts scarcely bother to deny the charge, although there is the type who will discriminate between the giant store or chain where 'they can look after themselves', and his favourite bookshop where it would be like robbing a friend! Regrettably, many do not even share this limited sense of honour. There is also the professional crook who has made a careful study of the value of certain books, whether they be £5 or £15,000 a volume. The audacity of all professional shoplifters has to be seen to be believed — size and weight being no deterrent, and 'seen' being the operative word, since managers forewarned have had suspicious customers under observation and still lost valuable books. Browsers, apart from keeping an eye open, can help by depositing hand luggage with the management.

15

Thefts also have a stultifying effect on the trade generally; a leading West End antiquarian bookseller had an important book stolen from a strongroom to which only 20 or 30 customers were ever admitted, and since the thief was never identified, the strongroom had to be placed out of bounds to everyone. Famous shops, such as Bernard Quaritch, with a large selection of expensive books on show — in addition to really valuable items under lock and key — have been forced to limit browsing, their receptionist directing customers to specific shelves of interest. The Antiquarian Booksellers Association has its own secret 'chain' system for alerting the trade to stolen items, but this operates only among members of the association and apart from those who are not protected there are always people who will buy dubious material, innocently or otherwise. Certain books have distinguishing marks, perhaps a book-plate or an error on page x, and may be rare enough to be known to belong to one specialist dealer. But when a book in less than fine condition is broken up for its valuable contents, old plates, maps, aquatints and steel engravings, they cannot normally be identified. Many of the top-echelon antiquarian bookshops also lose heavily through inadvertently buying stolen material. Some larger shops have in desperation partitioned-off sections to house their higher-value books, available only to special customers and collectors. One bookseller hit on the idea of clearing his 'junk' stock by pricing every copy at £10 +, placing them at strategic points, and relying on indiscrimate shoplifters to do the job for him!

In addition to the economic burden, the bookseller faces increasingly tough competition within the trade from paperbacks and 'remainders' which, whatever the trade thinks of them, provide the book-buying public with excellent value. (A remainder is a fairly recently published book 'cleared' by the publisher to make room for better-selling titles. Occasionally remaindered books have soared in value to considerably more than the original published price.)

One hardly enters conventional bookselling today to make a fortune, but even so the monetary rewards for most are barely adequate. No self-respecting trade union would allow members to put in the time most booksellers do — if one includes out-of-hours buying and replenishing stock. Some booksellers with the right blend of foresight, expertise, luck and money manage to prove everyone else wrong. Blackwell's of Oxford, and Heffers of Cambridge, both previously well established, are glittering examples of what larger bookshops should ideally be like. Heffers now sell only new books, of course; but in the purely antiquarian and secondhand field, Peter Eaton of Holland Park, London, opened the world's first stately home bookshop, Lilies, in 1969 at Weedon, in Buckinghamshire — a 60-room country mansion in superb surroundings, with nearly half-a-million books on view in a unique setting.

The bookseller operating on the grandest scale of all is Richard Booth, based at Hay Castle, where approaching one million books spill over into the best part of all the available space in Hay-on-Wye, Powys. This is scarcely browsing territory, unless one is free of the necessity to work for a living. But Mr Booth has even overcome some of these problems, by providing flats as overnight accommodation for browsers.

Richard Booth, justifying his claim to run the world's largest secondhand 'bookshop', does at least have the space, but booksellers cannot always expand their interests without moving, and with a long established business that is not usually desirable. An ingenious solution to this fairly common problem was found by Fisher & Sperr, of Highgate. Highgate Village, along with neighbouring big brother Hampstead, is steeped in period atmosphere and charm, and the premises of Fisher & Sperr in the High Street, dating back to the time of Charles II, are probably the oldest in London used as a bookshop. His large stock was arrayed on four floors, including the basement, but John Sperr had for several years dreamed of finding more room; there was apparently no way of doing so without altering the frontage or spoiling the skyline. However, Camden Council eventually gave planning permission to *excavate* the back garden and extend the back of the shop below ground level another 44 feet. The additional shop area completed in 1974 was even low enough for a small flat to be built on top with beautiful views across north London.

Spectacularly large bookshops are not an innovation of the 20th century. In his *Shadows of the Old Booksellers*, published in 1865, Charles Knight recalled how at the age of 10 (in 1801) his father had taken him to the rather pretentiously named 'Temple of the Muses', a singularly offbeat bookshop in Finsbury Square, Moorgate, belonging to a bookseller with considerable flair, James Lackington. Knight describes the scene:

> A dome rises from the centre, on top of which a flag is flying. This royal manifestation proclaims that this is no ordinary commercial establishment. Over the principal entrance is inscribed 'Cheapest Booksellers in the World' . . .
>
> We enter the vast area, whose dimensions are to be measured by the assertion that a coach and six might be driven round it. In the centre is an enormous circular counter, within which stand the dispensers of knowledge, ready to wait upon the country clergyman, in his wig and shovel hat; upon the fine ladies, in feathers and trains, or upon the bookseller's collector, with his dirty bag . . .
>
> We ascend a broad staircase, which leads to 'The Lounging Rooms', and to the first of a series of circular galleries, lighted from the lantern of the dome, which also lights the ground floor.
>
> Hundreds, even thousands of volumes are displayed on shelves running round their walls. As we mount higher and higher, we find commoner books, in shabbier bindings; but there is still the same order preserved, each book being numbered according to a printed catalogue.

Even Lackington, had he been alive today, might have hesitated at such an investment with present-day rents in that area of £25 a square foot, plus soaring rates. So progressive booksellers use their ingenuity in other ways: they take a lesson from history and attend book 'fairs'; they offer coffee, even snacks. They lecture on books and allied subjects to schools and evening classes. They issue catalogues supplementing the unpredictable passing trade. A few even explore modern marketing techniques. Triers like these will not go down lightly; but there are too few of them.

THE BOOKSELLER
AND THE DEVELOPMENT
OF THE BOOKSHOP

This book is predominantly concerned with where to buy, but it would be well to dwell for a moment on the person who influences the return we get from browsing — the bookseller. Personally I find it hard (admitting to a certain vested interest) to imagine anyone connected with the book world being anything but a highly cultured person of kindly disposition. But even those who do not wear rose-tinted specs would agree that bookselling is a gentle trade — some might even say 'soporific' — and some booksellers are diffident to the point of indifference. One 'elder statesman' who is friendly enough to those he knows is openly rude to casual customers — an indication of his reluctance to part with a diminishing stock. Fortunately, a more sensitive assistant is usually on hand to soothe ruffled feathers.

With a few exceptions, booksellers are friendly and helpful, although I still wonder why many of them bother. Accepting that their remuneration is a pittance, what else motivates them? A desire to spread the gospel of literature? A relationship with the public? R. M. Williamson, in his *Bits from an Old Bookshop*, recalls a bookseller called Don Vincente who '. . . had a shop in Barcelona fifty years ago. His love for books became madness of a most extraordinary and terrible kind. When he sold a rare manuscript or book, he followed his customer and secretly stabbed him to death. He never took money from his victims, but murdered them for the sole purpose of regaining the books he had so recently sold.'

Quite a few booksellers who obviously have a special regard for books nonetheless consider their stock as secondary to the act of trading and providing a service. Single-mindedness, often synonymous with an outstanding track record, leaves less room for diplomacy and conforming to Establishment standards. There are several booksellers today whose contribution to the trade has been considerable, or at the very least stimulating, who are frowned upon by their colleagues. Certain booksellers seem to regard the manipulation of vast stocks as a display of vulgarity, if the offending party has had less than 25 years in the business.

This restrained back-biting is not new to the book-trade, and practically every innovator has to face a prolonged barrage of small-arms fire. But the rumblings seldom result in punitive action — possibly because in the past such measures have backfired. James Lackington, who opened 'The Temple of the Muses', incurred the wrath of the trade nearly 200 years ago when he pioneered the market in 'remainders'. At trade sales, he discovered it was common practice to *destroy* a half, even three-quarters, of the remaindered stock, but to charge full publication price for the rest; he resolved not to destroy copies, but to sell them off at half or a quarter of the publication prices. The trade tried to boycott his activities, but he quickly became too successful to ignore. In 1791 he estimated that *four times* as many books were being sold as only 20 years before. Lackington also saw the beginnings of the vogue for book clubs and libraries, which were resisted by the trade Establishment — vehemently, and ineffectively.

Bookselling often gives people a 'second chance' to fulfil their dreams. The days of apprenticeships are past and only a minority of booksellers have been in the trade since leaving school or college. Indeed, a fair number of talented individuals who have made their mark in other spheres have used that success to finance a new career in bookselling. Most of the early booksellers were, in fact, printers and publishers, and the retail trade as we know it did not emerge until very late.

The history of the printed word covers only a few hundred years, (although 'books' as the Romans knew them were plentiful and cheap, because, in the days of slave labour, manuscripts were both inexpensive to produce and quick to copy). In the Middle Ages the only people with any time — the monks — had so *much* that their work became increasingly elaborate; indeed, they might have been classified as painters more than writers. Initially there was no trade in books, but gradually a system of barter evolved between monks from the different monasteries. Booksellers of this period were called *stationarii*, either from the practice of stationing themselves at booths or stalls in the street, or from the other meaning of the Latin *statio*, depository. It has been suggested that these booksellers did little but provide a place to which private persons could send their manuscripts for sale. In due course, the term became anglicised to 'stationers'.

However, the milestone in English history and literature was 1471, when printing was introduced here by William Caxton. Not surprisingly, the presses were first used for the dissemination of existing knowledge, principally the inheritance from Greece and Rome. Throughout educated Europe, these first 50 years witnessed a gigantic 'salvage' operation aimed at preserving the priceless content of scattered and vulnerable manuscripts, in danger of being lost to posterity. The printed versions of the classics were, of course, expensive and were ravenously consumed by the rich, and the even richer church libraries. Literature's true debt is to printers such as Aldus, Stephens and Plantin who started the next cycle by producing cheap volumes for the ordinary scholar. Until then printers had been subsidised by rich patrons. It is ironic that today, because of soaring production costs, some publishers have turned the clock back and invited sponsorship in certain areas of non-fiction.

The first evidence of 'mass' book-buying (in the context of the 16th century) was the demand for cheap copies of the Bible, and the demand actually caught printers by surprise. In 1540, Richard Grafton cautiously printed 500 copies of his complete edition of the scriptures, yet between 1526 and 1600 there were 326 editions of the Bible (or parts) printed.

Fear of the real and imagined power of the press is not the prerogative of 20th-century governments. Throughout the Elizabethan and Stuart periods printers were regarded with some suspicion and their activities curtailed (a decree of the Star Chamber in 1637 actually limited the number of type-founders in England to four). Inevitably, these restrictions resulted in a fall in the quality of both print and paper, and it was not until the 1660s that a new edition of the English Bible, cheap but well produced, became what we can genuinely describe as a best-seller. This was due to the foresight of one man — Thomas Guy, founder of the famous teaching hospital. Being a bookseller turned printer, and making a fortune in the process, Guy persuaded Oxford University, which had a monopoly in theological work, to let him print for them in London, using better type imported from Holland.

Despite the snowballing growth of printed books, the industry might not have survived but for the interest and patronage of the nobility. For the first half-century of printing, the presses were kept running by their appetite for translations and abridgements of the classics and foreign literature. Indeed Caxton, speaking of his *Boke of Eneydos*, says: 'This present book is not for a rude uplandish man to labour therein, nor read it: but only for a clerk and a noble gentleman, that feeleth and understandeth in feats of arms, in love, and in noble chivalry.' Fortunately for the history of browsing, that 'rude uplandish man' was about to go to school, and so create a fresh demand for the educational book. In England and Scotland between 1471 and 1600 there are records of 350 printers, and nearly 10,000 separate titles, although many were only single sheets.

The classics may be an acquired taste, but in the 17th century politics arrived with a snarl and a roar — 30,000 'political' tracts being issued between 1640 and 1660. However, because printers were still hamstrung, the effort expended on this political activity left little room for other new work. And although Charles II and the Restoration trendsetters provided a powerful incentive to the theatre, progress began to slow again through lack of encouragement from above. There was little incentive to produce written work, it seemed, for anyone — Milton's reward for *Paradise Lost* being £15. For a period, an Act of Parliament restricted the number of printers allowed to practise to 20. However, the Great fire of London in 1666, which destroyed an immense number of books stored in church vaults in the city, stimulated fresh activity, and the number of new books published yearly until the end of the century rose to nearly

100, with nearly three times as many reprints, pamphlets, single sermons and maps. Gradually, too, politically orientated 'intelligence' began to take on a more distinctive form — to be reborn as the regular newspaper or magazine. By 1724, despite the imposition of stamp duty, London had three daily papers, six weekly, and 10 three times a week, and in the provinces too the numbers were growing.

A new mode of bookselling — the auction — gradually became established towards the end of the 17th century. The first recorded in England was tried by a bookseller called Cooper in 1676, when he prefixed his catalogue with: 'Reader, it hath not been usual here in England to make sale of books by the way of auction, or who will give most for them; but it having been practised in other countries, to the great advantage of both buyers and sellers, it was therefore conceived (for the encouragement of learning) to publish the sale of those books in this manner of way.' The idea spread to the provinces; a leading auctioneer, Edward Millington, known for his style and wit, once rounded on his audience with the words 'Who but a sot or a blockhead would have money in his pocket, and starve his brains?' Raph Thoresby in his *Diary* described what he says was the first book auction ever held in Leeds, on 7 January 1693.

> The large chamber, being overcrowded with the press of people, in an instant sunk down about a foot at one end; the main beam breaking gave so terrible a thunder-like crack, and the floor yielding below their feet, the people set up such a hideous noise, apprehending the fall of the whole house, at least the sinking of the room (which, in all probability, had been the death of most present), as was most doleful and astonishing, though I, sitting upon the long table by the books was at first not apprehensive of the danger; but being informed, I hasted out with what expedition I could.

Under William and Mary, bookselling attained a freedom denied to authors and publishers under the Stuarts. The liberty of 'unlicensed printing' advocated by Milton was eventually established, although there were still certain restraints; a special overseer was appointed, the Surveyor of the Press. This was hardly the most incorrupt of periods in British history, and these 'surveyors' or licensers interpreted their role according to different standards: one would 'wink at unlicensed books, if the printer's wife would smile on him'. But the system did protect the copyright of books.

Tastes in reading matter were also beginning to change, though one of the most popular adventure stories of all time, *Robinson Crusoe*, was persistently rejected until William Taylor took a gamble with it in 1719 — by which time Daniel Defoe was 60. In the days before book editors and graphic designers, the need for short 'punchy' titles had not been impressed on authors, which might account for Defoe's original title: *The Life and Strange Surprising Adventures of Robinson Crusoe, of York, Mariner, who eight-and-twenty years all alone in an uninhibited Island on the coast of America, near the Mouth of the Great River Oroonoque, having been cast on shore by Shipwreck, wherein all the men perished but himself; with an Account how he was at last strangely delivered by Pirates. Written by himself.* Taylor sold four editions in as many months before publishing a second volume. In 1722 came the third volume, and it was only then that an abridgement of the three was carried out, some say pirated, by another bookseller, Thomas Gent.

Bookseller John Dunton described the country book scene at the time: 'Of three hundred booksellers now trading in country towns, I know not of one knave, or a blockhead among them.' But some of them must have been stallholders on market days and, although restrictions on the trade had been lifted, bookselling at this level was often considered degrading by later generations. Michael Johnson, father of the great Dr Johnson, ran a bookstall in Birmingham and other towns and Boswell refers to Samuel's youthful embarrassment, and his penance in later years.

In a *Complete Catalogue of Modern Books* published in 1757, new works from the beginning of the century (excluding pamphlets and tracts) totalled 5,280, still less than 100 a year, although it may well be that the later editions had a higher print run. By the time of the accession of George III (1760), another pattern had emerged — publishers limiting the number of books printed, but running larger impressions. With their rise in status and influence publishers began to sell through regular commercial channels. The reign of George

III heralded a mini-boom in popular literature and, to extend the market to the relatively poor, publishers began to produce books in parts. The opportunity to buy books in 'installments' was evidently welcome and Smollett's *History of England*, one of the most successful 'number' books, sold 20,000 copies — enormous for those days.

Figures for the years 1792–1802 reveal that the new yearly average publication of new books had risen dramatically to 372. Another 25 years saw the yearly average rise to 588. Prices, in relation to size, had also been rising, eg the octavo edition was costing as much as 14 shillings, and the larger quarto 2 guineas. But the fact that at the start of the 20th century prices had dropped sharply, and that they remained low for many years, does not encourage the belief that the all-time ceiling prices of the 1980s could subside again: the traditional hardback is in danger of dying.

Comparatively recent trends are touched on in the following regional breakdown, but, first, a few of the more successful booksellers who had some influence on the development of trade. One normally defines success as the attainment of wealth, fame or position, but the three do not of course go hand-in-hand. There are those who prize respectability, men like Thomas Guy (1644–1724), not only the founder of Guy's Hospital, but an eminent figure in the Company of Stationers and MP for Tamworth. Guy made his money by printing and selling Bibles — a trendsetter but dull.

In contrast, John Dunton (1659–1733), who probably earned as much money, spent it at a faster rate; he gained notoriety rather than fame. A strong personality, Dunton made up in flair for what he lacked in business acumen. The elder Disraeli described him as a 'cracked-brain scribbling bookseller, who boasted he had a thousand projects, fancied he had methodised six hundred, and was ruined by the fifty he executed'. Dunton possessed an instinct for selling books, and from the start it came to his aid in building up his initial stock — without any cash. The son of a clergyman, he started by confining his activities to the works of nonconformist ministers, friends of his father, for which there had to be a steady theological audience. But he used the first book, in place of cash, to barter with other booksellers. 'This book fully answered my end', he wrote later, 'for exchanging it through the whole trade, it furnished my shop with all sorts of books saleable at the time.' At the end of the 17th century, he turned with customary versatility to the new art of book auctioneering, and made a name for himself in Dublin.

Jacob Tonson (1656–1736) was known as the Prince of Booksellers, mainly because of his association with eminent men of the time, but his contribution to literature was considerable. As well as publishing the best contemporary writers, eg Dryden and Pope, he is regarded as the first bookseller to make Shakespeare available to the reading public. He was also the first person in the trade to appreciate the merit of Milton's *Paradise Lost* and, by selling it successfully must take some credit for establishing its place in English literature.

Samuel Richardson (1689–1761), the novelist, became a master-printer, publisher and bookseller. One of the first bestselling authors, Richardson began writing at the age of 13, when he was contracted by three separate young women to write love-letters for them — an experience which, he considered, gave him the basic training for his novel writing. In 1706 he became an apprentice to a City printer, and worked for seven years for a master who 'grudged every hour to me that tended not to his profit'. Authorship came almost by accident when two bookseller friends persuaded him to write a small volume of 'letters' — advice and etiquette for young ladies, dressed up in fictional form to make them more readable. The result, *Pamela, or Virtue Rewarded*, immediately became a bestseller, and started a trend in popular fiction.

Many notable booksellers led a bitter existence before making the grade. William Hutton (1723–1815) was placed in a silk mill at the age of seven. Never a person to indulge in self-pity, Hutton nevertheless described his first job with some bitterness. 'I now had to rise at five every morning, summer and winter, for seven years; to submit to the cane; to be the constant companion to the most rude and vulgar of the human race . . .' This seven years left him physically scarred for life, and as a man of 14 he found another equally

26

gruelling job, working for his uncle, a stocking-maker. He gradually acquired a taste for reading, and because the only books he could get were tattered, he tried his hand at binding. From this start he improved his skill and knowledge, and at 21 set up as a bookseller in Nottingham. Then in 1750 he made an exploratory journey to Birmingham, where he found only three booksellers — and stayed, hoping 'I might escape the envy of the three great men'. He had no problem obtaining premises — half of a little shop for 1s a week — but he had no money for stock. A friendly clergyman offered him 2cwt of books at his own price — payment to be postponed to some future date. The contract read: 'I promise to pay Ambrose Rudsall £1.7s *when I am able.*'

His skill in binding made its contribution, and by the end of the first year Hutton had saved £20. From then on he steadily prospered, starting a circulating library, and writing books himself. His best-known work, *History of the Roman Wall*, was published in 1802 after some incredible research. Until then, no one had bothered to make a personal inspection of the wall, so at the age of 75 he started off on foot for Northumberland. He walked 600 miles in one pair of shoes, and claimed later that he could still walk 40 miles a day at the age of 82!

Finally, a man who died in his 81st year, bequeathing to the 20th century bookselling's most distinguished name — Quaritch; a man who made such an impact on the international book world that an American obituary notice credited him with 'making' the modern market for scarce books. Bernard Quaritch earned this reputation, not through entrepreneurial flair or showmanship, but through unrivalled knowledge and courageous buying.

Born in Prussia in 1819 (on the anniversary of Shakespeare's birth), Quaritch served a bookselling apprenticeship in Germany, and came to London in 1842 armed only with two letters of introduction. He started on his own in 1847 and almost immediately launched the first of the catalogues that were to become famous, although these little resembled the later editions. The first four, published in broadsheet and printed on both sides, were entitled *Quaritch's Cheap Book Circular: Selling for cash at very reduced prices* (ie from 1s to 1 guinea). The shop attracted a good clientèle from the start — one of the first customers being Gladstone — but within a few years Quaritch's buying had started in earnest. In 1858 he bought his first Mazarin Bible for £596, buying it back in 1887 for £2,650; it finally went to the United States after his death for £9,500.

Each year Quaritch catalogues became more impressive, and the issue for 1874, published in sections, was described by him as 'the greatest effort of my life'. No such catalogue of valuable books and manuscripts — classified and accompanied by a three-column index running to 109 pages — had ever before been attempted by a bookseller: 1,889 pages covering 23,000 titles. Indeed, the extent to which Quaritch dominated the trade in the last 20 years of the century is illustrated by some of his spectacular purchases: over £33,000 worth of a £56,000 collection from the Sunderland Library of Blenheim Palace; a £44,000 share of £86,000 from the Hamilton Palace Library; and the acquisition of nine out of eleven Caxtons from the Osterley Park Library. After his death in December 1899, his obituary in the *Daily Telegraph* called him 'King of Booksellers, incomparably the greatest, wisest, best informed, most liberal and munificent bookseller of his age, or any age'; and *The Times* added: 'It would scarcely be rash to say that Quaritch was the greatest bookseller who ever lived.'

In the following pages are many fascinating characters — unspectacular, perhaps, next to Hutton, less authoritative than Quaritch — but equally interesting.

RICH PASTURES

Recollections of favourite bookshops are frequently clouded by nostalgia. Why do we prefer one bookshop to another? Although this book is a guide, the responsibility of 'grading' shops is rejected. Restaurant and hotel guides do at least have established criteria: one can deduct marks for dirty cutlery, lukewarm soup, or bed bugs. But in the absence of a British Standard for bookshops, any evaluation must be personal. The bibliophile responds not only to the number or quality of the volumes on the shelves, but to environment and atmosphere; and fortunately we do not all function on the same wavelength.

Even in the limited category of 'great' shops, those important for the quality or size of their stock, or with a particularly fine history, one should differentiate. Unless he is a serious collector, the browser generally will not idly wander into the hallowed precincts of the famous antiquarian bookseller. This is not to say that casual customers are unwelcome; indeed, the staff are invariably helpful, and many bibliophiles tend to assume that all their books must be too expensive, when in fact it is often possible to buy a very attractive old book for little more than one recently out-of-print.

Most would find a visit to one of the better general booksellers, a more rewarding experience. The right atmosphere does heighten perceptiveness, and one can often 'sniff' out books. Yet some people get as much enjoyment in wading through packing-cases full of books in an old cellar.

Who could resist this vivid picture from *Riceyman Steps*, by Arnold Bennett, himself a compulsive collector?

There were more books to the cubic foot in the private room even than in the shop. They rose in tiers to the ceiling and they lay in mounds on the floor; they also covered most of the flat desk and all the window-sill; some were perched on the silent grandfather's clock, the sole piece of furniture except for the desk, a safe, and two chairs, and a step-ladder for reaching the higher shelves . . . Mrs Arb had to step over hummocks of books in order to reach the foot of the stairs. The left-hand half of every step was stacked with books — cheap editions of novels in paper jackets, under titles such as 'Just a Girl', 'Not Like Other Girls'. Weak but righteous and victorious girls crowded the stairs from top to bottom, so that Mrs Arb could scarcely get up. The landing was also full of girls . . . The massive mahogany table was piled up with books; as also the big sideboard, the mantelpiece, various chairs. The floor was carpeted with books . . . Coming out of the bedroom, she perceived . . . a long, narrow room. Impossible to enter this room because of books; but Mrs Arb did the impossible, and after some excavation with her foot disclosed a bath, which was full to the brim and overflowing with books . . .

The shop in question is supposed to have been inspired by Arnold Bennett's frequent visits to the forerunner of the Southampton branch of the excellent Hampshire booksellers, H. M. Gilbert. But the fictitious Mr Earlforward is still true to life and people readily identify booksellers with this image. Yet, there have always been men of vision who have left their imprint on the trade. One such personality, standing at the forefront of booksellers today, is Peter Eaton; as mentioned earlier, he opened the world's first stately-home bookshop. A bookseller for nearly 30 years, one might think that Mr Eaton had been universally accepted, but since he opened Lilies, a 60 room country mansion at Weedon, near Aylesbury, to house half a million books, much of the trade has tended to be critical. Dealing in books on this scale, his most obvious Achille's Heel is quality, and because of constant turnover the standard can vary considerably from month to month. The serious collector might be disappointed once in a while, but the average book enthusiast should regard Lilies as a must.

The stately-home bookshop concept sounds inspirational, but Mr Eaton admits that the decision to buy was motivated by necessity. Throughout his business life he had, like the majority of serious booksellers, bought in quantities — sometimes just to get two or three items of interest. In addition to a well established and popular browsing shop in Holland Park, London, he was paying rent for three ware-houses and considered taking a fourth, when he decided to look for an alternative. On trips to the United States, he had been impressed with the fact that, because of rent, parking problems, etc, many of the better new shops were outside the cities. He gives credit for finding Lilies to Frank Weatherhead, owner of the fine bookshop in Aylesbury.

Depending on the length of journey involved, it can be worth spending a whole day on a visit to Lilies, because the surrounding area is so attractive — Weedon frequently wins the country award for the best-kept village, and has a charming old pub, the Five Elms. Books occupy 35 rooms, more than enough to absorb my full attention in a dozen or so visits, so that I have only been partly aware of other attractions, such as the paintings and drawings and a small museum of literary and historical knickknacks. Indeed, one of the problems of visiting Lilies, as of all giant bookstores, is time. Peter Eaton still retains his small shop in Holland Park which was restructured in 1974, with a completely new layout tailor-made for the browser.

The outstanding individual bookseller in the United Kingdom during the second half of this century is Richard Booth, who, in a few years, has established what must be the world's largest 'bookshop' and put a beautiful but obscure Welsh village on the map for tourists, and especially librarians, from many countries. Bookselling in Hay-on-Wye is something of a cottage industry (apart from Booth's one million volumes, there are now other bookshops in healthy competition), but there is nothing 'folksy' or traditional about the business. Indeed, a large measure of Booth's success is due to the fact that he is one of a tiny minority of booksellers in Britain who use modern marketing and management techniques.

Having decided to live in Hay-on-Wye, Mr Booth began operating on the premise that size was necessary for survival in a village which had no passing trade — or, for that matter, any trade. In business terms he was handicapped by his belief that a book has an intrinsic value — fine old book or paper-back. He suggests that *in theory* booksellers have the same

31

commitment with every book. Consequently his main interest is in books selling at under £10. In this area, he believes, there is little point in following the pattern of most booksellers, who buy in lots and accept the fact that they might have to take several hundred volumes to acquire half-a-dozen they really want, and then get rid of the 'rubbish'. Booth believes that every book has a market, although the problem of identifying it has become increasingly complex because of the huge numbers being published. His solution has been to sort incoming stock into subject categories, with the object of building collections; an 8th impression of someone's war memoirs might be near-worthless as a single item but valuable to a collection. Thus a marketing commitment, even an artificial value, is created. Marketing (say) 500 books on the Cold War is called *horizontal* selling and the Booth team work to this end, influenced by what they call decision factors, ie the fewer decisions needed before selling, the more efficient the operation. Obviously, cataloguing at random would involve several decisions, so it pays to make just one at the beginning — to create saleable units. Organisation is the strong feature of the Booth operation.

Returning to the more traditional life-style, competing with Foyles for an unsolicited position as the most impressive company bookselling operation in the United Kingdom, is Blackwell's of Oxford. While there is little to choose between them in size, Blackwell's undoubtedly has the edge in scholarly tradition and associations, and has the distinct advantage (to you) of having the larger antiquarian and secondhand business just a few miles away at Fyfield Manor. Benjamin Henry Blackwell opened his first shop, dealing mainly in secondhand volumes, in Broad Street in 1879. A year later he took on an apprentice; but success brought his first headache, because the shop area was only 12ft square, and whenever more than three customers were inside, the apprentice had to go out! Eighty years later the company installed a computer which alone took up three times the space of young Benjamin's original shop; and in 1973 Blackwell's, now with a staff of 750, built a separate administration centre — a futuristic-looking building with around 70,000 square feet of landscaped office space. But this unique firm remains more than ever a family business. Blackwell's has been able to keep its original (expanded) frontage in Broad Street by moving backwards and sideways, a process culminating with the construction in 1966 of a giant bookroom *beneath* the neighbouring Trinity College. According to *The Guinness Book of Records*, the Norrington Room, named after the president of the college, with 160,000 volumes on 2½ miles of shelving, constitutes the largest display of books anywhere in the world in a single room.

There cannot be a less conventional operation than Eric Morten's shops in Didsbury, Manchester, where the fairly constant acquisition of cottage after cottage in a tiny street not much more than 8ft wide gives a rabbit-warren effect so complex that late browsers are in danger of being locked in for the night. Books by the thousand, from 16th-century works to the cheapest fiction, fill 17 separate rooms and 6,000 square feet of warehouse in what at first appears an 'old-fashioned' bookselling venture but has in Eric Morten a very 20th-century driving source. It is destined for further expansion in the north — Mr Morten already has a shop at Macclesfield.

Josephs, at the corner of Charing Cross Road and Great Newport Street, by London's Leicester Square, claims two proud distinctions — being one of the *busiest* second-hand and antiquarian bookshops in the country, and being owned by a family with the longest tradition of any in bookselling. Sam Joseph, at 86 a doyen of the trade, has traced the family involvement with books to the 1780s, and has seen an engraving of one of his ancestors at this time peddling books from a tray. There is reason to believe that this bookselling tradition goes all the way back to 1516. Although the shop itself is not large, the stock is interesting and of a high standard, attracting an impressive passing trade. Turnover is huge by bookselling standards, and the shop, attractive though it is to the browser, is like the tip of the iceberg; below ground are five storerooms.

Ironically, our oldest bookshop — and possibly the oldest retail business of any kind — Bowes & Bowes of Cambridge, now only sells new books; although in practice the 11 shops in the group, mainly university campus bookshops, do handle secondhand books — buying back from undergraduates for resale. The premises at Trinity Street was a shop in 1581, and attracted special attention even in those days when the owner, William Scarlett, was charged before the Court of the Star Chamber with pirating the Countess of Pembroke's *Arcadia*. The business, remaining a bookshop, changed hands a number of times until, in 1843, it was bought by Alexander and Daniel Macmillan (the grandfather of Harold Macmillan), who became founders of one of the largest publishing concerns in the world. With growth, and a new London office, the Macmillan publishing operation gradually broke away, so that the shop became Macmillan & Bowes, after a nephew Robert Bowes. Robert was joined in partnership by his nephew, the name of the firm being changed to Bowes & Bowes in 1907. In 1953 the business was taken over by W. H. Smith & Son and, although it was allowed to remain a separate limited company with its own policy and administration, the sale of antiquarian books was discontinued.

A bookselling giant of the West Country, George's of Bristol, probably has the highest ratio of secondhand and antiquarian to new in the major league. Despite the inevitable incursion of new books, the shop still has a thriving second-hand department housing about 100,000 volumes, of which one-third are antiquarian. Blackwell's of Oxford happen to own a majority shareholding in the firm, and by coincidence there are similarities in the early history of the two shops. The father of William George died in 1836 when the boy was six; Benjamin Henry Blackwell was the same age when his father died in 1849. George was apprenticed at 12; Blackwell at 13 — although young William was forced by circumstances to take the plunge with his own shop at 17, and by the time Blackwell launched out on a borrowed £150, the Bristol bookseller had a stock worth over £4,000, a considerable sum in those days.

H. M. Gilbert & Son own two of the most attractive book-shops in the country, within a few miles of each other at Winchester and Southampton. Each shop, oozing with old-world character and stocking about 50,000 books, is a bibliophile's dream. Both obviously stock new books but have very large secondhand and antiquarian sections: the Winchester branch is in the Cathedral Square, in an old part-Elizabethan building with rooms laid out in such apparent confusion that every doorway seems to offer a further surprise. The 'treasure-hunt' atmosphere made it inevitable that most of the firm's antiquarian trade would be done from here although in 1978, as the result of a complete restoration, the ground floor was extended (see regional section) and the upstairs rabbit warren let off. But the antiquarian books are now housed in a newly discovered medieval banqueting hall. At Southampton the shop's address — 2½ Portland Street — should itself give promise of delights to come. Indeed, the relatively small frontage, concealing three floors above as well as a basement, in a protected Georgian terrace has attracted and retained as customers many famous names in the world of literature, although it was the earlier shop in the High Street (Above Bar) that is supposed to have provided background material for *Riceyman Steps*.

One of the trade's outstanding personalities is Charles W. Traylen, whose business at Guildford, Surrey — housed in a pre-16th century building — is almost entirely antiquarian, although of around 50,000 volumes less than 10,000 are what he describes as 'fine' books. After more than 50 years in bookselling, Mr Traylen not only has a wealth of experience, but a fund of anecdotes. My favourite is the story of how he found and sold to the State Archives an original Charter of North Carolina, for which he was feted in the United States and even presented with a medal. Shortly after he had opened in Guildford, he bought some books from a couple of men who found him more generous than London booksellers and promised to come again. On the next occasion, among their books for sale, they produced the rolled-up charter. Mr Traylen, not knowing its value, paid £25 but said he would increase the amount if the document proved to be genuine. After research, the item was catalogued for £2,500 (it is probably worth 10 times that amount now) and sold to the appreciative Americans. The irony of the transaction is that some years before Mr Traylen had been asked to look at a quantity of books stored in wine cellars in Hertfordshire; they were practically worthless, and the visit was a waste of time. In due course, when the house contents were disposed of, one of the lots, a rolled-up piece of vellum thrown in with some china, was sold for 9s to one of the men who eventually turned up at Traylens. While he had searched despairingly through a mass of unwanted books, the charter had been lying unrecognised and ignored in the house!

The latest arrival in the big league, certainly in terms of versatility, is the Society for Promoting Christian Knowledge (SPCK). As I mentioned in the preface, the purchase of the Charles Higham business in 1976 provided the launch pad for SPCK's entry to the secondhand trade. With its headquarters at Holy Trinity Church in Marylebone SPCK has secondhand departments at bookshops in Bath, Bristol, Canterbury, Durham, Exeter, Norwich, Winchester and York. The size of stock ranges from only 2000 at Canterbury to 30,000 at Durham where SPCK is also the university bookshop. All except Bristol and Canterbury carry literature, history and topography, as well as theology. At five other shops in Bradford, Cardiff, Chichester, Leicester and Salisbury, the secondhand material is limited to theology.

Although SPCK has been in publishing since the early 18th century, using different publishers to produce its books — from the middle of the 19th century with its own imprint — it opened its first bookshop at the end of that century. Today it has 47 bookshop units, which could not happen without a dynamic approach to bookselling. The secondhand involvement is relatively small, but the policy is encouraged.

Small bookshops close or change hands constantly, but on the rare occasions when one of the 'giants' among the antiquarian booksellers is sold the ripples spread throughout the trade, and when, in 1979, Francis Edwards Ltd (see 'Central London') came on to the market, several interested parties competed for the debatable privilege of finding more than £300,000 for the business/stock, and initially even more for the lease of the building. The successful bid came from Alan Mitchell, in his early 30s, yet one of the country's leading authorities on Africana and hitherto very much a lone operator, with financial backing from the ICFC. Within a short period the first of the many necessary changes became apparent — and it stunned the trade. This was a decision to hive off one of Edwards' major sources of income, the sale of maps and prints, to concentrate on what the new management considered the better long-term potential, antiquarian books.

Another major change in policy was not so apparent to outsiders. Mitchell turned Edwards' into one of the very few antiquarian booksellers to run its business on modern commercial lines, with common-sense systems to monitor almost every aspect of trading, especially buying and selling performance. Too many firms find that even a healthy profit margin is eroded by the time a book remains on the shelves and, more particularly, the time it takes for customers to pay. A £500 (or even £50) invoice unpaid for three months may not seem significant to a large business, but multiply that figure by several hundred to represent the number of customers taking extended credit, and the amount of capital tied up becomes significant. Mitchell had the guts to ask for payment in advance (except for institutions) and cut down a major cash-flow problem overnight. He also cut down on the number of books bought at auction (the easiest, but hardly the most economic way to buy), asking his sales staff instead to make periodic trips to the provinces in search of suitable material. A revitalised company produced 16 catalogues in the first year, followed by 10 per year after the introduction of a customer profile system.

Some of the shops listed in the guide from Penzance to the Orkneys will be known — or should be after a 100 years or so of trading — and many others will provide new browsing pastures. Big, small, old, new, there are bookshops for every taste, whether your interest be in the location and its history, the premises and their architecture, or just 'ordinary' bookshops . . . 12th-century Beeleigh Abbey, the oldest site of a bookshop; Deighton Bell, the oldest booksellers trading under the same name; 15th-century settings galore; converted coach-houses, bake-houses, inns, cinemas, chapels and even a slaughterhouse; bookshops with their resident ghosts — 'identified' or mere sightings; stainless-steel edifices to ramshackle old shops that seem set to collapse if you lean against one of the shelves. What they all sell is a unique merchandise, a mirror for dreams as well as reality.

Guide to Bookshops

NOTE

The guide records most secondhand and antiquarian bookshops in England, Scotland and Wales. A small number may have escaped the net, but a few were deliberately omitted — eg businesses about to close or move, and those that for reasons of their own do not encourage the casual customer. Every effort has been made to ensure that material is correct and up-to-date, but we cannot accept responsibility for omissions or changes that may have taken place.

As before, I have included a few booksellers who operate from private premises but are willing to see members of the public by appointment, having a warehouse nearby or a large or specialist collection easily accessible at home. These (marked *) have been selected with considerable care, so that there is no obligation to buy: however, mere sightseers would obviously not be welcome.

After lengthy consideration I have, despite the drawbacks, retained the regional listings. The main reason is that it is sometimes more convenient when travelling to disregard county borders. However, I have compromised by providing a cross-reference in the index, where entries are included under their counties.

Shop times are generally taken to be normal business hours (9.30–5.30 or 10.00–6.00 Monday to Friday, and 9.00–1.00 approx on Saturday) unless stated otherwise.

CENTRAL LONDON

One of the pitfalls of an established reputation is the need to live up to it; industries, like people, become complacent on past glories. For many years the book trade has been proud of the fact that London has more secondhand and antiquarian bookshops than any other capital city. Yet with each succeeding year the claim becomes more difficult to justify, and sooner than we think it will be discovered that it is no longer true.

Having already described bookselling as a gentle art, it is apparent that the more dynamic management and marketing-conscious members of the trade — those who are *able* to compete — are in the minority. Many have moved out of the city and suburbs, and those who stay have the steepest uphill struggle of all. Some are good businessmen by any standards, others survive by luck more then judgement, and by clinging to the loyalty of old customers. Central London is the hardest hit, and certain traditional browsing areas are today almost denuded of bookshops; although fortunately for the book trade in general, chain stores such as W. H. Smith have increased the space devoted to (new) books. More specifically, the three most important areas have been the City, West Central London (particularly around the British Museum) and Mayfair, the home of the more exclusive antiquarian bookshops. At the time of the establishment of the book trade, the City *was* London. But apart from the inevitable shift in the balance of administrative power within the capital, caused by natural growth, the heavy bombing in World War II and subsequent large-scale redevelopment changed the whole character of this once all-important area.

There are only two bookshops left at the very heart of the City of London. Until 1980 there was only one — **J. Ash (Rare Books)**, 25 Royal Exchange, EC3 (01 626 2665). I described it as such in the first edition when the shop was located three minutes' walk away in Cullum Street, but the present site is an integral part of the history of the book trade in London, and the proprietor Laurence Worms has compiled a list of over 60 names of booksellers who operated from the Royal Exchange between the 17th and 19th centuries.

The business was formed as Jon Ash in 1946 — deriving its name from the founders, Hugh Jones and Cyril Nash. Their assistant, Laurence Worms, who came to bookselling straight from university, took over in 1971 and eight years later took advantage of an opportunity to move to the present premises which not only symbolise the long bookselling tradition, but are considerably less cramped. It consists of four small floors connected by the original Victorian spiral staircase, in which the ground floor and basement are devoted to books, while the top floor gallery, with a floor to ceiling round window, is given over to antique maps and prints. The books are mainly antiquarian with a slight emphasis on literature (1st edns) and London topography, but with a reasonable selection of travel, sporting, natural history and other subjects.

The history of the Royal Exchange which has stood on the site between Cornhill and Threadneedle Street for over four hundred years, is worth relating. The original Elizabethan building described by John Stow, the 16th-century antiquary and chronicler, as 'The Eye of London' was destroyed in the Great Fire of 1666. The replacement building, equally admired, was also burned down on a bitter night in January 1838 when the water froze in the firemen's hoses. The present one was opened by Queen Victoria in 1844. The bookshop is situated on the northern, Threadneedle Street side of the building, opposite the Bank of England and the Stock Exchange. Cl Sat.

Timothy Shaw arrived at 1 Telegraph Street, EC2 (01 920 0961) in the second half of 1980 after running a bookshop in Finchley Road, Hampstead for a few years. A former free-lance writer before becoming a bookseller in 1975, Timothy now has two rooms on the *first* floor of a charming red-brick, bow windowed building built as a tea room in the last century. There is a sandwich bar and tobacconist on the ground floor, but the bookshop is signposted from the three approach positions. The stock of general antiquarian books and modern firsts is small but interesting. 11am—5pm.

Having described the Shelley Bookshop as shining like a 'beacon in the wilderness of the EC1 postal district', I was disappointed that it had to close in 1979 because the building threatened to fall down! However, the proprietor Reg Read (who also owns the Southwood Bookshop, Highgate) managed to find alternative premises just round the corner, alongside the stage door of the Sadler's Wells theatre. Now called **Divertissment**, 19 Arlington Way (01 837 9758), the shop specialises in modern 1st edns and all the performing arts, especially ballet, dance, and Gilbert and Sullivan. It also offers a large selection of theatre and other programmes. Hours 3—7pm five days; noon—7pm Sat (other times by appointment).

I must confess clichés come in handy when compiling a guide and the writer is pushed for space, but if I compare **Paul Minet's Bookshop** to an oasis it is because it is the only secondhand bookshop around, and the address happens to be Ivory House, St Katherine's *Dock*, E1 (01 481 2849). It is situated at Tower Bridge, between the World Trade Centre and the famous Charles Dickens public house, and faces the marina. The shop, relatively new in the sense that it is part of the complex converted from an old warehouse, is quite tiny but packed with books. Because of the tourist attraction of the Tower and the marina which has given the area a new lease of life, two of the specialities are sailing and English topography (especially London), although there is also a fair number of general books, reasonably priced in keeping with the company's marketing policy (see World of Books p. 71).

The London branch of **Thomas Thorp**, one of the country's largest booksellers, moved in 1973 from the West End to 47 Holborn Viaduct, EC1 (01 353 8332), almost opposite Holborn Viaduct station; it could be missed quite easily, possibly because one does not expect to find a bookshop here and because there are seldom many books in the window. Apparently the landlords do not allow the shop to use a sunblind, and understandably Thorp's is not prepared to risk leaving books unprotected. However, once inside, there can be little doubt that this is one of the better bookshops in London, the 60–70,000 titles covering most subjects, but with particularly strong sections on early law books and angling.

The company's history is fascinating. Founded in 1883, it began to win its reputation in the early 1920s in Cecil Court when that locality was approaching the first peak of success. In the early '30s, Thomas Thorp went to Guildford to establish a large shop there, and returned to London to make his mark in the West End, with a shop in Old Bond Street. The London branch moved to Jermyn Street, twice suffered extensive bomb damage, and finally moved to Albemarle Street after the war. It remained there for close on 30 years, until exorbitant rent increases and other considerations forced it to move. In 1977 Thomas Thorp's earned an unenviable place in the record books — being victim of the bulkiest book theft of all time when thieves broke in over a weekend and systematically ransacked the shelves, using a van or lorry to make off with many thousands of volumes.

Even allowing for rents being among the highest in the country, it is surprising that bookshops in the environs of Fleet Street, a locality so steeped in literary tradition, have disappeared so rapidly; apart from newspapers and the fact that the thoroughfare has been associated with printing since 1500, there are a number of places that browser visitors to London will find worth viewing, eg Dr Johnson's house in Gough Square and St Bride's Church where Samuel Pepys was baptised; it is identified by the much-quoted sentiments of Richard Lovelace, 'Stone walls do not a Prison make, nor Iron bars a cage' (*To Althea from Prison*, 1642).

J. Clarke-Hall Ltd, Bride Court, EC4 (01 353 4116), a charming shop which moved to its present site in 1967, is now run by Sally Edgecombe, a partner in the business. The shop, split almost down the middle between new books which have gradually increased their foothold to cope with the passing trade and s/h and antiquarian for established customers, specialises in Johnson and Boswell, and prints of London; also some modern 1sts, and a reasonable stock of illustrated books with a leaning toward the 1925–1940 period. Justin Clarke-Hall, a barrister by profession, spent only a year in law before making bookselling his career. Having tried Cecil

Court for a spell, he moved to Fleet Street in 1935, when, supplying libraries principally, he and his wife concentrated on review copies. When the shop was destroyed during the blitz, the business was transferred to Wine Office Court where it began to blossom. Specialisation in Johnsonia began by chance because of the number of tourists who called in after visiting Dr Johnson's house, only a few yards away; now the shop issues periodic catalogues on the subject. Sally Edgecombe joined the firm 15 years ago; her own speciality is illustrated children's books.

In 1978 a print shop was opened across the Court at 22 Bride Lane (01 353 5483), selling 19th-century maps and prints, and offering a framing service. Hours of this shop are limited: noon–4pm.

L. Simmons, 16 Fleet Street, EC4 (01 353 3907), is a popular and very busy shop which only just reaches this guide because the stock is predominantly new; but because Mr Simmons is ruthless in taking 'old' stock off the shelves, there is always a constant supply of volumes at reduced and bargain prices. These are not remainders, simply books that are slow to move. Ironically, for most of his bookselling career, Mr Simmons has dealt in s/h books, opening his first shop in Islington in 1928. He moved to a first floor office in Fleet Street in 1938, evolving a business with the emphasis on libraries and mail order. The business at 16 Fleet Street — a small building on four floors, almost opposite the Law Courts — was started in 1945, the first time in more than a 100 years it had been used for books, having been built as a coffee house. Among the booksellers on this site earlier was the famous Bernard Lintot (1675–1736), who opened his shop in 1700 and established his reputation as the publisher of Alexander Pope.

A few minutes' walk away, across the road, through Bell Yard into Carey Street, is one of the most attractively situated bookshops in London, albeit the specialisation is limited to law books. However, no booklover should miss **Wildy & Sons, Ltd**. Lincoln's Inn Archway, Carey Street, WC2 (01 242 5778), strategically placed between Lincoln's Inn and the Law Courts. The shop has been on the same site — on either side of the historic archway — since the business was established in 1830 by John Wildy, after a partnership in another law booksellers. Largest stockists of early English law books in the world, Wildy's display of new and old books totals more than 10,000 vols if one includes the warehouse in south London. There is nothing stuffy about the firm, and the s/h department encompasses a range of books on allied subjects, eg criminology. Inevitably it is this department which contributes most to the shop's character.

Though now open only five days a week, director H. A. Goss recalls the days when distinguished judges, living in chambers in Lincoln's Inn, would call in on Saturdays, in mufti, to browse, expecting not to be recognised — an unspoken understanding respected by the efficient and discreet shop staff. Another feature of the firm's history has been continuity, the company staying in the Wildy family, followed by the Sinkins, ever since. John Wildy's granddaughter died only a few years ago, following the death in 1951 of Mr W. W. Sinkins who had worked for the company since 1895. His sons maintained this tradition — William E. Sinkins, the present managing director, has been there for over 45 years, and Kenneth K. Sinkins for 39. Wildy's has been tenant of the Honorary Society of Lincoln's Inn for 150 years, and has retained some of its customers, such as the Bar Library, and the Royal Courts of Justice, as well as several generations of individual families in the legal profession, since the beginning. In 1980, in recognition of the 150th anniversary, the managing director was awarded the Freedom of the City of London.

The Chancery Lane Bookshop, 6 Chichester Rents, Chancery Lane, WC2 (01 405 0635), run by Mr E. C. Nolan, is the last good general s/h bookshop in the area — not only in terms of stock but for its pleasant browsing atmosphere. Situated in a pleasant alleyway leading from Lincoln's Inn with a healthy passing trade, the shop has picked up considerably since the last edition, at which time half the space had been partitioned off. Mr Nolan has a very large number of books of Irish interest — with a few rarities not on show — and is also strong in law to accommodate the lawyers on his doorstep. The stock is varied, with something to appeal to most people.

A 10–15 minute walk to the top of Chancery Lane and through Gray's Inn brings you to **The Bloomsbury Bookshop**, 31 Great Ormond Street, WC1 (01 242 6780), near the famous children's hospital; a cramped but cosy shop, specialising in jazz, run by Teresa Chilton. Because of the small size there are only a few thousand volumes on display, but interestingly mixed and reasonably priced. Hours 10–3pm (10–4pm Sat).

The Marchmont Bookshop, 39 Burton Street, WC1 (01 387 7989), which had become synonymous with one of the doyens of the trade, Stanley Smith, was taken over by former schoolmaster Don Holder in 1977. Naturally the character of the shop has changed somewhat because of Mr Holder's own speciality — modern firsts and literary criticism. At the time of going to press Mr Holder has a second, small shop a few yards away at no 45, housing a small general s/h stock. 11am–6pm. Cl Sat.

Only a few hundred yards or so away — immediately south of the noisy Euston Road — is a tranquil precinct called Woburn Walk, where at no 10 is **Frank Cass (Books) Ltd** (01 387 7340). This pleasant shop, opened on this site in 1966, originated in the basement of Frank Cass, the publisher, then in Great Russell Street, in front of the British Museum. In fact books had been sold from this site in the 1940–50s when the shop was very much a literary haunt because of the owner, a larger than life character called Charlie Lahr. In the early days the accent was on African and Oriental history, subjects identified with the publishing house, but gradually the area of interest has expanded to cover many subjects. Several thousand books are divided roughly 50/50 s/h and antiquarian. The shop is slightly off the beaten track so it has less passing trade than it merits, although regular customers come from all over. Cl lunch and Sat.

Moving diagonally south across Russell Square into Bloomsbury proper, into bookland, the atmosphere is steeped in literature, despite the declining number of shops devoted to s/h books. The area south of the British Museum has always been one of the delights of London. The 'village' community, with Museum Street the main artery, lives off trade stimulated by the museum, but it has a character of its

47

own. The British Library Reading Room is really outside the scope of a browsers' guide, but every book enthusiast should visit the place. It is used by 150,000 scholars every year, following in the footsteps of such famous students as Disraeli, Dickens, Lenin and Karl Marx. George Bernard Shaw left one-third of his estate in gratitude for its help when a struggling author, which means it has received over £1 million as its share of royalties on *My Fair Lady*, with another small fortune to come.

To the north of the museum, in the shadow of the University of London, is **Dillon's University Bookshop Ltd**, 1 Malet Street, WC1 (01 636 1577), often considered to be the best academic bookshop in the country (although as general booksellers they rank only second in London to Foyles, and are in the same league as Blackwell's and Heffers), but stocking predominantly new books in 19 rooms on four floors. There is, however, a thriving s/h and antiquarian department which is likely to continue expanding over the next few years, on the first floor. Started by Miss Una J. Dillon in 1936, it became a joint venture operation with the University of London 20 years later, eventually being purchased by an industrial holding company in 1977. From its humble beginnings, Dillon's now employ 220 people — 40 of whom are based in branches at universities in the provinces. Students of architecture would be intrigued by the interesting Edwardian building, designed and built by Charles Fitzroy Doll, 1908–10, but there is nothing Edwardian about the bookselling philosophy of the present management. Miss Dillon, who retired in 1967, set an exceptional standard and was awarded the CBE for her services to the book trade.

The number of bookshops in Great Russell Street itself has diminished, and today they are limited to specialist subjects. Starting from the Tottenham Court Road end, the first is **The Cinema Book Shop**, 13–14 Great Russell Street (01 637 0206), exclusively concerned with all aspects of film. Obviously, in justifying the claim of having 'Europe's largest collection' on the subject, the stock ranges from new through out-of-print to rare, and includes comprehensive 'stills' archives available for hire as well as sale. The owner, Fred

Zentner, is friendly and understandably has an encyclopaedic knowledge of his subject. Small though it is, the shop has character, and despite the 20th-century subject is in keeping with a wall plaque on the outside of the building which reads 'Here lived Charles Kittenbell, as related by Charles Dickens in *Sketches by Boz*'.

Stock at **The Museum Bookshop**, 36 Great Russell Street (01 580 4086), which opened in 1978, is dictated to some extent by its position opposite the museum, being strong in archaeology, classical studies, history, travel and lit. New and s/h are placed side by side in two rooms. There is a wealth of books on travel and topography because the owners, Ashley Jones and David Mezzetti, run a travel business specialising in the Middle East. Sat opening variable.

It is ironic that the Wimpey Bar next door was once the famous Poetry Bookshop run by Harold Monro between the wars.

Arthur Probsthain Ltd, 41 Great Russell Street (01 636 1096), directly opposite the museum, deals in Oriental and African books (history, art, politics, literature etc) and has a large s/h stock, as well as new books. The business was established in 1902, and is run today by the founder's nephew Walter Sheringham, his wife and daughter. A cosy shop. Open Sat until 3.30pm.

When you see customers prepared to endure minor 'discomforts' to browse, you know you've found a good bookshop. This is typified by **The Bookshop**, 32 Coptic Street (01 636 8206), just round the corner, which must be one of the tiniest in the country but enjoys a turnover worthy of many larger businesses — because it is never empty. The secret of Arthur Page's success, apart from the friendly atmosphere, is that the general stock is surprisingly large for the small display area, yet carefully selected and reasonably priced from 50p to £500. Mr Page had a varied career until he found his niche in bookselling in 1972, moving to his present premises at the end of 1977. Normal hours but open until 7.30pm on Th and open Sun 11.30–6.30pm. In 1981 Mr Page opened a second shop round the corner at 29 Museum Street, with similar opening hours.

Stanley Crowe at 5 Bloomsbury Street (01 580 3976) is

considered to be one of the country's leading authorities on the topography of Great Britain and Ireland, with a stock to match; the shop is vital for those interested in the subject. Mr Crowe opened his first shop in the City in 1927, but it was destroyed by bombs in 1941. Within three weeks he had reopened nearby, but in 1946 he moved to Bloomsbury. For most of this time he had been a general bookseller, veering by inclination towards topography, old prints and maps, but from the 1950s he specialised. Other fringe subjects, representing about 15% of his stock, include genealogy, archaeology and architecture. Catalogues issued.

M. Ayres, 31 Museum Street (01 636 2844), founded by art expert Maurice Ayres who died in 1979, naturally enough specialises in art books of a high standard. Once claimed to be one of the best in the country, the art section is divided into works of reference and illustrated books, but there are also private presses and modern firsts, together with a large range of prints. Six days.

Although the **Atlantis Bookshop Ltd**, 49a Museum Street (01 405 2120), ostensibly specialises in the occult, it carries an interesting and varied stock which includes a large section on microscopy. Towards the end of 1980 most of the general stock was hived off to a new shop in Waterloo. (see 'South London'). The shop's association with the occult goes back 45 years when it was a meeting place for many of the well known figures involved in the study. The present owner, Mrs Kathleen Collins, took over in the early 1960s after running a bookstall in Victoria with her late husband, and she has been joined by her daughter Geraldine. 11—5.30pm. Six days.

In adjoining Little Russell Street, **Louis Bondy Ltd,** at no 16 (01 405 2733) is run by an ex-journalist who turned his hobby of collecting miniature books into a full-time business, opening the shop in 1946. Although the speciality is miniature books, caricatures, juvenalia and illustrated books, the shop's small stock manages to offer an interesting variety, and I have bought the most unexpected items here.

Four minutes' walk to the south in Barter Street is **Andrew Block** at no 84 (01 405 9660). The premises come as near to the traditional image of the bookshop as any I can recall, with thousands of volumes spilling everywhere in apparent disarray, although Andrew Block, 88 at the time of writing, still refers to a much-thumbed card index that seems to have been started with the acquisition of his very first book. The shop specialises in theatre and music hall, offering a vast collection of posters, programmes and photographs, although the general stock, especially history, is also comprehensive and interesting.

Andrew Block began bookselling in 1911 with a shop in West Hampstead, although for some years his time was divided between books and writing. He was joint author (with Charles Stonehill) of the four volume *Anonyma Pseudonyma* in 1926, and his other titles include *The Book Collector's Vade-mecum* (1932). Over the years he has had as customers and friends many of the great names in English literature, and he has been one of the foremost authorities on the subject. It is not unusual to find film or TV production executives rummaging for period ephemera as background material for their sets, and the library of miniature books at Disneyland was supplied by Andrew.

Charing Cross Road, a natural border separating the truly antiquarian bookshops west of Soho, from general secondhand stores, is itself one of the last strongholds of the trade, although even here the display is being whittled away, as old-established family businesses close. The bookselling tradition goes back to the 1900s, reaching its height in the 1920s and 30s. It all began in 1899, when Holywell Street, known as Booksellers' Row, was demolished as part of the Aldwych construction programme. Those who could afford the higher rents moved to the lower end of Charing Cross Road. Ironic though it may seem today, in 1900 the activities of the newly arrived booksellers were considered to threaten the tone of the neighbourhood. Westminster City Council informed one of the booksellers that he must remove the shelves outside his shop, as they constituted an obstruction and were illegal. In the ensuing Battle of the Bookstalls, booksellers dug in their heels, with the support of the media and the public. One was actually fined 1s at Marlborough Street magistrates court, but the display of books remained.

At the north end, by Tottenham Court Road station, is **W & G Foyle Ltd**, 119–125 Charing Cross Road, WC2, probably the largest single bookselling premises in the world, claiming to have more than 30 miles of shelving, carrying over 4 million volumes. The name Foyle has become as synonymous with books as vacuum cleaners with Hoover, but unfortunately it no longer stocks s/h books. The vast s/h section was closed when the guide first appeared but more recently the large room on the second floor housing antiquarian and better s/h items has been given the kiss of life.

However, the Foyles story is too impressive to overlook. In an era when the merchant banks have moved into big-time bookselling, it is refreshing to reflect on the success of an enterprise due entirely to the genius of the founding family. The business was started, almost as an afterthought, by the brothers William, then 19, and Gilbert, only 17; frustrated at having failed their Civil Service entrance exams, they decided to sell their textbooks, taking a small advertisement in one of the educational journals. After working from home, their first proper commercial venture was a small warehouse in Islington at 5s a week. Next came a slightly larger shop in Peckham where they worked a very full seven-day week, wrote their catalogues by hand and asked for their return.

By the time they moved into Cecil Court they were able to hold their own in any company, and a few years later (1929) the Lord Mayor of London opened their new premises — one of the present five-storey buildings, handsomely extended in 1966 with the erection of Goldbeaters' Hall at a cost of £250,000. Escalators and a redesigned layout incorporates additional features such as the Foyles art gallery and records shop. Another well known feature of an organisation which includes 10 book clubs are the literary luncheons, started in 1930 by the present managing director, Christina Foyle (daughter of William), when she was only 19. A third generation is now represented by William's grandson, Anthony. Open all Sat and until 7 Th.

Almost opposite is the **Hellenic Bookshop**, at no 122 (01 836 7071), specialising in Greece and Turkey, although its coverage of new, s/h and antiquarian material within these areas is so extensive that one might almost call it a general bookshop. Subjects covered include history, literature, theatre, religion, art and architecture and all aspects of

Hellenic culture. The shop was opened in 1966 by Mrs Photini Constantinou who had been selling books on Greece and Turkey for over 20 years, and had even acted as a cataloguer in her speciality for the British Library. Her daughter, Monica Stoddart, who worked with her from the start, subsequently became a partner. It is always worth asking here for a title that cannot be seen on the shelves — because behind each row of books is usually a second row, not immediately visible.

Literally around the corner, in direct competition (although the shops probably complement each other) is **Zeno**, 6 Denmark Street (01 836 2522), known as Tin Pan Alley, the home of the music publishing trade. Zeno, open until 6.30 every day (5.30 Sat) is a friendly shop and has been described as 'not just a bookshop, but a centre of Greek literary activities where most Greek scholars have met'.

Collet's London Bookshop, 64—66 Charing Cross Road, WC2 (01 836 6306), with its emphasis on left-wing books, reopened the s/h department after a lapse of some years, and today offers an interesting collection in the basement. Starting on this site in 1931, Collet's now have several shops each with its own speciality, but at this branch s/h material covers Marxist philosophy and economics, working class and industrial history, trade unionism, women's lib, race relations and black studies.

On this south side of Charing Cross Road are a number of bookshops, although only one in the middle of the cluster still deals solely in s/h material: **Albert Jackson & Son**, at no 68 (01 836 9144). Run by Bryan Jackson, a fourth generation in the family business started by his great-grandfather at Great Portland Street in 1873, the shop has always been strong in fiction, although these days the bulk of the books on display are paperbacks or review copies. Jackson's is typical of the friendly shop that has been penalised for its encouragement of browsers — losing not only cheap hardbacks but even paperbacks. Cl Sat.

E. Joseph, 48a Charing Cross Road & 13 Great Newport Street (corner site), WC2 (01 836 4111), a jewel in the somewhat lacklustre conglomeration in Charing Cross Road, has a good general out-of-print stock with the accent on literature, art, history and sets. The most expensive antiquarian books can only be seen on request, although the shop is usually so busy that browsers should not expect to wander through to that section without some specific interest. Like all good bookshops, Joseph's is plagued by book thieves, although it has tried to minimise the risk by keeping cheap books outside, philosophically regarding certain losses as a way of clearing old stock.

Although the family is descended from a long line of booksellers, it did not trade under the Joseph name until 1902 when Mr E. Joseph started the exodus from Holywell Street to Charing Cross Road, after serving a useful apprenticeship working for his aunt, Mrs Lazarus. She employed three bright young assistants who went on to make their own names — her nephew, a Mr Myers (father of Winifred Myers, specialist in autographs), and Mr Sawyer, father of the present Charles Sawyer. Mr Joseph's business was passed on to his two sons, Jack and Sam, and now the line is continued by Jack's grandson, David Brass, a specialist in illustrated books, and who solves one of the problems of diminishing stock by buying extensively abroad. ½ day Sat.

Immediately south of Leicester Square is the pedestrian precinct of Cecil Court, overlooked with a few exceptions by booksellers leaving Holywell Street and taking over the mantle of Booksellers' Row in the 1930s. Until World War I, Cecil Court was known as Flicker Alley, a pre-sound era Wardour Street, although the first bookseller arrival was John M. Watkins in 1900.

Watkins Bookshop, 19 Cecil Court, WC2 (01 836 2182), is probably the country's leading specialist in theosophy, philosophy and allied subjects. The founder, setting up as a publisher and bookseller in the 1890s, was a scholar of mystical and antiquarian interests, who had previously been secretary to Helena Petrovna Blavatasky, founder of the Theosophical Society, well-known medium/author of such works as *Isis Unveiled* and *The Secret Doctrine*, and obviously a major influence on him.

During 70 years of trading, the Watkins, father and son, have had as customers and friends men of the stature of Yeats, Crowley (if stature is the right word), Waite, Mead,

Ouspensky, D. T. Suzuki, Krishnamurti, Kathleen Raine and Alan Watts. Present managing director Richard Robinson, in describing the shop as a nonsectarian centre where the best literature of its kind is available in extensive and balanced selection, says that the firm's policy is to be concerned with 'inner *and* outer worlds — including the environment and current affairs — to balance the escapist tendency of much so-called spiritual literature at the present time'. Open Sat cl Mon. There is a second shop at Dulverton, Somerset (see regional entry).

When the last edition of the guide appeared, Cecil Court seemed to be suffering from the malaise that affected the trade as a whole, but more recently there has been a marked revival resulting in a Cecil Court Booksellers' Association — part of the Covent Garden Association. There are not only more bookshops in the passage, but an agreement that any leases that expire are to be offered only to booksellers — for which it has again become a most desirable quarter. The lift in morale is immediately apparent from the alleyway's generally brighter appearance. Most operate normal hours, starting at 10am, and are closed on Sat.

Alan Brett, who took over Harold Mortlake's shop at the Charing Cross Road end at no 24 (01 836 8222) in January 1978, appeared in the last guide under the Open Book which he ran for seven years. This is probably the most eye-catching of the surprisingly different shops in the court — and has featured in several films including Graham Greene's *The Human Factor* — having a minstrel gallery in the main shop, as well as a map 'gallery' in the basement. In his business in Surrey, Alan claimed to have the largest stock of moule (county) maps in the world and still buys and sells in enormous quantities, although prints cover most subjects and all periods. Although books are still mainly concerned with topography and transport, Alan 'inherited' some of Mortlake's speciality — Gothic horror, and Victorian double and triple-deckers. Other minor specialities include fine bindings (he qualified as a bookbinder after a seven-year apprenticeship and the stock reflects his expertise) and early cycling books — his hobby being the collection of penny-farthing bicycles.

Peter Stockham at Images at no 16 (01 836 9661) achieved a lifetime's ambition when he arrived at the court in January 1977, after 20 years at Dillon's Bookshop, latterly as managing director. For much of that time he had his name down on the waiting list for a shop here. Peter specialises in material with visual appeal, the shop bulging at the seams with a mixture of new and s/h illustrated books of all kinds, but also taking in novelties, eg book-toys, as part of what may be the largest stock of printed ephemera in the country. Even the occasional catalogues he issues are tiny novelties in their own right. A most pleasantly eye-catching shop with glossy art books rubbing shoulders with Victorian fiction, books on dolls with those on circus. Peter Stockham has written and compiled a number of books including facsimile reprints of famous 19th century children's books and chapbook ABCs and Riddle books. His latest, the definitive *A History of Children's Book Illustration* (from 1750 until the present day), was published in 1980. Hours T–F 11–6pm, and the first Sat of the month 11–2.30.

On the south side of the court, where the shops are larger than those facing them, is **H. M. Fletcher,** 27 Cecil Court (01 836 2865), which houses a large stock of antiquarian material, 95% pre-1850. The business is run by Bill Fletcher, who has spent more than 55 years in bookselling, and actually put up the shop's shelves in 1937 when he helped his father move from New Oxford Street and Porchester Terrace — and from Ramsgate where it had started in 1906. Today the third generation, Keith, helps run a fascinating shop which refuses to specialise because that would deprive it of the opportunity to handle so many other fine books. Instead it buys what it can, which means that at different times certain subjects are much in evidence, eg colour-plate books or French books. Bill and Keith Fletcher symbolise the spirit of true booksellers. Admitting that he could perhaps earn more money working from home, Bill Fletcher says 'A letter is not the same as seeing a customer's face when you produce a book you have found for him. If you are content to work from an office, you might just as well be a stock-broker.'

The most elegant-looking shop is **Quevedo,** at no 25 (01 836 9132), almost dauntingly so, but Justine Budenz, the

American manager, is friendly and knowledgeable, and the stock is not necessarily expensive. Formerly the premises of Mr Seligmann, the art specialist who died in 1976, the shop was taken over in the following March by Tobias Rodgers who had for several years run a postal business from his home under the name J. F. Rodgers. He called the shop after the 17th-century Spanish writer Quevedo whose books he collects. Not surprisingly there is a fair proportion of Spanish books among the varied stock — in the main pre-1850, including lit, history and travel, the emphasis being on text as opposed to illustration. Justine has had 14 years' experience with major bookshops and auction houses on both sides of the Atlantic, including Sotheby Parke Bernet, Christie's and Quaritch.

Frognal Rare Books, at no 18 (01 240 2815), run by Lady Edith Finer, moved to the court from much larger premises in Hampstead in 1977 and it was she who was the driving force behind the formation of the association, which had been talked about for some time but never got off the ground. Always a specialist in law and economics, she now puts most of these into catalogues, leaving the shop with a good selection of books on lit, art, travel and sets.

One of the most fascinating shops in Cecil Court — **Pleasures of Past Times**, at 11 (01 836 1142) — is run by an actor, David Drummond, although the stock is not restricted to books. What is now a flourishing business began as a sparetime interest, beginning in 1961 with a stall in Islington on Saturdays, then moving to Shepherd Market (Mayfair). At the outset Mr Drummond's stock came under the vague heading of 'interesting objects', but because of his involvement in the theatre and interest in stage history, he began to specialise — eventually arriving at Cecil Court in 1967. Now 50% of his trade is in books, several hundred, fairly evenly divided between those on the performing arts — with the accent on circus, music hall and conjuring, as well as 'legitimate' theatre — and juvenile books. The shop is also believed to have the largest stock of postcards in London, comprehensively classified, as well as photographs, posters and autographs — all are constantly used by TV and film companies for research and authentic background material.

He also provides a picture library service for students or anyone who wants to copy something small and out-of-copyright. Hours unusual: 11–6 M to F, but lunch closing 2.30–3.30 to accommodate middle-of-the-day browsers. Check for Sat opening.

Although there are a number of very good booksellers specialising in music, there is only one shop of any significance in the country, **Travis & Emery**, at 17 (01 240 2129). Valerie Travis has been in Cecil Court since 1956 when she managed Alec Clune's music book-store on the same site. In that year she married Walter Emery, probably the foremost English scholar on Bach, and in partnership they took over the shop in 1960. Mr Emery, also known in literary circles for his Icelandic studies (translating two of the sagas), died in 1974, but the business continues as before. The firm's comprehensive out-of-print and antiquarian stock — housed in the shop and basement — provides specialist collectors, musicians and students with their only opportunity to browse, and consequently includes many distinguished artists and celebrities in its international clientèle.

Harold T. Storey, at no 3 (01 836 3777), is another shop which has been here for over 40 years. The business, run by Norman Storey, has a large general s/h stock, with leanings towards certain subjects such as travel and naval history and fine bindings. An expansive, friendly man, Mr Storey has a wealth of anecdotes, mainly about customers, justifying a chapter in their own right.

Robert Chris, at no 8 (01 836 6700), has been here since 1934, and 48 years' involvement in English literature has equipped Mr Chris with more than a passing knowledge of the subject, although he dismisses his own occupation as 'cigarettes, coffee, stories and gossip'. Apart from English lit, the shop carries an interesting mixed bag, and is one of the better general-interest shops in the court.

Clive A. Burdon Ltd, at no 13 which opened in April 1980, is predominantly concerned with maps, prints and portraits of the 18th and 19th centuries. Only a handful of illustrated books stocked.

Griff's at no 4 (01 836 2793) stocks only books (new and s/h) related to Wales, including Welsh language titles, and as such is obviously of limited interest. The business was started in 1945 by four brothers from a South Wales mining village — incredible in itself that they imagined they could all make a living starting from scratch. Fired with idealism, they not only managed to survive, but created a business that has become famous in the bookworld, although it must be conceded that the nucleus of their operation became library supplies. The Griffiths brothers featured on radio and TV programmes because of their fascinating history (all being formerly professional musicians, and being at one time part of a family orchestra), and the surviving brothers Arthur (71) and John (79) must be among the best known names in the trade.

Smallest stock in the court is housed at **Edmunds** at no 1 (01 240 1683) because some of the space — which is in any case a small area — is taken up by bric-a-brac, mainly of a military and theatrical nature. Frederick Edmunds opened here in 1950 after a lengthy apprenticeship in books. The small s/h stock is varied, although the most eye-catching collection of fine bindings really belongs to Mr Edmunds and he is usually reluctant to sell them. The shop looks like a throwback to the last century but has a warm and pleasant atmosphere. Hours noon–4pm.

Although I have left them until last (at the St Martin's Lane end) it was the arrival of **Anglebooks** at no 2 (01 836 2922) in June 1976 that seemed to signal the court's 'revival'. The shop specialises in books on fishing, although it is also very strong on topography — having large selections that only specialists can provide (it also enables the shop to issue four catalogues a year on each subject). The owner, Michael Holman, a bibliophile who has worked in publishing, started the business at the end of the 1960s, running a successful postal operation before settling into the court.

Running parallel to Cecil Court is St Martin's Court, and at no 34 is the **Green Knight Bookshop** (01 836 3800) owned by Keith Nicholson MA, who took over in 1977 what had been part of Paul Minet's operation. In fact, Keith had worked there since coming down from Cambridge six years earlier, supplementing his income by writing on one of his special interests, book illustrators. The shop got its new name from the desire to be identified with English lit and illustrated books, but also to commemorate the original Green Knight Bookshop and Café in St Martin's Lane before and during World War I which was a meeting place for poets and writers such as Rupert Brooke, Edward Thomas, Robert Bridges and John Masefield. A stock of around 10,000 is fairly general, but particularly strong in the performing arts (partly because of the shop's proximity to the theatres), and with a reasonable coverage of biography, fine art, philosophy, archaeology and classical lit. Occasional catalogues. Hours flexible: 11am–6.30pm, sometimes later in summer.

The change in the character of Covent Garden which had been promised for several years following the departure of the fruit and vegetable market but which did not take physical shape until 1980 is too significant to deal with here. Suffice to say that the change gradually brought about an influx of shops relating to the arts, among them a number of booksellers.

One of the first to anticipate the revival was **Bertram Rota Ltd**, 30 & 31 Long Acre, WC2 (01 836 0723), a firm which seems to believe not only in stocking good books, and giving a good customer service, but in the right environment for browsing. After 12 years at their most attractive modern premises in Savile Row, they moved in 1977 to the very heart of the market area, into a building which is now one of the country's most eye-catching bookshops. While one is immediately taken by the character of the building with its Venetian style front elevation, in practical terms the restoration has capitalised on the *size* of the display areas — an open plan effect broken only by cast iron support columns. Light comes from a large open well around which runs a suite of offices. With the very large stock, the emphasis is on modern first editions and manuscripts. Because of its reputation, Bertram Rota manages to attract many of the important collections which come onto the market, such as the Cyril Connolly library of 10,000 books and pamphlets. Another speciality is association copies and private press books, but there is also a good stock of material from the 17th century onwards. In 1980 the company took over the business of George Sims, the author bookseller.

Bell, Book and Radmall, 80 Long Acre (near the junction with Drury Lane), Covent Garden (01 240 2161), which opened at the end of 1974 is also a large, almost 'open plan' shop (850sqft) specialising in modern firsts, with a heavy emphasis on detective stories and fantasy. The stock is not inexpensive but, in common with other firms carrying a large stock, there are a number of attractive items to be found on the miscellaneous shelves. The business has been elected to the ABA, and now issues five catalogues a year. Partners are Christopher Radmall, a collector who crossed over, and John Bell, whose father is Ian Bell of Bridge Conacher of Kent.

Since the last edition, **Jarndyce** have moved a stone's throw away to 68 Neal Street, Covent Garden (01 836 9182), two minutes from the tube and, while they can no longer claim to be housed in a garret above a fruit and vegetable warehouse, they still have one next door (a survivor from the old market). The premises are two first-floor rooms, approached through an alleyway, in a terraced house built in 1800. Jarndyce, run by former journalist Brian Lake, and Janet Nassau, deals only in late antiquarian material, ie 18th and 19th century lit, with a growing stock of economic, social and political history, and is particularly strong in early Dickensiana (esp 1st edns), three-decker novels, minor poetry, biography and London topography. Of around 6000 volumes, nothing was published after 1910. The business is mainly orientated to catalogues but visitors are welcome in 'shop' hours, although a phone call is advisable.

Throughout Covent Garden's transition period there was an influx of people from the arts, so it is no surprise to see *two* shops in Floral Street (running parallel to Long Acre) which cater exclusively for this broad interest. **Ian Shipley Books Ltd**, at 34 (01 836 4872) deals only in books on art and allied subjects (eg architecture, theatre design, photography) and is therefore able to offer an impressive range of books, new and s/h together in alphabetical order, according to subject. The shop opened in January 1979 when Ian Shipley jumped in at the deep end, his experience limited to working for publishers' distributors. The expertise in his chosen subject is based on four years at art college where his love of books was so evident that he was appointed 'honorary'

61

librarian. Today, a significant part of his business is the sale of new art books to libraries since Floral Street does not attract much of a passing trade, although now that the business is well established a greater effort is being made to build up the s/h and antiquarian side. Six days.

Bernard Stone — the Turret Bookshop, at no 43 (01 836 7557) a much bigger shop, has a wider selection, although the emphasis is heavily on poetry, illustrated books/prints, and small presses. Mr Stone, who opened the original Turret Bookshop in Kensington 25 years ago, moving to Covent Garden at Christmas 1979, has had his own publishing imprint since 1965 when he started producing limited editions of modern poets. Today, Steam Press is the vehicle he uses for publishing the works of such diverse talent as Ralph Steadman, the artist (his partner in the publishing venture), Ted Hughes and Alan Sillitoe. The two also produce the *Covent Garden Carrot*, an amusing broadsheet on the locality.

At the back of this attractively laid out shop, customers might find Mr Stone somewhat overshadowed by a very distinguished, white-haired gentleman, even more striking in the modern setting, and bearing a remarkable resemblance to Sigmund Freud. However, when he seems to ignore questions, the customer realises that 'Freud' is merely a lifelike wax dummy. Now something of a mascot, 'Freud' is the creation of ex-Madame Tussaud's sculptor Lyn Kramer to publicise Steadman's biography of the great man. Children's books and modern firsts are also available in a large and comprehensive stock of new and s/h books arranged side by side. Six days (open until 7pm).

Before leaving Covent Garden, we can include a shop which has no s/h books, although sometimes a handful of titles are reduced in price, but is worth a visit if one is interested in the theatre: **French's Theatre Bookshop**, 26 Southampton Street (01 836 7513). Once the home of David Garrick, the actor-playwright, French's was established in 1872, when Samuel French, an American, secured the works of almost every famous playwright. Today, amateur dramatic societies as well as actors from all over the country get their lines from this company, whose shop even has the appearance of a rather austere theatre foyer.

The **Economists' Bookshop**, Clare Market, Portugal Street, WC2 (01 405 5531), has the main shop for new books adjoining the London School of Economics, but a smaller s/h department nearby has a good stock in economics, history, politics and sociology.

The West End bookshops have a character unlike any you might find elsewhere in the country. There are so many distinguished names among them that I have given precedence to age, and started with the oldest: **Henry Sotheran Ltd**, 2—5 Sackville Street, Piccadilly, W1 (01 734 1150), founded in 1761 at York, where the annals of bookselling go back almost as far as in London and where the founder gained his experience, moving to the capital in 1815 to open a shop in the City. The reputation of this company, evidenced by superb catalogues, has been built on its purchase of many important libraries and collections, such as the libraries of Laurence Sterne, Charles Dickens and Sir Isaac Newton.

There has been no Sotheran in the company for many years, but the board of directors includes the Earl of Drogheda, Evelyn de Rothschild and Viscount Chandos. Today this exceptionally imposing shop, with its 40ft frontage, carries a comprehensive stock of 'important' subjects, with fine bindings, autographed letters, etc. Prints and maps are housed in an extended print gallery on the lower ground floor. Cl Sat.

In contrast, very much a small family business since it was established in 1894, is **Chas J. Sawyer**, 1 Grafton Street, W1 (01 493 3810), which proudly claims to sell only books you are not likely to find at 'ordinary' bookshops. The stock is thus relatively small but very select and includes fine bindings and sets, colour-plate books, private presses, 18th and 19th-century English lit, Churchilliana, autographed letters, etc. Also, apart from the main showroom, there is a superb department dealing with all aspects of Africana, probably the best in the country.

Charles Sawyer's interest in Africana started at the end of World War II, when Charles Raymond Sawyer, younger son of the founder and now in partnership with his son, Richard, decided to investigate the South African market for the sale of old English books. Research established that the best source material was in England and Holland, because many European travellers to India had stopped off in Africa, and bought pictures and contemporary art. Sawyer's started to build its collections, and commissioned a friend and expert, A. Gordon-Brown, to compile a *Pictorial Art in South Africa during three centuries to 1875*. Today the Africana section includes not only books but paintings, drawings, prints and even statuettes.

The company was formed when Charles (James) Sawyer, as a young bookshop assistant, had the good fortune to impress a retired American bookdealer who offered to back a West End venture. The business flourished to such an extent that in 1908 Sawyer's was in residence at nos 23, 29 and 31 New Oxford Street, moving to Grafton Street in 1922, where it has remained. Publishing is another interest, dating from 1927 when the firm brought out in two volumes a bibliography entitled *English Books 1475–1900: a signpost for collectors* (written by Charles Sawyer in collaboration with Harvey Darton). It also owns the Navarre Society and Argonaut Press imprints. Open Sat 9–11.30.

Sawyer's are associated with **Jonathan Potter Ltd,** which specialises in rare and antique maps, and trades from the lower ground floor with a separate entrance to the showroom on Hay Hill.

Bernard Quaritch Ltd, 5–8 Lower St John Street, Golden Square, W1 (01 734 2983), is famous for the tradition handed down by the founder, and maintained by successive talented managing directors, of acquiring important books. In 1951, the company bought the Gutenberg Bible which was subsequently sold for £1 million — a far cry from Bernard Quaritch's first catalogued offerings of from 1s to 1 guinea. In 1978 at auction in New York, it established a world record by buying on behalf of the University of Texas the Pforzheimer Library copy of the Gutenberg — the price was $2.4 million.

The shop is beautifully laid out on one floor — one of the criticisms of their previous premises in Grafton Street was that the two-floor showrooms were so imposing that even regular customers were too awed to wander upstairs to look around. Now, with the company aiming for a more informal atmosphere, the effect is somewhat wasted because of the need for stricter security. A receptionist seated just inside the main door directs all visitors to the section they need and there is consequently less scope for browsing, although one is never discouraged.

Bernard Quaritch's first shop was in Castle Street, Leicester Square, which he took on with a capital of well under £100, paying a rent of 16s a week. He moved to Piccadilly in 1860, to the site on which Swan & Edgar now stands, and the firm remained there until 1907 by which time his son was running the business. When Bernard Alfred Quaritch died in 1913 at the age of 42, the business was left to his two sisters and was run by the senior assistant Edmund Hunt Dring, who became managing director when a limited company was formed in 1917. The appointment of Mr Dring started a Quaritch tradition of rewarding long-serving members of the staff; many years later his son Edmund also became managing director, although he had to wait 50 years for the honour! Meanwhile, in 1907 the shop had moved to the lovely Georgian house in Grafton Street where it remained for 60 years.

In 1971 the company was taken over by a consortium of bankers but returned to private ownership four years later when one of the consortium's administrators, Milo Cripps, Lord Parmoor bought the business in partnership with Simon Sainsbury (of the grocery family). Lord Parmoor remains an active chairman and Nicholas Poole-Wilson became managing director on the retirement of Mr Dring. The business was reorganised, but one custom that seems to have disappeared at the beginning of the 1970s was the periodic clear-out of imperfect antiquarian stock — imperfect in not quite conforming to Quaritch's exceptionally high standards. A tea-chest was filled at intervals with damaged, although still fascinating material, and sold unseen for perhaps £20 to a provincial bookseller — many of the items later finding their way back to Quaritch's via would-be fortune-hunters. Today, the wide stock ranges from fine books and bindings to modern first edns (although this is not one of their strengths).

If one was able to establish a prestige league table of

antiquarian booksellers, the top of the first division would be contested by Quaritch and Maggs and the two businesses have much in common, although **Maggs Bros Ltd**, 50 Berkeley Square, W1 (01 499 2007), has always been controlled by one family. The firm was founded by Uriah Maggs, who came up from Somerset in 1860 to make his fortune, although it was the brothers Ben and Henry who prospered, initially at a shop in Paddington Green, then a pleasant London suburb. Frank Maggs, eldest son of Ben, who also became such a distinguished name in antiquarian circles, was born above that shop, although by the time he came into the business in 1915, they had risen in the bookselling world — to the Strand. The business moved to the West End at the end of World War I, and to Berkeley Square before the start of World War II. Frank Maggs was also an authority on navigational charts and instruments, and worked closely with the National Maritime Museum, indebted to him for the acquisition of many priceless old maps, globes and instruments. He was succeeded as chairman by his cousin, Clifford, while his son John is managing director, and his nephew Bryan Maggs, a specialist in English bindings and early English books, is also on the board.

Maggs have earned a venerable reputation on merit as dealers in fine books, but a less commonly appreciated feature is that while they offer a large range, eg incunabula, manuscripts, private presses, early travel, early English books and military books, they choose to accept an 'obligation' overlooked by most booksellers — to provide something for all pockets. Some of their catalogues carry 'cheap' books, and the firm numbers schoolboys among some very distinguished customers. Maggs also follows an 'old fashioned' moral code, behaving with such admirable discretion that they might be family solicitors. If a customer chooses not to divulge a purchase of a sale, the transaction remains a secret, even to his wife. This is noticeable in the reticence with which Maggs talk about their trading, and one is more likely to hear about transactions that have misfired, such as their purchase in 1970 of a Sarum Missal, a manuscript of around 1420, which they sold to an Amsterdam dealer for £1,000. When they realised it had been stolen it was recalled and the money refunded, but since the thief did not reveal where he had stolen it, they were still waiting several years later for the owner to claim it! In 1980 it was returned after someone read about it in my book *Antiquarian Books* and got in touch with Maggs. In a happier vein that year they issued their 1,000th catalogue which has in itself become a collector's item. Friendly and helpful staff; situated on ground and first floors.

A perfect illustration of the successful blend of tradition and modern business methods can be seen at **Hatchards**, 187 Piccadilly, W1 (01 439 9921) where the rare books department on the second floor is quite small but interesting. Hatchards is known world-wide and is the appointed bookseller to the Royal Family. Now the oldest of the London shops (ie not moved in from the Provinces), the business was started in 1797 by John Hatchard with a capital of £5. By the time of his death in 1849 he had not only become the most respected of London booksellers but had increased his original stake to £100,000 — which was worth something 130 years ago. The Duke of Wellington and most of the outstanding Victorian politicians frequented Hatchards. However, over the years the type of 'carriage' customer who would order fine bindings by the yard to complete a library of unread books diminished and the rare book department, depending more on collectors, became smaller and moved upstairs. Today, the ground and first floors house a wide selection of new books and the basement has paperbacks. Manager of the rare books department, Robert Lory, supervises an interesting stock which he describes accurately as 80% cheaper books (mostly under £10), and 20% antiquarian and collectors' items. Hatchards is a good-looking and well laid out shop by any standards.

The largest and most comprehensive stock among the West End booksellers is housed at **Francis Edwards Ltd**, 83 Marylebone High Street, W1 (01 935 9221). The present building, erected in 1911 with four floors and a basement, was designed specifically as a bookshop, immediately evident from first sight of the shop entrance and gallery at the back. In fact, the receptionist who directs visitors to the required department is employed not so much as a deterrent to bookthieves but because of the size and complexity of the shop. The ground floor and gallery house finely bound sets, literature, arts, military and naval history, transport, etc; the first floor, illuminated manuscripts, books printed before 1500, English books before 1800, fine bindings and autographs; the second, travel and topography. There is also a restoration and binding department.

The business dates back to 1826, although it did not take the name of Francis Edwards, son-in-law of the founder, until 1855. Five years later he opened a shop in Marylebone High Street, where the business flourished, but Francis died in 1875 and the eldest of his nine children — also Francis — was removed from school at the age of 15 to take over! The young man obviously had an aptitude for bookselling, and was largely responsible for the growth of the company. He remained as managing director until his death at 84 in 1944, when, because his son had other interests, the business (a limited company since 1927) passed into the control of other relatives and members of the staff rewarded for long service.

Alan Mitchell, who took over the business in 1979 (see 'Preface'), became a bookseller in most unusual circumstances. A geologist friend who had spent some years mining in South Africa and had acquired an extensive knowledge of books about that continent decided to become a full-time bookseller. His enthusiasm fired Alan, still at school, to come in and learn the trade. The plan might have been nipped in the bud when the geologist died from a heart attack while potholing, but the 19-year-old Mitchell decided to carry on alone. With the advice and encouragement of people in the trade, he learned the hard way, and eventually became an expert in his field. Throughout this period he worked from home, determined never to be 'tied' by a shop, but when the opportunity arose he realised that Francis Edwards was no ordinary shop. A staff of 22 includes nine booksellers and two trainee assistants.

Dawson's of Pall Mall, now **Dawson Rare Books**, 16/17 Pall Mall, SW1 (01 930 2515), is an impressive business started through an interest in old medical and scientific periodicals. Specialist collectors in the fields of science and medicine would find a visit rewarding because Dawson's carries one of the most comprehensive antiquarian stocks in terms of size and coverage. Dawson's also specialises in travel books, English literature (mainly of the 18th and early 19th century), natural history, economics, music, theatre and ballet — with outstanding stocks of early printed and manuscript music.

The shop is part of the William Dawson organisation, founded in 1805 as a newsagents and today one of the world's largest groups in the distribution of news media and books, incorporating its own publishing and advertising service. The organisation demonstrated its interest in Europe as long ago as 1925, when Dawson-France was launched to provide a two-way service in books and magazines.

The rare books business in Pall Mall was the brainchild of former group chairman Herbert Marley who in the 1930s, as an expert on old scientific journals, was frequently offered books from the same collections and decided he ought to learn something about them. Mr Marley's businesslike approach to this comparatively new sphere was typical of the drive and resourcefulness which took him in 40 years from office boy to chairman of a giant organisation. He has the distinction of being probably the only man in history who bought one million books in one bid. The drugs magnate, Sir Henry Wellcome, who through the Wellcome Foundation had amassed an incredible collection of principally medical and scientific books, decided in the 1950s to get rid of the books outside these categories. Stored at a warehouse in Willesden, this 'surplus' amounted to one million volumes. 'It was a ridiculously low offer alongside today's prices, and it was made without really expecting an acceptance, and without any idea of what to do with the books, or where to put them' Mr Marley recalls. Eventually, they were shipped out in three monthly instalments! The rare books department resided for some years in Wigmore Street, and then moved to offices above the present premises until able to get the shop. Other antiquarian shops in the group are: Bow Windows Book Shop, Lewes; and Deighton, Bell & Co, Cambridge, all issuing their own catalogues (see regional entries).

One of the virtues of having a good passing trade is not only to attract custom, but to bring in people with good books for *sale*. This is one of the ways that Barbara Grigor-Taylor of **Cavendish Rare Books Ltd**, 2–4 Princes Arcade, Piccadilly (01 734 3840) manages to maintain the high standard of her stock. About a half of around 4000 books, at an average price of £6, are general travel and voyages and there is a small but select literary section. An attractive long plate-glass frontage enables people in the busy arcade (running between Piccadilly and Jermyn Street) to see a cross-section of the books which are well laid out and effectively lit.

The shop was opened in 1974 under a different name with Barbara Grigor-Taylor as manager, and she bought the business three years later. Her own experience of antiquarian books is extensive, having served an apprenticeship with one of the doyens of the trade, John Howell of San Francisco. Then, having indulged her passion for sailing in the Pacific, she ended up in New Zealand where she opened and ran a bookshop for several years before coming to the UK. Still a keen yachtswoman, her love of the sea has been 'diverted' to a specialisation in mainly 19th-century books on maritime history, concentrating on the merchant service. The shop issues four catalogues a year, divided between travel and literature. ½ day Sat.

Appearances can be deceptive of course, and only a few yards away in Jermyn Street — the only bookshop in this famous street of shirtmakers — is **John Faustus**, at no 94 (01 839 3388), with a very sober frontage giving a rather daunting impression of exclusivity. Instead, the shop has a warm and friendly atmosphere, and of more than 15,000 books in the main shop practically all are general s/h and priced from £5, although some expensive items are kept separately. The emphasis is on fine bindings and literary sets. The shop opened in 1972 and is owned by Susan Hadidas of the Faustus Gallery just along the road at no 67/68, well known art dealers specialising in 16th and 17th-century Dutch masters. In recent years the bookshop has added a range of antiquities — largely Egyptian and Roman jewellery, bronzes and pottery, as well as etchings (eg Rembrandt), and although it has become a little more like a museum, don't be put off if you're interested in attractive books. Cl Sat.

Paul Minet is very much an innovator, an entrepreneur

with big yet realistic ideas. His **World of Books**, 30 Sackville Street (01 437 2135), just off Piccadilly, which he advertises as 'London's largest secondhand bookshop', is completely different to anything one would associate with a location as exclusive as Mayfair. It has 3,000 square feet of space divided between a vast L-shaped ground floor area with s/h books divided into sections by subject, and a basement for mainly non-fiction remainders, which Minet also sells by mail-order. This is the perfect contemporary browsing shop; no frills, no atmosphere to speak of, but thousands upon thousands of books. The shop has a sale of 3,000 volumes a week, the bulk under £3, and although this low figure may be helped by the large selection of fiction at 50p, the pricing policy also ensures good value in the non-fiction categories — predominantly travel, history, biography and cookery.

Paul Minet was brought up in a literary atmosphere and his mother used to sell books by post. By the time he was 21 he was following in her footsteps and operating from market stalls in towns around Devon. He was a well established bookseller, selling mainly by post from his home at Chichele, Newport Pagnell, when he became founder-publisher of *Antiquarian Book Monthly Review* in 1974, selling the company two years later. Meanwhile, having launched Piccadilly Rare Books, he opened what is now Cavendish Rare Books in Princes Arcade and, in the following year (1975), Minet's Book Emporium (now Green Knight Books) in St Martin's Court, before moving to Sackville Street in 1976, operating from next door to the present shop which opened a year later.

Turning over stock on such an enormous scale, one might imagine there were problems replenishing the shelves, but Minet has efficient links with specialist dealers who channel the unwanted stock bought at sales. Currently there are around 80,000 books in stock here, backed up by 300,000 in a warehouse at Wapping. There is also a smaller shop operating under the same policy at St Katherine's Dock, Tower Bridge (see separate entry).

Marlborough Rare Books Ltd, 35 Old Bond Street, W1 (01 493 6993), is on the second floor, so obviously not a conventional shop, but the offices are open to the public.

Started after World War II and run by Michael Brand, the company offers a smallish but select stock of pre-20th-century illustrated books, with impressive sections on fine printing, fine and applied arts and architecture. Mr Brand travels widely to keep his stock up to the standards with which he has become associated.

When Roderick Brinckman operated from Toronto I heard references to him as the best bookseller in Canada, but in 1980 Mr Brinckman, decided to settle his business, **Monk Bretton Books**, on the first floor of 107 New Bond Street, W1 (01 629 7084). Mr Brinckman started bookselling in 1972 after 14 years in publishing during which he built up a collection of private press books. Because of this interest he decided to specialise in finely printed books (roughly Kelmscott and later), and his catalogues earned him an international reputation; but after six years of trading he began to think about moving to the centre of things, New York or London. Being half-English and having spent a year at Hatchards in his first job, he decided to come here. Monk Bretton also carries a stock of illustrated books and something apparently out of character — a section on North and South America and the West Indies, together with American maps. Cl Sat.

Gray's Antiques Market at 58 Davies Street, W1 houses a few interesting bookdealers — such as **Mellor and Baxter** (01 629 7855), which deals only in antiquarian books, specialising in early printed books, scientific and medical works. The business is run by Douglas Mellor, formerly a scientist from Kansas, and Angela Baxter, and although it is possible to find the occasional volume for around £5, the stock, as one might imagine, is expensive. Cl Sat.

Also at Gray's is **M. & R. Glendale** (01 629 2851), specialising in illustrated and children's books, table games and ephemera. The business began 10 years ago with Victorian children's books, but mushroomed to encompass learning material dating back to the 18th and 17th centuries, and domestic history, ie fashion, cookery, herbals etc. Partners Monika Sears and Ruth Sands obviously take a deep interest in the period and subjects, and welcome browsers with like minds.

NORTH LONDON
(INCLUDING MIDDLESEX)

The fashionable transformation in the 1960s and 70s of what had long been run-down parts of Islington, Canonbury and Highbury did not, surprisingly, lead to an influx of dealers in the arts. In Islington, particularly near the Angel, there was admittedly an explosive growth in the number of antique shops and even art galleries, but no corresponding boom in books. The final straw came in 1981 when the popular **Compton Bookshop**, established in Upper Street, N1 since 1974, moved to Suffolk.

Just along the road at 186 Upper Street is **G. W. Walford*** (01 226 5682) which, although a shop in the conventional sense (Mr Walford having been on the site since 1948), is not open to casual browsers. A note in the window makes the point, requesting that would-be customers ask for any title in which they have an interest before entry. Solely antiquarian, the stock is quite large and is strong in plate books, travel and literary sets. *Strictly by appointment.*

No chance of getting lost looking for **Robert Temple: The King's Cross Bookshop**, 18 York Way, N1 (01 837 2711), because the shop is next door to the main line station. Run by Peter Allen, who obtained degrees in English and Philosophy before getting his initial bookselling experience with Henry Sotheran, the shop has a fairly large general stock (about 4,000 titles) with its main emphasis on lit but there is also a large warehouse where catalogue items can be inspected by appointment. These include specialities in modern 1st edns, detective (including Victorian triple-deckers) and science fiction and poetry — enough to justify nine catalogues a year. Robert Temple was founded in partnership with Andrew Carpenter in 1976 as a mail order operation specialising in antiquarian and modern 1st edns, and two years later when they took over the present premises, which had been run by Geoff and Anna Mullett since 1974, they retained the original business name. Unusual hours, designed to help workers in the area, noon–2.30pm and 4.30–7pm, six days.

A closer study of specialist subjects often reveals a permutation of interests. Quakerism, for example, interests not only the theologian but the sociologist and the historian, and indeed the **Friends Book Centre**, Friends House, Euston Road — directly opposite Euston Station — NW1 (01 387 3601), has a large clientèle. Owned by the Religious Society of Friends (Quakers), and originally started at Bishopsgate during World War I, the shop has a medium-size stock, including some new. Cl Sat.

Charles Higham (SPCK), Holy Trinity Church, Marylebone Road, NW1 (01 387 5282), under the management of Mrs Gill Thompson, with 'only' 20,000 volumes on show must still be the largest s/h theology specialists in London. I say 'only' in deference to those readers who remember the vast cavern of a shop in Charterhouse Street before SPCK took over in 1976, although it must be admitted that some of the stock in those days had been on the shelves from the beginning and would never move. Mrs Thompson is more conscientious about clearing out such material; quite apart from the economic factor, even the most fervent bibliophiles have to concede that *too* many unimportant books can be off-putting. Because theology is not easy to classify, the stock is helpfully set out in a number of bays, designated by letters with subject headings; within the bays are more detailed sections, all broken down into a wide variety of classifications.

Charles Higham, son of a printer and binder from Kent, entered the book business in 1869; it was founded seven years before in Farringdon Street. The construction of the Holborn Viaduct forced it to move and eventually the firm went to its famous basement premises in 1921. Having always specialised in theology and allied subjects, the emphasis at the start of the century was on sermons and hymnology. In 1905 Highams status was established by the publication of a catalogue of 4,000 vols exclusively on hymnology — a considerable bibliographical achievement (see also 'Rich Pastures').

In Bell Street, NW1, off the Edgware Road and a stone's

throw from Marble Arch, are three very traditional s/h book-shops: **Archives,** at 83 (01 402 8212), run by Timothy Meaker who took over from Edward Burns in 1978; **Greer Books,** a corner shop at 87 (01 262 7661) where Patrick Cassidy succeeded George Greer in 1975; and **Charles Duley** at 105 (01 723 8455), a couple of minutes from Marylebone Station.

Duley is really a misnomer since A. A. (Monty) Miles has been the proprietor since 1969, and has been associated with the shop since 1943 when, as a customer, he got into the habit of helping out. The traditional image of an old bookshop, it carries a small s/h stock, and is open six days. Mr Cassidy had been at W. A. Foster of Chiswick for five years when the opportunity came to buy **Greer's.** A small general stock in one room with a few prints and postcards. Cl M, and not open in the morning until 10.30. Mr Meaker spent a year at Quaritch before a spell in advertising and other retail areas to get a better idea of modern business. He sold books from a stall for several years before moving to Bell Street. Small general stock in one room; the shop also offers a bookbind-ing/restoration service. Six days.

The Hampstead Book Corner at Alfie's Antique Market, 13 Church Street, Marylebone, NW8 (01 724 2320) is so named because it began operations in Hampstead and the owners thought it would be even more confusing to change the name as well as their address. The present location is a six day 'supermarket' of self-contained shops or stands, which used to house several booksellers. However, Hampstead Book Corner alone is worth a visit if you are interested in children's books of all periods. In 1981 the partners went their separate ways, leaving Barbara Stone trading alone from this site. A second partner, Sheila Feller, opened **Unicorn Books** in an extension of Alfie's Antique market (01 724 2320), also specialising in children's and illustrated books. Both cl M.

To the best of my knowledge **Stephen B. Jones,** 46 Malden Road, Kentish Town, NW5 (01 485 6045) is the only bookshop in the country which sells *shelves* as well as books. Surprisingly large after the impression one gets from the street, the shop carries a medium-size stock, strong on lit and biography. Stephen Jones who began bookselling by post and with market stalls for eight years before moving to these premises in 1978, found that he was often asked where bookcases could be obtained, so started stocking them — with profitable results. Open Wed–Sat 11am–6pm and Sun 2pm–5pm.

The **Aviation Bookshop**, 656 Holloway Road, N19 (01 272 3630), near the Royal Northern Hospital, can justifiably claim to be the biggest aviation specialist operating from a shop — its only main competitor being a postal bookseller. Owned by Jack Beaumont who ran a similarly well known shop in Bath Street, EC until moving to Holloway in 1974, the shop carries several thousand new and s/h books on all aspects of flying (except fiction) in a main showroom, with a separate room for magazine back issues. The manager is David Hatherell who has been part of the operation since the 1940s when Mr Beaumont started on a part-time basis, opening up his garage to browsers. Today, the business has customers from all over the world. Six days.

Further along the High Road is **W. E. Hersant Ltd (The Cholmeley Bookshop)**, 228 Archway Road, Highgate, N6 (01 340 3869), founded in 1922 by the late Mr Hersant and carried on by his daughter Mrs Betty de Looy. Despite a colourful display of new children's books at the front, the shop specialises in aviation, military and naval history, and there is a good stock of s/h material in these subjects. Cl M and Th and lunchtimes.

Bonaventure, 259 Archway Road, N6 (01 341 2345) is run by Mr R. O'Farrell, an ex-oilman who opened in 1967 with a general s/h stock but specialising in oil and petroleum, Central and South America and travel. Cl M, Th pm and usually lunchtime.

At the top of the hill by Highgate Underground Station, the **Southwood Bookshop Ltd**, 355 Archway Road, N6 (01 340 6264), which is owned by Reg Read of the Divertissment bookshop (see 'Central London'), has a fairly large s/h stock with a few modern firsts. Prices very reasonable apart from 'bargain' section. Six-day week.

A few minutes' walk from the station along Southwood Lane — uphill but worth the effort — takes you to one of my favourite bookshops, **Fisher & Sperr**, 46 Highgate High

Street, N6 (01 340 7244), which has everything the bibliophile seeks — from a first-class stock to premises so steeped in atmosphere there is even, admittedly unsubstantiated, talk of a house-ghost! I have already mentioned the partially sunken annexe at the back, although the additional space has not noticeably increased the number of books on display so much as provided more room for the browser. The stock of some 50,000 items — virtually no new books — ranges from incunables to paperbacks, and those who have a wide interest can have a field-day. I have been in the basement, which houses cheaper fiction and part of a range of good topography, countless times — and found it a trifle chilly, although never eerily so; but the proprietor John Sperr maintains that customers' dogs object to going down and his own Siamese cat avoids it like the plague. Claims of psychic manifestation have never been proven, although a number of customers have testified to 'something' unusual; a woman cleaner left because of it, and indeed on one occasion a doctor had to be called to one man who was overcome by an allegedly ghostly experience in one of the upper rooms. However, to put things in perspective, John Sperr has never in 30 years' occupation experienced anything untoward, and if there is a resident from the spirit world he must be a kindly soul, because the premises are extremely pleasant.

The building, under a preservation order, is a timber structure dating back to the days of Charles II, and so is probably the oldest in London being used as a bookshop. The main beams throughout are original ships' timbers. Earlier known as the Cooper's Arms, and one of the 19 inns that were once open in Highgate Village (there are still 11), it became a bakery at the beginning of this century. Over the years, additions of architectural interest have included a fine 18th-century fireplace in the first-floor front room and a bow window installed in the 1920s. It did not become a bookshop for another 10 years or so, and was taken over in 1946 by a demobbed John Sperr, in partnership with T. E. Fisher. After 20 years, the partners went their own ways, with Mr Sperr retaining the Fisher & Sperr trade name. Six days but cl lunch.

One of the best collections purchased by Fisher & Sperr

was the result of an elderly clergyman calling in merely to use the toilet. On leaving, perhaps in less of a hurry, he noticed he was in a bookshop, and casually mentioned that he had a few books he might be prepared to sell — the 'few' needing two lorries to move them. But probably the most intriguing purchase was an antiquarian book with an integral lock, kept as part of a collection in a garden shed. It took several days to find a key to fit, when the contents were found to be a superb series of engraved erotica. The book, with lock intact, is now in the possession of a famous overseas library.

John Sperr, now living in the modern flat above his annexe which, because the shop is on top of a hill, has a spectacular view of up to 20 miles across north-east London, has a very broad knowledge of English literature and can be most helpful.

A most distinguished name in the antiquarian book world, **Peter Murray Hill (Rare Books) Ltd*** no longer has its well known shop in Chelsea, having moved to private premises at 35 North Hill, Highgate N6 (01 340 6959) in 1975 where visitors can be seen by appointment. One of the few firms to provide two presidents of the Antiquarian Booksellers Association, and certainly the smallest to do so, the business was founded by the actor Peter Murray Hill. In 1956, the year that he became president of the ABA, Mr Murray Hill was joined by the present owner Martin Hamlyn, who had been with one of the great names in bookselling, Robinson's of Pall Mall, until it closed. He too became president of the ABA (1972–3). Specialising in English 18th-century literature and social history, depicting the English character (very little is later than 1850), the firm became known for its attractively produced and interesting catalogues. Today the business is almost entirely by post. *Strictly by appointment.*

In view of its traditional associations with the arts, Hampstead could do with a few more bookshops, although shop rents are even dearer than in some parts of central London. The few that remain are very attractive and well worth a visit despite the parking headaches around the Heath and the High Street. Two are in Flask Walk, literally next door to the Underground station, a charming part-paved, part-cobbled passageway. **Stanley Smith & Keith Fawkes**, at nos 1–3 (01 435 0614), was opened by Mr Fawkes in 1972 on a smaller scale but in due course he was able to take over the shop next door and convert them into one. The 'new' shop has considerable character, being set a little below pavement level, and the floor to ceiling bookshelves are set out in corridor fashion throughout two very large rooms, housing more than 20,000 s/h and antiquarian books in most areas from fine bindings to paperbacks. In August 1977 Mr Fawkes, whose background is in antiques, was joined by Stanley Smith, a doyen of the trade, who had owned the Marchmont Bookshop (see 'Central London') for many years. The two had been friendly for more than 20 years, Mr Fawkes admitting that he acquired much of his knowledge of antiquarian books from the older man. The stock coverage is wide, but particularly strong on art, early theology and philosophy and early science. Six days.

Stanley Smith has obviously bought many collections in the years since he started bookselling in 1935, but the most unusual belonged to a good friend and customer who died 10 years ago. On arrival at the man's small flat, Mr Smith discovered over 35,000 books piled up in every nook and cranny, in places 10 deep. In addition there were 100,000 loose prints, as well as a wealth of books and photograph albums in the cellar, ruined by damp. The main collection, volumes dating back to 1750, took three months to clear.

Opposite, at no 6, is **The Flask Bookshop** (01 435 2693), run by Joseph Connolly since 1974 when he took over premises that had housed a bookshop since before the war. The stock of about 8,000 volumes, mostly concerned with the arts, modern firsts and review copies is housed in front and back rooms and a basement. The period lettering style on the black and gold fascia was designed and painted by the owner, formerly in publishing, who is the author of *Collecting Modern First Editions, P. G. Wodehouse: An Illustrated Biography & Bibliography*, and a critical biography of Jerome K. Jerome (1981). Cl M and Th.

The expiration of a lease forced Bernard Harrison to move from Hampstead proper down Rosslyn Hill to a site some people feel to be equally attractive in a different way, and in January 1980 open **The Village Bookshop** (so named because of the village atmosphere) 46 Belsize Lane, NW3 (01 794 3180). Mr Harrison and his partner Myrtle Smith, have a medium-size general stock but in recent years they have specialised in German language books with a stock of some 10,000 mainly of the 1900–1930 period. Art is among the other subjects carried, although surprisingly not a speciality since Mr Harrison was a professional artist who moved into books because he was tired of being asked by galleries to paint to order. He ran a stall in a West End antiques market before opening the Rosslyn Hill Bookshop which was very popular with browsers. Six days.

Although **Eric & Joan Stevens** open their shop at 74 Fortune Green Road, NW6 (01 435 7545), opposite Fortune Green, on Fridays and Saturdays only, they can be seen there by appointment for the rest of the week, since they use the whole building as offices and storehouse. Joan, a librarian by training, and her husband started full-time bookselling from their home in 1961, and opened this, their first shop in 1974 — although for a time they kept it as offices for a catalogue operation (they produce about six a year) and sold from another small shop in the same road. Three years later they decided to concentrate on the one outlet. The shop has a small but selective stock of 20th-century literature and 19th-century illustrated works. The latter interest was developed with their own publishing imprint, reprinting specialist books — the first a biography of the Victorian landscape painter, Samuel Palmer. Another strong section is feminism. Hours 10–6pm.

Before leaving the district (or on your way back to town) you might find it worth calling on **Albion Books***, 72B Fellows Road, NW3 (01 722 6708), run from a third-floor flat near Swiss Cottage by Richard Lucas. Normally I only list postal booksellers who have well laid out bookrooms, or are highly specialist, but Mr Lucas has a stock larger than many shops (10–15,000 vols) — tailor-made for enthusiasts who don't mind rummaging about in cartons and in odd corners. The other attraction is the low prices, cheap enough to draw a constant stream of dealers. *Strictly by appointment.*

Less than 10 minutes by car from Highgate — or from the opposite direction by bus from Finsbury Park Underground station — is the **Crouch End Bookshop** at 2 Topsfield Parade, Middle Lane, Hornsey, N8 (01 348 8966) which has been run by Marsha Carters since 1974. The shop consists of one large room housing a small but interesting general stock, but the size offers scope for development. Normal hours, although Mrs Carters divides her time between this shop and another with the same name 100 yards away at 22 Crouch End Hill which sells only new books.

Edna Whiteson, 343 Bowes Road, N11 (01 361 1105), which opened in 1974, is directly opposite Arnos Grove tube station. Mrs Whiteson, whose links with literature began when she worked for a publisher, started operating as a postal bookseller from home 15 years ago, keeping the bulk of her stock of modern firsts and local topography in the garage. In addition to her original interests, the shop carries about 10,000 volumes to include signed and limited editions, private press items, local material, railways, etc. She exhibits at most of the international book fairs, including four in the United States. Edna's husband Maurice, who concentrates on prints, runs a stall at the Dolphin Arcade in Portobello Road on Sat. Cl W.

Bibliophiles should not be put off by the name of **The History Bookshop**, 2 The Broadway, Friern Barnet Road, N11 (01 368 8568) because this shop, on two floors with over 2,000 feet of shelves, carries a good general stock of over 20,000 volumes. The business was established in 1964 by Graham K. Scott, but taken over by the present partners, Jonathon Prickett and Martin Gladman, in 1976. Because of its traditional strength in military, marine and aviation (equipment and uniforms as well as history), the shop issues several catalogues a year to customers all over the world, and in 1980 another specialist, David London, was brought in to concentrate on shop sales in these areas. Also strong in social sciences and topography. Six days. (NB The Broadway is not listed in street guides, so look for it between Macdonald and Stanford roads.)

Elliott Greenfield of **Ergo Books*** at 65 Salisbury Road, Barnet is one of our leading authorities on Sherlock Holmes — despite the fact he is not British but American. He also has a large stock of detective fiction, although as part of a gradual change towards 'better' books, and trying to contract his stock from three floors to two, the emphasis over the past year or so has been children's illustrated books, fine and allied arts, architecture and photography and modern firsts. However, Elliott does not neglect his interest in Sherlockania, or more particularly Conan Doyle. Having arrived in London after a four-year study spell in Paris following service in Korea with the US army 20 years ago, Elliott does much of his business at book fairs but will see people *strictly by appointment* at almost any time. Why is the business called Ergo? If you're interested I suggest you ask Mr Greenfield . . . (01 440 0240)

About five miles to the west and almost opposite Mill Hill railway station is **Lionel Halter**, 7 Hale Lane, NW7 (01 959 2936), who got into bookselling almost by accident. Mr Halter and his wife Hilary had run a printing service from the same premises since 1971. Like many others one day in 1975 Mr Halter decided to put a few old books from his own collection on the shop counter — for 15p each. They sold so quickly that customers asked for others, so the Halters put up some shelves . . . Today there is a general stock of approx 3,000 vols, plus a collection of signed limited editions. Printing is still carried out on the premises, but the emphasis is now the other way about. Cl in the week for lunch, and cl Sat but open Sun 10.30–1pm.

Literally round the corner are **John and Judy Trotter***, 16 Brockenhurst Gardens, NW7 (01 959 7615), who for the past five years have specialised solely in comparative religions and Middle East studies, although they do issue catalogues in other subjects also. But for visitors *strictly by appointment* (the Trotters spend much of their time at provincial book fairs) the stock available for inspection comprises Holy Land travel and Middle East (1,000–2,000 items), Egyptology, North Africa, Arabia, Near East and some Far East (500–1,000); Judaica, Hebraica, Old Testament studies and comparative religion (1,000–2,000). They also stock prints, maps and general ephemera of these areas and do their own binding when they have time. John specialises in a little known skill — the production of hand-marbled papers to his own design. These are usually required for the insides of half and quarter calf bindings, but some of his larger abstract designs have been bought to frame and hang as works of art.

Carnegie's, 37–39 High Street, Harrow-on-the-Hill, Middlesex HA1 (01 422 2179), opened by collector turned bookseller Ian H. Carnegie in October 1979, stocks only antiquarian books, apart from a small bookcase of modern firsts. A double fronted shop which used to be a branch of International Stores and still has some of the original shelving, which adds a touch of character to the place, Carnegie's carries a small but select stock — originally an 'overflow' from the owner's collection. A pleasant shop, attractively fitted, featuring sporting books, travel, topography and fine bindings; there is also a selection of prints. Six days.

Social sciences and the humanities seem to be a feature of bookshops in Middlesex, on the perimeter of north-west London, which might have something to do with the (relatively) clean air! Certainly one of the largest bookshops in the country devoted exclusively to out-of-print works on the subject is **Michael Katanka (Books) Ltd,** 103 Stanmore Hill, Stanmore, HA7 (01 954 0490), which has been established in its present building since 1968. It is a 10 minute pleasant walk from Stanmore tube station, through the interesting little 'village'. The atmosphere is one of efficiency, with never less than 70,000 items on display in 16 rooms, arranged by subject and in alphabetical order by author. The proprietor, a leading expert on his subject, knows his stock and can produce the book you want within seconds.

The shop, with two floors above, is of Victorian origin and was previously a bakery. 'Vertical' interests within the subject include social history, socialism and international affairs and there are large stocks of pamphlets and political ephemera, all of which attract visitors from throughout the world. Michael Katanka claims the shop is better known in countries like Japan than it is in the UK, probably because of the impressive catalogues issued from time to time. He is co-author of a number of books on the history of trade unions, including the Historical Association's *Trade Union Bibliography*. He has edited two volumes of Fabian Tracts and written (together with the poet Edgall Rickword) a life of Gillray and Cruikshank.

The Social Sciences Bookshop*, 74 Park Chase, Wembley, Middlesex (01 902 3659), is not a shop but private premises, although the owners Ray and Norma Feather do have a warehouse nearby. The business is included because a stock of 25,000 different out-of-print titles, all in the social sciences, can be inspected at the warehouse *by appointment*. Mr Feather is generous in his praise for the help and advice given him by Mr Katanka, and has developed his trade principally because of his own specialisation. His subjects include economics, politics, sociology, town and country planning, anthropology, the history of education (on which he has possibly the best collection in the country), criminology, psychology and psychiatry.

The business was started in 1968. Mr Feather was a social worker by profession, a book collector since he was 12 and had been a 'runner' (a scout) for friends in the trade. Realising the need for a specialist service, Mr and Mrs Feather set up on their own, selling mainly to libraries and the trade but also dealing with collectors. Nearest tube Wembley Park. From the M1, leave motorway at Edgware and take A40 through Stanmore.

Thomas Barnard Rare Books, 11 Windsor Street, Uxbridge (89 53829), a minute from Uxbridge Underground station, with its period box-window frontage, carries a large stock of general s/h material, prints and maps. Cl W and Sat pm. Mr Barnard, who ran an export remainder business from London between 1952 and 1972, also owns the **University Bookshop** farther along the road at no 50, which sells only new books and remainders.

WEST LONDON

Quality is the hallmark of **Baynton-Williams**, 18 Lowndes Street, Belgravia, SW1 (01 235 6595), which is really two shops in one: the firm's original speciality, prints made before 1860, is housed in one part (and unlike most print galleries this means no reproductions, no watercolours, drawings or paintings), and antiquarian books in the other.

The firm's founder, Lawrence Baynton-Williams began dealing in prints in 1926 in the vicinity, although after war service he started up again in Leatherhead before returning to London in 1954. Joined by his son Roger, who runs the business today, he moved again in 1972 to the present premises — only a few hundred yards from the original shop. It was not until three years later that the neighbouring premises were acquired to use as the book department. The stock is limited to what might be called 'important' atlases, colour-plate and illustrated books.

Roger Baynton-Williams, author of *Investing in Maps* (1969), was elected to the committee of the Antiquarian Booksellers Association and currently takes a particular interest in the fight against book thefts.

Peter Eaton (Booksellers) Ltd, 80 Holland Park Avenue, W11 (01 727 5211) reopened in November 1974 as possibly the first antiquarian bookshop purpose built in London for 50 years. Peter Eaton began bookselling in the area 30 years ago and the existing premises next door to Holland Park Underground, originally two small shops, were rebuilt as one large shop. The new showroom has extensive shelving on three sides to display a large range of s/h material, and a gallery roughly head-high covering approx one-third of the space for antiquarian books. Because it has been designed as a bookshop, one of the features is security; browsing among the general stock is unrestricted but access to the gallery is by electronically operated doors controlled by an assistant, placed in a position from which any part of the shop can be seen. The shop is managed by Susan Harvey, who joined the firm after a spell with Quaritch. Air-conditioning and carpeting, as well as the imaginative design, make this a model for modern bookshops. Six days.

Booksellers open one day a week, even if that day is Saturday, would not normally be eligible for the guide but when they are clustered together, as in the famous Portobello Road market, the site is obviously worth a visit from bibliophiles. **Books & Things** in the Dolphin Arcade, 157 Portobello Road, W11 is run by Martin Steenson, a cartographer by profession, who started the operation in 1972. Here he has a small general stock, with a bias towards 20th-century illustrated, decorative and graphic arts; also a selection of original posters and original book illustrations. In common with most of the stallholders, he closes around 4pm. The same arcade houses Edna Whiteson (see 'North London'), with husband Maurice specialising in prints.

In the Westbourne Arcade, where Westbourne Grove intersects Portobello Road, the biggest selection is offered by **Demetzy Books**, run by Paul Hutchinson who used to have a shop in Old Amersham, Bucks. This operation occupies a large corner of the arcade and offers an impressive stock ranging from fine plate books and general antiquarian to bound sets and general s/h. Nearby is another full-time bookseller, John Walwyn-Jones of **Questor Rare Books**, who spends the rest of the week dealing by catalogue. John, who went straight into bookselling from university, with spells at Richard Booth and Piccadilly Rare Books before setting up on his own, has a general stock of antiquarian, fine plate books, fine bindings, reference books, miniature books, panoramas, early photography and ephemera. **B. L. Bailey**, who also sells books from home, has a small but varied display in bookcases against a wall, taking in art and architecture, illustrated books, children's, travel and topography.

A fascinating innovation of 1980 was the concept of several young booksellers (some with shops, others mail order specialists) getting together to share large premises at **320 Portobello Road** (at the extreme northern end). Large numbers of inexpensive books are displayed under subjects, and with only the dealer's initials inside to identify them. This was obviously a break from the market tradition of separate stalls, and hopefully will catch on in different parts of the country. Open F and Sat, 8am–8pm.

Just around the corner from Barker's of Kensington an art gallery, **The Space,** opened on the first floor of 5 Young Street, W8 towards the end of 1980 to exhibit the works of young, unknown artists. However, in addition to the paintings there are approx 1,000 s/h books on modern art, design and related literature, art catalogues and artist monographs. Six days.

The Studio Bookshop, 123 Kensington Church Street, W8 (01 727 4995), started operations in 1946 not far from the present premises in a shop measuring 9 × 6 feet, without the bookshelves! At that time Jack Sassoon, who runs the business with his mother, was feeling his way in bookselling, having been trained in Egyptology and later working as an artist. However, they moved to the present main road site five years later and have filled two fair-size rooms (and a basement store) with an attractive mix of books, prints and selected greetings cards. The books range from 19th-century illustrated to selected quality remainders, although Mr Sassoon's speciality is Japanese books from the mid-18th century, a subject he collected before becoming a bookseller and in which he is something of an expert, although he finds the stock increasingly hard to replace. The small, carefully chosen range of greetings cards includes some hand-painted and, since many of the illustrations are of cats, this interest has spread to the book stock. Paperbacks are relegated to an outside shelf. Cl M.

Grey House Books*, at 12a Lawrence Street, SW3 (01 352 7725) which runs between King's Road and Cheyne Walk, occupies one of the delightful Queen Anne houses in the road, with 5–6,000 books distributed over four floors. The speciality is detective fiction, Victorian to the present day, true crime and criminology, with even paperbacks in the basement. The premises are open every day, but *by appointment only.* Readers interested in history will find the location fascinating. Apart from Tudor and Stuart associations, one can find the home of Tobias Smollett (marked with a plaque), while around the corner on the left in Upper Cheyne Row is the house of Leigh Hunt and nearby (in Cheyne Row itself) that of Carlyle, also both marked. William de Morgan's pottery stood on the corner where the two Rows meet, now occupied by a church.

Only a stone's throw away, on the other side of the King's Road, is **Lesley Hodges: The Costume Bookshop**, Queen's Elm Parade, Old Church Street, SW3 (01 352 1176) which specialises in fashion and related subjects, eg needlework and textiles. Lesley Hodges began as a postal bookseller in the same subjects in 1977, but opened the shop two years later. Although it has a double bay frontage the shop is quite small and the stock correspondingly so, although as with any specialist collection one can expect a reasonably comprehensive coverage. The shop is attractively laid out; walls lined with fashion or fancy dress plates and some original fashion designs of the Edwardian period. Apart from books and illustrations, there are also fashion magazines from the mid-19th century onwards. Cl lunch and ½ day Sat.

The dividing line between antiques and books is often a very thin one, which is why there are so many bookstalls in antiques markets up and down the country. Most bookstalls stick solely to books, but with others the transition is blurred; none more so than **Follies**, stands M6–M7 at Antiquarius, 135 King's Road, SW3 (01 352 1129), run by Melody and Harold Carlton (a novelist who writes under the name of Simon Cooper). The Carltons began operations from this site in 1974 intending to concentrate on the 1930s, selling everything from books to ceramics. First books took over, but in turn made way for ephemera. Today **Follies** claims to be the only retail outlet in England that mixes Victoriana with what might be called 'moderniana', ie Beatles, Disney etc. The books cover children's illustrated, woodcut books from the 1930s and photography. Journals include rare film magazines dated back to 1920. The sub-heading 'Fun and Fantasy of the 19th and 20th centuries' seems to sum up admirably the stock and scope of **Follies**. Six days.

Market trading is a way of life, and some people prefer the informality to the restrictions of running a bookshop. Peter and Adrian Harrington enjoy the atmosphere of Chelsea and the business they run, **Harrington Bros** has been at Chelsea Antique Market, 253 Kings Road, SW3 (01 352 5689) since 1972. Having begun their business lives as booksellers, they eventually concentrated on purely antiquarian material and today a stock of approx 10,000 volumes has no s/h or new at all. Because of the risk of damage caused by careless browsers only a few hundred books are displayed on their large stall in the body of the market, the bulk being available in a room upstairs. Apart from some general interest stock, specialities are illustrated travel, natural history, children's books and bound literary sets. Six days.

Chelsea Rare Books, 313 King's Road, SW3 (01 351 0950), was taken over in 1971 by Leo Bernard, another ex-publishing executive who dealt privately in books before taking the plunge with a shop. Approx 6,000 books on the ground floor range from modern firsts to English lit of the 18th century, although there are some older books. The basement carries art and architecture, prints and maps. Six days.

The large bookshop bulging at the seams with s/h books seems to be little more than a memory because of soaring rents and overheads. Fortunately there are still a handful about, and one is Nigel Burwood's **Any Amount of Books**, 103 Hammersmith Road, W14 (01 603 9232), 200 yards west of Olympia. Mr Burwood, who came to this site in 1976 after running a stall in the Portobello Road, believes in giving the browser a fair chance of finding the little 'pot of gold' tucked away, since virtually everything is priced very reasonably and the turnover does not give him time to spend hours 'screening' his stock. Outside are two stalls, with books on one priced at 20p and on the other at 10p (OAPs can take one free). Inside the stock is priced between 30p and £3, with a small section of scarcer books near his desk. There is a large basement full of 'forgotten' novels, what might be called 'slow moving' non-fiction and foreign books — but even this is turned over with a one-third off sale every three months. Mr Burwood's hobby is figurative book-plates, and he is sometimes tempted into selling or swapping items from his own collection. Cl M, hours 11am–7pm.

In terms of turnover in s/h and antiquarian books, the **Guildhall Bookshop**(s) is one of the country's most impressive operations. The main shop, an early Edwardian terraced building at 25 York Street, Twickenham, TW1 (01 892 0331) carries 60,000 volumes in various rooms on three floors and a basement and this is supported by a warehouse in Surbiton (see 'South London'). The business was started in 1956 by former interior decorator Alfred Wallis and his wife Berthe, operating from home. Their first shop at Kingston (Surrey) near the town hall (hence the name) was opened three years later, but when the area was redeveloped they moved across the river to Twickenham (1970). The stock had grown to giant proportions because in the early days Mr Wallis found it more practical to buy books in bulk, ie more cheaply. Gradually his coverage of most subjects became more and more comprehensive, so that eventually bibliophiles knew there was always a chance of finding what they wanted on his shelves. There are, for instance, 10,000 fiction titles arranged in alphabetical order and several thousand foreign language books, as well as large sections in most categories. Six days.

Specialist booksellers tend to have small albeit select stocks, but **Anthony C. Hall**, 30 Staines Road, Twickenham TW2 (01 898 2638) carries a large range of 50,000 volumes dealing with Russia and Eastern Europe, Middle East, Asia, Africa and European social history. Mr Hall set up on his own in 1966 after a 10 year 'apprenticeship' in the trade. He has a degree in Russian, and the stock includes a large number of books in that language. Much of this trade is carried on by catalogue, and as a conventional shop in other respects Mr Hall also has a small general stock. Cl W and Sat afternoons but available at those times by appointment.

Chater & Scott Ltd, who moved from Syon Park next to the motor museum to 8 South Street, Isleworth, Middlesex (01 568 9750), specialise in motoring and motorcycling books. The shop is run by Frank Stroud who took over a general s/h business 26 years ago after running a travelling lending library. Better known in the motor racing fraternity, Mr Stroud has small shops at Silverstone, Brands Hatch and Oulton Park which are open on race days. Now in a purpose built shop, browsers interested in this speciality will find a comprehensive range of some 2,500 different titles (English and foreign) in the new section, several hundred s/h and antiquarian books and 15,000 magazines. Six days.

Seal Books, 2 Coninsby Road, Ealing, W5 (01 567 7198), started in 1970, was the fulfilment of a dream of Elizabeth Lewisohn, an enthusiastic book collector for many years who persuaded her husband, a City businessman, that they should open a shop; a medium-size stock of predominantly out-of-print books (some antiquarian) in the fields of English lit, history, topography, travel and natural history. The shop, in a pleasant backwater of South Ealing, is open normal hours from W to Sat and closed in August. Mrs Lewisohn also has a bookroom in her house nearby, and this can be inspected *by appointment*.

G. L. Green, 104 Pitshanger Lane, Ealing W5 (01 997 6454), specialises in naval and maritime books, covering all aspects of the sea except yachting. The stock, in three rooms, consists of new as well as s/h, antiquarian, ephemera and postcards. Cl M and T.

SOUTH LONDON
(INCLUDING SURREY)

A bookseller to whom the shop is more important than the books — because it gives a tangible pleasure to so many people — is **Jane Gibberd: Secondhand Books**, 20 Lower Marsh, SE1 (01 633 9562). And this attitude is communicated by the general atmosphere, which is why people go back. Ms Gibberd aims to sell her stock as cheaply as possible, although she realises that it is the combination of desirable book and price that sells and not cheapness alone. The result is a turnover of around 20% weekly, which is high. The shop, with its small general stock, is situated in a busy lunchtime street market next to Waterloo station and opposite the Old Vic, although because of its close proximity to the South Bank complex it attracts early evening custom too. As well as s/h she carries a few remainders and s/h paperbacks. Cl. M, T and S to allow Jane time for buying, which she regards as almost more important than selling. Opening hours 11am—7pm.

In November 1980 the proprietors of the Atlantis Bookshop, Bloomsbury, opened a more general retail outlet, **The Well Read Bookshop**, 61 Roupell Street, SE1 (01 928 1828), partly to display their non-occult stock and partly to play their part in plugging the drain on disappearing s/h bookshops in London. The one roomed shop is set in an attractive Victorian conservation area — the road runs between Waterloo and Blackfriars Roads, thus attracting a healthy passing trade. The policy is to let demand influence the stock, but initially 10,000 vols (approx) cover a broad range of interest, strongest in lit, biography and science. Although the derivation of the shop name seems pretty obvious, the decision was taken because at the time the premises were found the Collins family actually discovered a well in the basement of their home. Open W—F, 11am—7pm.

For a shop specialising in maritime subjects, what better site could one find than close by the National Maritime Museum and the *Cutty Sark* at Greenwich? This was the conclusion of William Blackmore, founder of **Meridian Books**, when he opened at 7 Nelson Road, SE10 (01 858 7211), in 1968 — just 150 yards away. Mr Blackmore, a senior executive with a leading publishing house, had collected maritime books for many years, and hence his speciality. Today less than 15% of over 8,000 specialist books are new; the rest include a large section of 19th-century works, although occasionally one might find an interesting 17th-century volume. After a year Mr Blackmore and his partner A. M. Smith launched their own publishing imprint, Conway Maritime Press Ltd.

The Bookshop Blackheath Ltd, 74 Tranquil Vale, SE3 (01 852 4786), a corner site overlooking the Heath and one minute's walk from the railway station, has grown and is now three shops in one. Ownership was taken over in 1969 by Louis Leff, formerly a clarinet player with the London Symphony Orchestra, who runs it with John Beaumont who has his own specialist postal service in modern firsts. A typical browsing shop, the stock of approx 20,000 mainly s/h books is strong in travel, with London and Kent topography, lit and literary criticism. The basement offers fiction and theology. The shop has also published a couple of books on the district. Catalogues issued. Cl Th.

A bias towards the sciences at **The Bookshop, Crystal Palace**, 89 Church Road, SE19 (01 771 9719), is hardly surprising since the owner, J. S. H. Collins, was a laboratory technician before opening the shop 12 years ago. Situated between Crystal Palace and Gipsy Hill railway stations, less than 100 yards from the better known shop from which he moved in 1979, the shop carries approx 10,000 volumes of which less than a quarter are new. Despite the large section on scientific subjects, the contents can best be described as general out-of-print. Hours somewhat uncertain, so unless in the vicinity a telephone call is advisable.

Norman Shaw*, 84 Belvedere Road, SE19 (01 771 9857), near Crystal Palace station, has the largest stock of old boys' books in the country; a private house bulging at the seams with journals, comics, annuals and books housed in five storerooms on two floors. Mr Shaw, who spent the first part of his business life running shops on passenger liners, developed his collecting hobby into bookselling after the war. Having always been interested in boys' books, he gradually amassed a stock as a collector, eg buying whole runs of magazines and comics to get one or two special issues. Within a few years he was able to run the operation full-time. A fascinating stock, but *strictly by appointment.*

Terence Hillyer is an antiques specialist whose interest in books grew almost by accident when he began to examine the contents of libraries he had been buying automatically. His business, **Hillyers**, 301 Sydenham Road, SE26 (01 778 6361), has been operating for 30 years but the book stock, originally supplementing the antiques, has grown to approx 4,000 vols. Now, apart from 15p trays outside the shop, the books inside vary in quality and content; half the fun in this situation is finding items of interest among the chaotic assortment. Six days.

The shortage of out-of-print material and soaring rents are headache enough for booksellers these days, but W. S. Reading of the **Croydon Bookshop**, 304 Carshalton Road, Carshalton (01 643 6857), had to contend with a compulsory purchase order and close a well established business to make way for a new flyover — which is why the shop has a name slightly incongruous in Carshalton. In fact, Mr Reading opened his first shop in the town in 1958 before moving to the busier Croydon two years later, and is now only a few hundred yards from his first shop. Medium-size general stock of s/h and antiquarian books. Cl W.

The **Take Five Bookshop**, 5 Prince of Wales Terrace, Hartfield Road, Wimbledon SW19 (01 947 4850), near Wimbledon station, is owned by Paul Giuliani who was running a bookshop in Glasgow when in May 1980 his father died and he came south to take over. Take Five was already a bookshop when Mr Giuliani Snr arrived in 1976, although he introduced a bookbinding and repair service. A small shop with approx 5,000 general s/h books. Six days.

Relatively few booksellers in this country specialise in antiquarian books from France and Germany and **Nicholas**

Meinertzhagen*, who operates from private premises, 82 Ritherdon Road, SW17 8QG (01 672 2288), next to Tooting underground station, is obviously worth a visit from bibliophiles interested in foreign language books and Continental history. Although the stock is limited to between 2–3,000 items the subject categories are varied and (depending on the demands of his catalogue business) there are usually quite important books to be found. The business was started in 1978 after nearly 10 years in Europe where, in addition to historical research work, Mr Meinertzhagen was enlarging his collection, much of which went into stock. Collecting was obviously in the blood because previously he had amassed what was believed to be the second largest private collection of pre-1850 British railway books — which was also subsequently sold. *Strictly by appointment.*

In July 1974 **Michael Phelps** opened a new business at 203 Upper Richmond Road West (part of the South Circular Road), Barnes, SW16 (01 878 4699), after spells with a postal book service at Uxbridge and with Dawsons of Pall Mall. A general stock of several thousand volumes in a couple of rooms is biased towards Mr Phelps' special interest — the history of medicine, science and technology — and ranges from antiquarian to lower-priced items. ½ day W.

To many bibliophiles, the most enticing description one can give to a bookshop is 'chaotic', and from that point of view **The Baldur Bookshop**, 44 Hill Rise, Richmond (01 940 1214), is a browsers' delight. The large stock is, in fact, of a very high standard, taking in illustrated books, art and literary ephemera, including a number of items dealing with true murder cases — the owner, Eric Barton, being something of an authority on Jack the Ripper. The shop, just off Richmond Hill, was established in 1933, since when its reputation has grown on the personality and literary knowledge of Mr Barton. The hours are inclined to be unpredictable, so a phone call is advisable, although there are other interesting bookshops in the immediate area so that a trip (on spec) need not be wasted.

A few doors away at no 28, **The Book Bay** run by Jeanette White (01 948 0583) in the back room of an antique shop has a very small stock of children's books of the 19th and 20th centuries with some ephemera, including card games. Cl W but open Sun afternoons, although a phone call is advisable.

The problems of finding suitable staff made John Prescott of the nearby **Richmond Bookshop,** 20 Red Lion Street, TW9 (01 940 5512), experiment with a two-day week, Friday and Saturday. The result is that the shop, opened in 1965, is now busier and more profitable. A general stock of approx 15,000 volumes, predominantly 20th century, includes a fair number of review copies which, at first glance, makes the shop seem remainder-oriented, which is far from the truth. The theme is arts and humanities, with particular interests in history, philosophy, music, theatre, cinema, literary criticism and biography, art, poetry and architecture.

Within a few minutes' walk, in an attractive pedestrian precinct, is **W. & A. Houben,** 2 Church Court, Richmond (01 940 1055), which sells new books concerned with the arts but which has a small s/h department in the basement also. Dr William Houben and his wife Anne have owned bookshops in Surrey for many years; in 1960 taking over this shop which had been selling s/h books since the 1940s. In the new book section there is also a stock of 19th-century topographical prints, mostly of London and Surrey. ½ day W.

Derrick Nightingale, 32 Coombe Road, Kingston-upon-Thames, KT2 (01 549 5144) opened in 1977 near Norbiton station, after eight years of postal bookselling and still issues a monthly catalogue. A good s/h stock of approx 10,000 volumes restricted to the ground floor consists of about one-third antiquarian, but it is this section that pleases the Nightingales most. The shop specialises to some extent in 19th-century fiction, with an unusually large number of three-decker novels on display. However, coverage is wide and ephemera, prints and postcards are also stocked. Six days, cl lunch.

The Guildhall Bookshop (warehouse), rear of 8 Victoria Road, Surbiton KT6 (01 390 2552), which is also the administrative offices for the Twickenham shop (see 'West London'), is housed in two rooms and a cellar of converted banqueting rooms. Because of the requirements of office space, there are 'only' 30,000 volumes on display and, although this stock is quite diversified, it is what might be called 'better quality' than the bigger range at Twickenham, eg modern firsts and collectors' items. Alfred Wallis took the warehouse to accommodate his 'overflow' in 1964, five years after opening the first shop in Kingston. Although his policy of bulk buying was initially dictated by finances, Mr Wallis preferred a wide variety of books. Gradually he was able to acquire better items so that today this shop offers quality even more than quantity. Cl M.

The Cheam Book Shop, 32 Station Road, Belmont, Surrey (01 642 1234), in a quiet shopping precinct by Belmont station, scarcely merits a second glance — especially as the larger of two bay windows is crammed with antiques and novelties. But these unprepossessing premises (that is, from the outside) conceal one of the largest stocks of s/h and antiquarian books in the south of England. The proprietor, Bill Carter, ran the original Cheam Book Shop for eight years until August 1979, moving because the site was due for demolition. At a time when most men of his age (he is approaching 80) are thinking of the quiet life, Bill and his wife practically started again from scratch, not only gutting the new shop and installing bookshelves but laying out a rock garden area where customers can sit and have coffee between breaks in browsing — and breaks are needed because there are over 80,000 books on the premises and many more in store to bring the total stock to around 250,000 volumes.

The window of antiques is designed to invite interest because, unlike the previous shop, there is not much passing trade and initially Bill reasoned that he had to get people inside to attract others. Now that news of the enormous stock has spread, dealers and bibliophiles come from all points of the compass. Practically every subject is well covered and those in the shop and back room are merely an appetising selection. Outside at the back, separated by tables and chairs, is an attractive sign *The Book Shop*, which Bill managed to buy for 25p before he ever had a shop, affixed to the first of four air raid shelters (13ft × 8ft each). All were painted white, fitted with metal shelves and eventually carpeted. One is full of children's books, one entirely fiction, and the others of general interest. Any few inches of 'spare' wall are filled with paintings.

Bill did not start bookselling until he retired at 66 after a distingushed career in engineering (during the war he was assistant to the Director of Scientific Research). At first most of his books were technical, but because of the limited demand he gradually broadened the range of interest. Today there is little he does not sell and with books coming and going so quickly, fun can even be had delving into boxes not yet sorted. Obviously a 'must' for browsers, the shop is just outside the boundary of the London A–Z street map, so look for it a couple of miles south of Sutton railway station, just off the Brighton road at Belmont station.

The Antiqu'airy'un, 443 Stroude Road, Virginia Water, Surrey GU25 4BY (099 04 2749), was opened by Reginald Heath in January 1977 when he retired as a foreign exchange broker and, because he is not concerned with making his fortune in books, prices are usually attractive. Many thousands of s/h books — ranging from paperbacks at 10p to antiquarian items at £200 — are housed in the shop's one large room. As well as books, Mr Heath has a large selection of sheet music. The relative prosperity of the area enables Mr Heath to do most of his buying locally; because of his reputation of paying reasonable prices he is frequently able to pick up large private libraries. The stock is general because he tends to put vertical interest books, eg gardening or fishing, on one side for specialist dealers who will take the lot. However, it is quite strong in 19th-century art, foreign language books (not on display) and academic books. Cl W and for lunch.

Thomas Thorp, 170 High Street, Guildford, Surrey GU1 (0483 62770), was established in 1932 after the founder had become known in bookselling circles through his lively business in Cecil Court. He returned to London soon afterwards to smart premises in Old Bond Street, leaving his younger son Hugh to run the Guildford operation, which is found at the top of the famous High Street.

There is little to indicate from the small frontage, with the name 'Constitutional Hall' above the front door, that the shop is one of the largest in the country. Rambling rooms and corridors stretch back and open into a large hall which was used during the 19th century for public and political meetings among other things — hence the name. Spread about the shop is a huge stock of around 100,000 vols, comprising a mixture of s/h in various subjects, new books and remainders. Catalogues containing about 2,000 items chosen from recently acquired stock are occasionally issued. Visitors to Guildford will be interested in the famous Royal Grammar School nearby. Six days (also see 'Central London' section).

Substantial losses of antiquarian books have meant that visitors to **Charles W. Traylen,** Castle House, 49–50 Quarry Street, Guildford, Surrey GU1 (0483 72424), these days need to ring the front doorbell. Collectors are still welcome and the stock is first-rate but 80% of the shop's trade is by catalogue. The business was started by Charles Traylen, who began in bookselling as an apprentice with Galloway & Porter of Cambridge more than 50 years ago and started on his own in 1945. He has become one of the most distinguished names in the trade, respected throughout the world.

Castle House dates back to before the 16th century when it was included in the grounds of Guildford Castle, and a court was held here in 1555 during the reign of Queen Mary. Little is known of its history during the next 200 years but in 1826 it was a gentlemen's boarding academy. After World War I it became an antique furniture gallery and remained so until 1959, when purchased by Mr Traylen. Today the large stock fills 21 rooms in an attractive, rambling house which still retains many of its original oak beams and a very fine stair-case. Stock is arranged under subjects, and in alphabetical order, so that the small staff can tell within a minute or so whether a book is available. Mr Traylen's son Nigel, who used to run Beeleigh Abbey Books, has now joined the business. To the rear of the shop is a pleasant garden directly beneath the Castle mound, and nearby is the house where Lewis Carroll, creator of 'Alice', died in 1898.

With the town so well served with major shops it might seem surprising to add a postal bookseller but **Trevor Coldrey***, 8 Recreation Road, Guildford, Surrey GU1 1HE (0483 33177), is worth a visit from those interested in lit criticism and biography in which he carries a stock of around 15,000 vols. All are modern (mainly academic) books which might be described as sources of ideas as opposed to *objects* *d'art*, but coverage is broad — from Greek tragedy to contemporary satire. Trevor gave up lecturing for full-time book-selling in 1976 and the books, all reasonably priced, are in three rooms and a hall. The house, near the College of Technology, is reached from Chertsey Street which starts at Thomas Thorp. *Strictly by appointment.*

THAMES, CHILTERNS
AND COTSWOLDS

Even in university towns antiquarian and s/h books are being muscled out by new books, paperbacks and remainders. However, although the icy trade winds have been felt in Oxford, the city's bookshops are still vigorous, rich hunting-grounds for book enthusiasts.

Blackwell's are so large that the main shop is in Broad Street, Oxford, while specialist shops (art, music, children's) are in separate buildings and the Rare Books department has moved eight miles away to a 14th-century manor house at Fyfield. The move, in 1979, was part of a comprehensive review of the company's policy and signalled a new era in its history. For some time the massive Blackwell's operation had been dominated by new books, and there was a danger that, in common with other giants such as Foyles and Heffers, there would eventually be no room for s/h and antiquarian books. Fortunately, the directors stopped to reflect on the future and took some very positive steps not only to stop the slide but actually develop the s/h and antiquarian activities as two 'new' and separate entities.

Although the present business was founded by Benjamin Henry Blackwell in 1879, the true history of the family's involvement in bookselling goes back another 30 or so years to the time when his father ran a shop in High Street, St Clement's, in addition to his duties as first city librarian — the strain of two jobs contributing to his death at the age of 42. His young widow was determined that the name should be restored to the list of Oxford booksellers. After giving her eldest boy the best education she could afford, she apprenticed him at the age of 13 to a local bookseller, where he received a wage of 1s a week, with an annual increase of another 1s. For nine years, young Blackwell learned about books — while continuing his own education.

The potential of the young man so impressed one old lady that she lent him £150, and he opened his shop at 50 Broad Street. A company history records that credit was very elastic in those days, and the earliest ledger shows that in November 1879 Dr Jowett, Master of Balliol, bought *Diodorus Siculus*, translated by Cogan, folio, 7s 6d, and paid for this in March 1881! But despite such cash-flow problems Benjamin prospered, took over no 51, and from that time until 1938 when nos 48 and 49 were rebuilt and joined to the existing shops the frontage remained unchanged.

Not surprisingly, over the years Blackwell's became a meeting place for dons and undergraduates, and the many Rhodes scholars returning home sowed the seeds of the company's vast overseas postal business. The guiding genius for so many years, Sir Basil Blackwell (known to most of the staff as 'the Gaffer', and in his early 90s still reputed to get to the office at least 20 minutes before the rest of the team) was born above the original shop in the room which is now the chairman's office. Today there is a third generation of the family in the business.

Like other major bookshops in university towns, Blackwell's has been happy browsing ground for men of eminence standing alongside young men and women whose academic future lies ahead. John Masefield commemorates the shop:

> There, in the Broad, within whose booky house
> Half England's scholars nibble books or browse;
> Where'er they wander blessed fortune theirs . . .

The most impressive change was the move in 1979 to what is now **Blackwell's Rare Books**, Fyfield Manor, Fyfield, Abingdon, Oxon OX13 5LR (0865 390692), a pleasant and historic village which boasts a famous restaurant converted from a 15th-century chantry. This is a complete contrast to the cramped operation at Ship Street with its attendant parking problems, which housed the department for many years. Peter Fenemore, the manager, regards his adapted manor house with its large stock of antiquarian and modern collectors' books displayed in such comfortable surroundings as 'one of the finest bookshops in the world' and, even

102

allowing for parental pride, it must be worth a visit from any bibliophile. The manor house has extensive grounds in which less dedicated members of the family could pass the time after looking round the village. Six days.

A large 'purpose built' (converted office area) second-hand bookroom is now housed on the second floor of Blackwell's Broad Street premises (0865 49111), holding general and academic books from various parts of the Blackwell's operation. Naturally, in a university town and by tradition the business is very strong on academic texts, but the stock is comprehensive and covers most subjects.

In addition to this 'new' department, some of the specialist sections in the Norrington basement room (see 'Rich Pastures') also hold stocks of s/h books, notably oriental and Africana, theology and philosophy, psychology and education. S/h and antiquarian books on music and sheet music can be found in the **Music Shop** in Holywell Street nearby.

What used to be part of the Blackwell's operation, known for many years as the Turl Cash Bookshop (the 'Cash' part is a relic of the days when it was common for customers to have accounts, and an owner who broke with tradition and offered discounts for cash), was taken over and extensively altered in 1980 by Ken Swift who had run the popular shop in Cowley Road for the previous seven years. The new shop, at 3 The Turl, Oxford (0865 40241) called **Swifts of Oxford**, is likely to acquire an even greater reputation because of its 'new' character and Mr Swift's style of bookselling (eg despite its size, the Cowley Road shop had armchairs installed so that browsers could read in comfort). Mr Swift, motivated by his own experience as a browser, has always set out to make customers feel at home, and has an obvious instinct for business. The shop has a general s/h and antiquarian stock, with an emphasis on Oxford material, English lit, and illus books.

The story of the conversion is fascinating. In 1978 it was discovered that the medieval building — originally comprising two small shops and living accommodation on three floors above — was unsafe. Having been built on the vaulted cellars of the 13th-century Mitre Hotel, it was slowly sinking down and forward into the street. The front and the roof of the building are listed, so all internal floors and walls had to be removed very carefully, a web of steel supports introduced and new floors installed. Student accommodation was provided on the upper two floors. When Lincoln College granted Mr Swift the lease to the two-storey shell beneath he decided to redesign the interior, creating a gallery on the upper floor using oak shelving from an old private library round the walls and a balustrade, staircase and panelling in new oak from nearby Bagley Wood. The waist-high shelves, which serve as a balustrade round the central well, also support a picture rail from which framed engravings are hung. Six days, cl lunch.

Diana Burfield took over Ken Swift's shop at 76 Cowley Road (0865 726909) in September 1980, renaming it **Artemis Books** — an association with her christian name. Diana's career has been divided between academic study and publishing, and to some extent her stock reflects those interests. After her first degree in psychology and anthropology she worked on the famous *Argosy* magazine in the 1950s, later becoming editorial director of Tavistock publications, producing books on the human sciences. Although she took over a good general s/h stock of around 10,000 volumes from Ken Swift, she has attempted to strengthen the human sciences and introduce books by women writers and covering feminism. Cl M, cl lunch.

If a visitor returning to the city after an absence of several years called on **Sanders of Oxford Ltd**, 104 High Street (0865 42590), another old-established business, he might be forgiven for assuming it was no longer a bookshop. Almost the whole of the ground-floor gallery is taken up with old prints, maps, drawings and watercolours (some good bindings remain). However, on the first floor the antiquarian and s/h range is larger than ever, with a large well stocked folio room, a second room for 19th century and later, including modern firsts, and a third for rare volumes. The original business changed hands when the founder sold to Lord John Kerr of Sotheby's, who in turn sold to the present owners in 1963.

The premises were originally a 16th-century pilgrim's

hostel, later to become known as Salutation House. The basement reveals vestiges of a blocked underground passage believed to have been connected with the Crown Inn in Cornmarket. The darker recesses of this and other parts of the ground floor are viewed by the staff with some apprehension in view of the building's age. Startled cleaning ladies have been tapped on the shoulder by 'someone' who was not there, while on the upper floor — among the books, readers will be pleased to know — assistants have reported seeing a blurred monkish apparition. However, there is no valid evidence of a ghost, and bibliophiles are unlikely to be allowed to stay the night to prove the point. Three catalogues a year. ½ day Sat.

One place that never changes is the scholarly (as befitting university booksellers) but charmingly Dickensian **J. Thornton & Son**, 11 Broad Street, OX1 3AR (0865 42939), established in 1835 by a nonconformist minister, the Rev John Thornton, for his son Joseph — whose own sons inherited the bookselling bug. The brothers operated from separate shops with James in the High Street also publishing a literary journal, *The Spirit Lamp*, with contributors of the calibre of Oscar Wilde, Lord Alfred Douglas and Max Beerbohm. When James died at the turn of the century — reputedly through overwork — his stock was transferred to the Broad Street shop run by his brother, grandfather of the present owner John Thornton. The disordered mass of books in the front window is enticing enough and a journey into the interior is no let-down as one wanders through a pleasant rabbit-warren of book filled rooms on three floors. A very large stock specialises in the humanities, and is particularly valued for its collections on Arabia, Persia, Turkey and Ethiopia and of Hebraica. In addition to the large shop there is a warehouse at the back to which some customers are admitted. ½ day Th.

Robin Waterfield, one of the most distinguished names in antiquarian bookselling, has retired but **Robin Waterfield Ltd**, 36 Park End Street, OX1 1HJ (0865 721809), provides an impressive legacy. The shop with its deceptively small frontage is actually part of a furniture warehouse and occupies only part of the ground floor of the building, but with three floors above full of books it offers the browser a general stock of approx 75,000 volumes, with specialities in English lit, academic books and modern firsts. It was opened by Mr Waterfield in July 1977 after a colourful career which began as a partner of David Low in Cecil Court between the wars, after which he had his own shop in London before deciding to spend several years as a missionary in Iran. On his return he resumed bookselling by post from Abingdon while the stock grew and another shop became inevitable. Today it is run by eight full-time staff (plus several part-timers) led by directors James Fergusson and John Stephens. Six days.

A relative newcomer, although he had lived in Oxford for many years, is **Brian Carter**, 43 High Street, OX1 4AP (0865 726466), who opened in September 1979. The shop specialises in theology and because of the limited space stock is restricted to about 3,000 titles of mainly scholarly books and church history, as opposed to devotional works. There are also a few general interest titles. The business is run by Brian and Elizabeth Carter, who have both been involved in the antiquarian and s/h trade for many years and have written on collecting theology and novels. They returned to the city from Hay-on-Wye where, with larger premises, they carried a much wider stock. Many of the rooms in this area were once occupied by students later to become famous; Compton Mackenzie once lived above the book shop. Regular catalogues. Six days.

Elgin Court Bookshop, 2 Market Place, Woodstock, Oxon (0993 812 888), on the first floor of an 18th-century listed building next to the Town Hall, has unusual origins. It is owned by Elgin Court Designs, publishers of greetings cards specialising in Edwardian and Victorian themes, which had amassed a collection of reference books used as inspiration for its designs. Since it already had a gift shop on the ground floor it was decided early in 1979 to open a bookroom above using the reference books as a nucleus. The stock, only s/h and antiquarian, is obviously strong on illustration, and specialities are children's and other illustrated books, local Oxfordshire history, field sports, coaching and inns, highwaymen and smugglers, old England and country life in general. Woodstock is, of course, identified with Blenheim Palace, the birthplace of Winston Churchill who is buried in nearby Bladon. Six days.

Jenner*, The Manor House, Church Enstone, Oxon, OX7 4NL (060872 273), is probably the only bookseller in the country specialising exclusively in old and rare medical books — as opposed to a few competitors who also deal in scientific books. The business has been run by Dr Nicholas Dewey (ironically a doctor of philosophy not medicine) since 1975 after his return from the United States where he had lectured and written on the history of medicine. It started when he issued a catalogue of his own collection. The stock is still small because of its very nature, and even those with an interest in the subject are advised to check first with Dr Dewey. The business is named after Edward J. Jenner (1749–1823), the physician who originated the practice of vaccination and whose family is believed to have occupied the property, a late 17th-century early 18th-century manor house — if that is not too grand a word for what is a tiny hamlet. *Appointment necessary.*

Shops in towns which are tourist attractions tend to gear their activities accordingly and **The Cotswold Bookshop**, High Street, Burford, Oxon, OX8 4QD (099 382 3308), has its busiest day on Sunday. Opened in 1971 by S. E. and B. J. Taubenheim, who had operated as postal booksellers for some years, the shop carries a wide stock, the only speciality being a fair-size collection of German books. The latter category is for the benefit of tourists, although coincidentally Siegfried Taubenheim is a German prisoner-of-war who settled here at the end of the war. His interest in books was started by the need to 'educate' himself and learn English, and developed into a deep affection for literature. Working as a head gardener in a convent, he began to buy — one of his early purchases being a Newton 1st edition — until the time when, with his wife Jean, he started selling unwanted copies. Usually open all week.

The **Banbury Bookshop**, White Lion Walk, Banbury, Oxon, OX16 8UD (0295 52002), is built on the site of the stables of an old coaching inn, the White Lion, which still stands, its walls adorned by a 300-year-old wistaria. With new books on the ground floor, the s/h department is upstairs and offers a general stock, strong in topography, modern fiction, Victorian children's books and illustrated books. Owned by Dianne Coles, the shop is situated in a traffic-free precinct just off the High Street, a minute's walk from her previous shop in Church Walk. ½ day T.

Gillian and Ralph Stone are booksellers with a reputation for doing things in style and when they moved from their lovely surroundings at Totnes, Devon in August 1979 it was not surprising that they found a place with even more atmosphere. **Titles: Old Post Bookshop**, Church Street, Shipton-under-Wychwood, Oxon, OX7 6BP (0993 831156), is on the site of the oldest registered post office in England, which until it ceased to be a post office three years ago was listed in the *Guinness Book of Records*. The present building, overlooking the village green, replaced a cottage destroyed by fire in 1909 and is therefore only Edwardian but the buildings nearby have historic associations — the church is mainly 12th century and the Shaven Crown pub with its perpendicular windows was once a rest house for the monks of Bruern Abbey; it also has links with Queen Elizabeth I who is supposed to have stayed and enjoyed herself there when hunting in the Royal forest of Wychwood.

Mrs Stone is a founder-partner in the Quarto Bookshop (see 'Scotland') and in 1972 joined forces with her husband, formerly in industrial management, to open a shop in Torquay. Two years later Titles moved to Totnes where the Stones began to specialise in the environment and agriculture. Today this represents the largest section of their stock of around 10,000 s/h and antiquarian books, and includes important 18th-century agricultural books, domesticated animals, organic farming and country books, geology, natural history, topography, travel, major constructions (docks, bridges etc) and town planning. However, there is also a good stock of books of wider interest, eg art, lit, history, children's etc and maps and prints. Located 4 miles north of Burford on the A361, the Old Post bookshop is open six days a week.

Compared to abbeys and stately homes, a World War II air raid shelter cum ARP control post may not sound very romantic, but when it carries a stock of 60,000 s/h and antiquarian books in six rooms one has to sit up and take notice. This is the 'shop' of **Checker Books**, 2 Checker Walk, Abingdon, Oxon (0235 28172), run by Mr and Mrs O. Weir who owned the popular Dene Bookshop in the town for 20 years. When the Weirs realised that the new owner was only interested in new books they bought the air raid shelter, complete with its own private parking, and started up again. However, the 'store' is only open in the mornings when Mr Weir puts up a board with a single word: 'Books'. Checker Books carries on a postal business and is therefore not dependent on the passing trade, although there happens to be a healthy custom due to the Weirs' reputation locally and because people have to walk past to get to the River Thames and the medieval remains of Abingdon Abbey. Those who cannot get there in the mornings should ring for an *appointment* (I suggest playing safe and check in advance for mornings too).

The Invicta Bookshop, 8 Cromwell Place, Northbrook Street, Newbury, Berks (0635 31176), consists of two 18th-century cottages joined by the demolition of part of an interior wall, set in one of the relatively unchanged corners of the town, 10 minutes' walk from the railway station. Started by Peter and Dorothy Hall at the end of the 1960s, the shop carries a general s/h and antiquarian stock of some 5,000 vols. Friendly atmosphere. Cl M, W and lunchtimes (except Sat).

I cannot think of any county that has more antique shops per square mile than Berkshire. The historic town of Hungerford alone has 25, but thankfully the bibliophile is not completely neglected. **Blakeway Books**, 13 Bridge Street (04886 3581), is a pleasant shop in an 18th-century building by the Kennet and Avon canal bridge in the town centre. Mr Michael Blakeway, a retired teacher, has written several popular books on history so it is not surprising that the stock should have a bias towards history and lit. Coincidentally, the Blakeways supplement their income by letting rooms for bed and breakfast — what greater attraction to browsers than to stay above a bookshop! Cl M and Th, although on these occasions it is usually worth ringing the bell since the Blakeways also live above the shop.

A bookshop which has everything — a first-class stock, a romantic history, a fascinating old building and even an 'identified' ghost — is **William Smith (Booksellers) Ltd**, 35–39 London Street, Reading, Berks, RG1 4PU (0734 595555). A serious fire at the end of 1973 devasted the antiquarian section of the building, reducing the stock from 12 rooms to just one long room and a catalogue room, so that currently about 50% of the books are new. However extensions, handicapped because the premises are scheduled for preservation, were carried out in 1974 and the antiquarian side gradually rebuilt. Today it has a good stock of non-academic books but confined to the same small area.

The business was established in 1832, although its origins go back another 100 years, but parts of the building date from the 17th century when it was used as a meeting house for Quakers, one of the congregation being William Penn. The ghost was first spotted a few years ago: the manager of the antiquarian department at that time was walking up the stairs leading to the old meeting house (then used as a storeroom and now accounts) and saw a figure at the top. The apparition, tall, dressed in black Puritan clothes with steeple-crowned hat and large white collar, looked at him but did not move. Gradually it became indistinct and faded away. The same figure, somewhat hopefully believed to be William Penn, was seen a second time; and although there have been no other witnesses, several members of the staff have since complained about feeling 'something uncanny' when walking through the room.

Before the present company was established, one of the early proprietors was John Newbery (b1713), an intimate friend of Dr Johnson and of Oliver Goldsmith and 'the philanthropic publisher' of St Pauls' Churchyard in Goldsmith's *Vicar of Wakefield*. In 1832 the business was bought by George Lovejoy, who moved with it to its present site. It was he, establishing a lending library, who developed the company, winning as customers and friends literary figures of the calibre of Dickens, Thackeray and Browning. The name of the shop changed in 1910 when it was bought by William Smith, who had for many years been associated with Mr Lovejoy. Today it is owned by Blackwell's and Oxford

University Press. Ten minutes' walk from the railway station through the town. Six days.

Quick turnover is the policy of the **Bargain Book Centre**, Bristol and West Arcade, Friar Street, Reading, Berks (0734 594263), opened by David and Diana Clarke in the centre of the town in 1974. Approx 5,000 s/h vols are displayed round the walls of a single-room, modern lock-up shop, with a similar number of remainders on a unit along the centre. David Clarke, formerly operations manager for the London Assay Office, and Diana, deputy librarian with the Royal College of Nursing, had plans for expansion and four years later opened another, similar shop in Bristol. Six days.

The attractive adjoining towns of Eton and Windsor, with their array of tourist attractions, are surprisingly lacking in s/h bookshops but there is a small but select display to be found at the **Eton Antique Bookshop**, 88 High Street, Eton, Berks (95 55534), which opened in 1975. A few thousand volumes, mainly turn of the century but usually fine leatherbound, are arranged in one smallish room in charming black and white double fronted premises. Open six days plus Sun pm, but cl ½ hour lunch. The proprietors, Danielle Kernec and Frank Savage, formerly book collectors who moved into selling six years ago, opened a second shop, the **Crown Antique Bookshop**, 5 Crown Lane (off the High Street) High Wycombe, Bucks (0494 40959), in 1976. Because these premises are slightly larger the shop tends to be a 'sorting house' for new stock, with the better quality items going to Eton; the stock here tends to be general s/h, with no specialities. Antique and modern prints are mounted and framed on the premises for sale in both shops. Six days, cl lunch 2–3pm.

Peter Bullimore Books, The Broadway, Farnham Common, Slough, Bucks (02814 4979), has really been two shops in one since September 1980 when it absorbed the shop next door — The Little Bookshop owned by Jean Pratt the specialist in cat books, who continues to operate from an office at the rear (to view her stock, however, a phone call is advisable 02814 3144/4979). Peter Bullimore MA, who gave up teaching for bookselling and opened on this site in the centre of the town in March 1978, has developed the business considerably, keeping the interest as broad as possible and now offering a mixture of antiquarian, s/h and new books, with a selection of prints and postcards etc. His policy is not to specialise in any way. ½ day M, W and cl lunch.

Another family business which has grown impressively in a comparatively short time is **Weatherhead's Bookshop Ltd**, at 58 Kingsbury, Aylesbury, Bucks (0296 23153), although the shop is in fact situated on the edge of the town's attractive main square. The founder, Frank Weatherhead, opened his first shop in Folkstone, Kent, after a career in the trade mainly with B. T. Batsford in London. He was joined by his son, also Frank, in 1931 and when the seaside town was evacuated he moved back to his home town. In 1948, two years before the death of the founder, the much expanded business moved to considerably larger premises where it has remained. Nicholas Weatherhead joined the firm on leaving school in 1956 and has concentrated on expanding the antiquarian side. Like many of the larger bookshops, Weatherhead's does not have the time to keep tabs on the exact size of its stock, but a recent estimation is around 150,000. Many of these are new, although it is the racks of cheap items by the front door, as well as the selection of s/h books in the window, that draw the bibliophile inside. The antiquarian department is upstairs and there is also a range of s/h books under subjects, down to a large collection of 'cheap' fiction — something increasingly rare now that the cost of shelf space is so high. In addition a well laid out storeroom a few minutes' walk away can be seen *by appointment*. Six days.

Lilies*, Weedon, Aylesbury, Bucks (029 664 393), with books in 35 rooms from basement to second floor, is well worth a special visit. With such a vast stock, subjects are housed in separate rooms with modern English literature and cheap fiction, at least, in alphabetical order. In 1980 Mr Eaton upgraded his stock — getting rid of around 30,000 volumes (to charity) but keeping one room of fiction, about 4,000 titles, at 50p. A rare book room was made available to selected customers. Peter Eaton has a detailed outline history of Lilies, in which he records not only the cultural background but the fact that the first dinosaur remains found in England were dug up in the woods here.

There have been a succession of houses on the site, dating back to pre-Domesday Book (1085), and many illustrious owners. It was the home for many years of the Lee family — ancestors of the famous American General Lee — and Lord George Nugent, author and authority on North American Indians. Lord Nugent and his wife had a large circle of literary friends, whose visits are commemorated in the stone seats and Latin inscriptions in the spinney; among them Harrison Ainsworth, Douglas Jerrold, first editor of *Punch*, and Robert Browning. Other literary associations are provided by Dickens, who planted some of the trees in front of the house, and John Cowper Powys, whose death mask is one of the 500 miscellaneous items in the small museum on the second floor of the house. *Appointment necessary.*

The Cottage Bookshop, Elm Road, Penn, Bucks (049 481 2632), is a delightful place, attractive enough to feature on the dust jacket of the last edition. Fred Baddeley, always a book enthusiast, started the business almost by chance in 1950 when the premises were partly let. He put a couple of dozen books in a home-made bookcase in the central passage of the cottage and offered them for sale at 1s each. He was not even sure who, apart from his tenants, might buy, but at the end of the day a dozen had been sold and the bookshop was launched. During the next few years the Baddeleys undertook the conversion of the first floor for storage and eventual opening to the public and of the roof area to form a second floor; and an extension to the main building. Then, as tenants made way for books, the whole of the ground floor was redesigned, an old beamed fireplace being uncovered and shelving built around. Today the stock of 50,000 good general s/h books, with a healthy trade in paperbacks, is open for inspection six days a week. The shop is indeed a picture, and a must for booklovers. A day-trip from London by car could easily take in Penn with (say) Weatherhead's or the Lilies.

Almost next door in Elm Road (the address is 'By the Pond') is the **Penn Barn** 049 481 5691) run by Paul Hennings, who is principally a print specialist but now stocks a couple of thousand good quality antiquarian books. A converted barn, the shop which opened in 1979 is basically only one room and tiny in comparison with the Cottage Bookshop but worth a visit for those interested in 19th-century illustrated books, travel and topography. Indeed the two shops complement each other. Mr Hennings is a cricket enthusiast (he plays for the Antiquarian Booksellers team) and as such carries a large stock of prints on the sport, so inevitably the interest spills over into books. Similarly, with a cookery-writer wife, cookery books are another minor speciality. Cl lunch.

Buckingham Books, 20 Market Hill, Buckingham (028 02 2800), is housed in a pleasant bay fronted 18th-century building with new books on the ground floor and s/h and antiquarian in two rooms above. The proprietor David Clegg, who moved here in 1976 from his former shop in Dunstable, at one time sold Georgian furniture and this had some influence on his decision to specialise in architecture and design, which includes furniture, interior and garden design — although this section is kept in a separate room and those especially interested are advised to telephone first to make sure Mr Clegg is on hand. The rest of the stock is very general, with approx 4,000 s/h and 500 antiquarian. Six day, ½ day Th.

In the bookworld there are several glowing examples of booksellers of prodigious energy in their 60s and 70s. **John T. Carr**, now 90, opened his business in Queens Road, Watford, Herts, in 1924 and has obviously enjoyed every minute. One of the problems these days is acquiring stock but as an almost compulsive buyer Mr Carr has filled his home to bursting point ('Stacked everywhere, even under the bed!') as well as the delightfully chaotic shop. Even so, Mr Carr says that it breaks his heart to sell certain items — although he manages to hide such feelings. Indeed he genuinely takes pleasure in the delight of others and it is compliments like 'what a lovely smell' (of books) which make it all worth while, because the financial return in this type of business can never truly compensate for the effort invested. Even a compulsory purchase order for the shop to make way for a road could not put an end to Mr Carr's career and he found a similar shop farther along the same road — at no 100 (92 38127). The crowded shop carries everything from paperbacks to rare signed copies and, not surprisingly, attracts customers from all over, even abroad.

Eric T. Moore, 24 Bridge Street, Hitchin, Herts (0462 50497), is a well established bookseller who has become an expert on local history and recently reprinted two important local history books, said to be models of their kind, *History of Hitchin* and *Hitchin Worthies*, both by Reginald Hine. Indeed, Hitchin has a past rich in antiquity, being one of the five towns in Hertfordshire designated as being of special interest by the County Council, while Bridge Street (three minutes' walk from the town centre) is a continuation of historic Tilehouse Street where the brilliant George Chapman, friend of Shakespeare and himself a prolific play-wright and translator of Homer, once lived.

Mr Moore, whose early career was spent in commercial art, changed to bookselling after the war, working for Hatchards of Piccadilly and a former City booksellers. In 1947 he joined the Countryside Libraries headquarters in Hitchin and 16 years later started his own bookshop on the present site, converting what was once the Post Boy inn, a building dating back to 1830. The transformation culminated in an attractive eight room shop, today carrying about 20,000 vols, plus a large number of antiquarian prints and maps. A picture framing and mount cutting service is also on the premises. Cl lunch, ½ day W, but open all Sat.

Two minutes' walk away, just off the main town square, is the **Woodford Bookshop**, 31 Bucklersbury, SG5 1BG (0462 50257), opened in 1979 by Tony Martin to specialise in military books. Housed in a 16th-century building complete with original oak beams, the shop occupies one large room although Mr Martin keeps additional catalogue stock in another room. On show are between 3–4,000 books covering military, naval and aviation subjects — concentrating more on man as opposed to machine — together with ephemera such as medals, models and prints. Mr Martin, a builder whose hobby was collecting medals, opened his first shop at Woodford (Essex) in 1974 and books came along as an ancilliary subject until they grew in importance to justify their own business. Six days.

Although most of our more historic towns and cities

manage to conform to what the tourist expects of them, it always surprises me that some of the most attractive remain something of a cultural desert. In St Albans, for example, there is only one, **Abbey Books**, 36 Sopwell Lane, St Albans, Herts (56 32514), which is only open Thursday–Saturday. However, the owner Jean Tulloch lives on the premises and if telephoned in advance will open to bibliophiles who can only come earlier in the week*. A former teacher, Mrs Tulloch took the shop, previously a general stores, in 1978 after a spell of postal bookselling. She has about 5,000 books covering almost everything except the sciences in two rooms and a basement; strongest subjects are English lit, and books on Latin America.

(*It is worth noting that St Albans has a covered market on *Monday* mornings, with one bookstall run by John Schroeder; an open street market in the Town Hall square all day *Wednesday* in which books are sold by Mary Hutchinson and another in the square on *Saturdays* when two or three stalls sell books.)

EASTERN COUNTIES

As one might expect, the bookworld of East Anglia is dominated by Cambridge and the big names in bookselling are at the very heart of the town, in Trinity Street, by the university centre.

Bowes & Bowes, which was a bookshop in 1581 and so the oldest bookshop in the country, is at no 1 but no longer deals in s/h and antiquarian material. Only a few doors away at no 13 is **Deighton, Bell & Co** (0223 353939), an equally distinguished name but a comparative newcomer — able to trace its origins only to 1700! The business established under the name of Deighton may well, however, be the oldest bookshop still operating under its original name. In the 19th century the business was partly owned by George Bell, who later (as did Macmillan of Bowes & Bowes) founded a publishing house in London. After various changes of fortune in the early part of this century, the business eventually became part of the Dawson group.

The shop, an early 19th-century protected building, displays a large antiquarian and s/h stock noted for its quality on the ground floor; while the first floor houses a separate catalogue section, and the floor above a classical department. Emphasis is on English lit of the 19th century and earlier, fine printing, book design and production, early Continental books and Greek and Latin texts; in the out-of-print category there is a large general stock, including larger sections on specialist subjects such as economics. Cl lunch (12.30–1.45) and Sat.

Very much a newer bookshop, in every sense of the word, is **W. Heffer & Sons Ltd**, founded in 1876, who moved into the present premises at 20 Trinity Street (0223 358351) and established a model — from the customer's viewpoint — for bookshops anywhere. Regrettably, Heffers no longer sell s/h or antiquarian books, and I have included them only because there are still regular exhibitions of modern private press books and fine books in general.

Not as decorative, perhaps, as some of the big names in bookselling but the most affectionately remembered business in Cambridge must be **G. David**, 3 & 16 St Edward's Passage (0223 354619). The shops, situated on each side of St Edward's Church, are the inheritance of Gustave David who founded the business in 1896 with a stall that was to become famous and on whose death in 1936 Cambridge University Press published a small volume of appreciation, compiled from tributes by distinguished men of letters, including Sir Arthur Quiller-Couch. The firm, run for many years by his son, Hubert David, still has a bookstall in the Cambridge market place on Saturdays. In 1980 the reins were handed over to Hubert's grandson David Asplin.

Gustave, a Parisian by birth and the son of a second-hand bookseller, came to England in the 1870s and settled in Cambridge 20 years later (via bookselling spells in Gorleston and London), where he was fondly remembered as bringing 'a flavour of the *Quais*'. The business in those days was predominantly antiquarian and countless now-famous people, during their undergraduate days, found material on the stall that gave them lasting pleasure. Gustave David earned a reputation over the years of passing on his good fortune at the London sales, being content with a small profit — not because he did not know the true value of the books he bought, but because he valued his relationship with his customers. In 1925 he was entertained at a lunch in his honour at Trinity College, in recognition of the 'conspicuous services he has rendered the cause of Humane Letters'.

Today about half the stock is taken up by remainders, but there are still several thousand volumes, including a large section of antiquarian, as well as out-of-print. Cl Th.

The history of **Galloway & Porter Ltd**, 30 Sidney Street, CB2 3HS (0223 367876), one of the most distinguished names in bookselling circles, is in fact closely identified with the Porter family since Mr Galloway left the company for health reasons after only a couple of years — 75 years ago. Charles Porter, known as something of a character and a founder member of the ABA, quickly established a reputation for the firm, so that the shop had already a certain prestige when young Charles Traylen (see Surrey regional entry) joined as an apprentice, at roughly the same time as George Porter, the second generation, who was to become president of the ABA (1970–71). Today there are two other Porters in the firm, David and his nephew Stephen (George's son). As a university bookshop, dealing not only with local colleges but universities and scholars worldwide, most of the stock on four floors is new these days. However, one floor is healthily taken up with antiquarian and s/h (mainly academic) material. Cl Sat.

Edward Searle's **Bookroom** (combined with John P. Gray & Son, the bookbinders) 10 Green Street (0223 69694), opened early in 1974. One would be hard put to find a more interesting location. The bookbinders have been established in Green street since 1847 and The Bookroom consists of a ground floor shop and a large panelled room above it. Legend has it that Green Street acquired its name during a time of plague from the profusion of grass and wild flowers which grew along the length of the thoroughfare when both ends were sealed up to contain the epidemic. Mr Searle's shop contains about 2,500 volumes ranging from voyages and travel (including Africana and Indiana) to natural history, medicine, topography and science. Although the lit section is limited, the stock does carry some manuscript material, limited editions and some private press works. Normal hours but by appt Sat, and occasionally Sun.

At the time of going to press it seemed unlikely that **Derek Gibbons**, the well established specialist in children's books, would renew the lease at no 12 (0223 312913) but since it is so conveniently situated it is worth a check since Mr Gibbons is one of the top booksellers in this field.

Jean D. Pain is a former schoolteacher who entered bookselling 'by accident' in the middle 1960s when she took over an antique business with a few books. She soon got rid of the antiques. After a spell of bookselling in Bedford in 1974, she opened in Cambridge at 34 Trinity Street (0223 358279), in what had been Bowes & Bowes' science shop. The stock consists of approx 8–10,000 volumes covering a broad area but very strong in English lit and aimed at people who like to read, not just collect. In recent years the print side has been developed considerably; with 2–3,000 mounted prints and several thousand unmounted, it must represent one of the biggest stocks in the region. Six days.

Postal booksellers **Siddeley & Hammond***, 19 Clarence Street, CB1 1JU (0223 350325), are given an entry in the guide because of the quality of the reasonably specialist stock. From my experience Kay Hammond, who started her first business in 1976 after 41 years in the trade (including 12 years with Bowes & Bowes and 24 with Galloway & Porter) is often able to provide a scarce title that one can never seem to find in a shop. She holds a medium-size stock, all in very good to fine condition, in the areas of theatre and drama, lit and modern firsts, private presses and signed limited editions. Operating from home, 10 minutes' walk from the town centre, Miss Hammond keeps normal business hours six days a week, but *strictly by appointment*.

J. C. G. Hammond's **The Bookshop*** at Crown Point, Waterside, Ely, Cambs (0353 4365), is a husband and wife partnership founded in 1970, specialising in books on all aspects of crime (except fiction) and cognate subjects. Five years ago it moved from London to a former smithy, part of a building that was patronised by Oliver Cromwell when it was a public house. Facing the River Great Ouse, a centre for boating and coarse fishing, it is about five minutes on foot from the Cathedral and a pleasant walk, partly by the river, from Ely station. The stock represents criminology; studies of crimes and criminals; trials (including a large collection of the out-of-print Notable British Trials series); police history and memoirs; medico-legal works on the detection of crime, including fingerprints, ballistics, and forgery; penology and prison memoirs. The shop is open each Sat but the rest of the week *strictly by appointment*.

If there is anyone still around who believes that bookshops must be dingy places heaped in dust and cobwebs and that their owners are as musty, with a pallor to match, his fantasy would be shattered by a visit to Brettons, Burrough Green, Newmarket, Suffolk CB8 9NA, where the antiquarian booksellers **R. E. & G. B. Way**, specialising in all field sport interests, have an incomparable collection of books on horses

120

in all their aspects. Mr Robert Way, who retired after a stroke, was a giant of a man looking more like a swashbuckling buccaneer than a bookseller and his son Gregory, who is now in sole charge, is a strapping 6ft 4in.

Newmarket is of course one of the homes of horse racing and Robert Way started the business in 1958 when he gave up farming and breeding racehorses. Bookselling began almost as a hobby but gradually occupied more of Mr Way's time, until in recent years the whole of the ground floor (six rooms) of what was once a rectory has been taken up with 50,000 books, which includes a fair-size stock of out-of-print and antiquarian volumes on subjects other than 'hunting, shooting and fishing' which have been acquired in the main through the constant hunt for books on horses. Mr Way nevertheless still found time to form, own and hunt the De Burgh basset hounds and, more recently, to write his first book *The Garden of the Beloved*, a philosophical allegory published in 1975. Such is the *joie de vivre* at Brettons that on one visit my two sons were 'lost' to the Way children for a tour of the exuberant family of dogs, cats and Welsh ponies; so entertaining that they were reluctant to leave when I had finished buying.

In 1973 the business was taken over by Gregory Way, who had been in the book trade since he was 16 and was with Heffers for six years. More recently the character of the business has changed. Gregory, who exhibits at many of the American book fairs, has broadened the stock considerably, so that current specialities also include Antarctica and good library sets.

The village of Burrough Green is about six miles from Six Mile Bottom, and Brettons is at the end of the road going straight across the middle of the green. If customers have no transport they may be collected from Dullington or Newmarket stations. Normal hours but to be doubly sure, since Brettons is slightly off the beaten track, visitors are advised to ring first (063 876 217).

Former architect Colin Lewsey obviously believes in keeping busy — he runs five market stalls during the week, as well as the attractive **Bury Bookshop**, 28 Hatter Street, Bury St Edmunds, Suffolk (0284 703107), which sells new books as well as s/h and antiquarian. The double fronted shop — originally a merchant's town house built of Suffolk yellow stone which is relatively rare in a shop and thus it is now subject to a protection order — was opened in October 1980, but previously Mr Lewsey had two s/h bookshops in Castle Hedingham. New books are displayed on the ground floor, but 15—18,000 general s/h vols, about half fiction, can be found upstairs. Cl M. If you happen to be travelling in Suffolk, Mr Lewsey's stalls — at each site he manages to show about 2,000 items from paperbacks to academic books — are at Bury St Edmunds (W and Sat), Newmarket (T), and Sudbury (Th and Sat).

Iain Graham* at Daws Hall, Lamarsh, Bures (nr Sudbury), Suffolk (0787 29 213) began dealing in books in 1979 as a logical extension of his lifelong interest in wildlife, field sports, travel and exploration. A permanent stock of around 1,000 books on these subjects is housed on a 5 acre waterfowl farm where he breeds rare and exotic waterfowl and pheasants. On the face of it this rules out anyone not interested in these subjects, but Major Graham is such a fascinating man that it is a temptation not to go and just look around (the farm is open to the public in the summer until late October); not only is he an authority on wildlife, but he has written several books on his experiences in Africa where he was once Idi Amin's commanding officer. Several years after leaving the army, he returned to Uganda for the Queen to plead for the life of Denis Hills. *Strictly by appointment.*

Assuming the stock is comparable, there are a number of advantages to book hunting in the country. Several of these benefits are apparent in a visit to **Trinder's**, Malting Lane, Clare, Suffolk (078 727 7130), a 16th-century timber framed building on the edge of a 20 acre country park, Clare Priory, and the River Stour. The premises were purchased in 1970 by Peter Trinder, a TV engineer with the IBA, and his wife Rosemary, a former computer consultant. Set at right angles to the road, it has a frontage of 90 feet with an archway in the centre. The building has been constantly restored by the Trinders and the double fronted shop opened in 1975 is on one side of the arch with a store on the other. Both book-lovers, when the Trinders decided to open the shop they jumped in at the deep end, building their stock slowly and learning as their fortunes developed. Today they have around 20,000 vols on a wide range of subjects, including 2–3,000 on British topography and another large section on architecture. Because they exhibit at a number of book fairs, a phone call is advisable for visits during the week, but open Sat and pm Sun.

The only thing John Rolph's shop, at **The Coach-House Bookstore**, Pakefield Street, Lowestoft, Suffolk (0502 2039), has in common with the pure air of the country is the healthy sea breeze. Otherwise it conforms more readily to the Victorian picture I had dismissed as fiction — complete with dust and the occasional cobweb! But while the elegant members of the trade compel our respect, the bookworld would be a poorer place without the treasure-trove character of traditional old shops like this — an old coachhouse.

Pakefield is the southernmost suburb of Lowestoft, two miles from the station, from which visitors can get a bus or walk along the front or beach right to the end of Pakefield Street (via the cliff path), or what remains of it, since half was washed away by the sea 75 years or so ago. The shop, on two floors, is much too small according to John Rolph (although would it have the same appeal in less cramped conditions?). To use his own description: 'The staircase is precipitous, and books and magazines are stacked in dusty heaps in front of the shelves and anywhere another couple of cubic inches can be found. Occasionally I have an onslaught on the cobwebs, but it's no use . . . When you stock things like old biscuit tins and cigarette packets and Victorian Children's shoes it's impossible'.

Mr Rolph does himself an injustice. While the stock of approx 10,000 vols is fairly wide ranging, he has specialised for 30 years in modern firsts. He also has an excellent collection of children's books from 1880–1950, as well as a comprehensive section on day-to-day life in Edwardian times and the 1920s — work and leisure, games, medicine, magazines, domestic economy and inventions. Mr Rolph is the author of the Dylan Thomas bibliography (Dent, 1956) and is founder/director of Scorpion Press, which poetry enthusiasts will know launched Peter Porter, Edwin Brock and others,

123

and has also issued the works of Christopher Logue, Doris Lessing, Henry Miller, etc. Hours are unusual: in summer 10–1 and 2.15–6 on T,W,F and Sat; in winter less reliable so phone call advisable.

Until fairly recently few people outside Suffolk had heard of the tiny village of Yoxford near Saxmundham, but its place in the world of the arts has since been established by a good local pottery and an art gallery. The latter quarter of 1974 saw the arrival of the first booksellers — the **Yoxford Bookshop,** in the High Street (072 877 309), run by Edwin and Phyllis Packer who had entered the trade as postal booksellers. The shop, almost opposite the village church, is in fact owned by the church. Built in 1912 with wooden walls and corrugated-iron roof supported by an antique bedpost, its architectural shortcomings are more than overcome by a pleasant setting and friendly proprietors who like books *and* people. Phyllis Packer was a schoolteacher for many years and Edwin a probation officer before becoming a journalist in 1960, since when he has written a couple of books. In 1980 they began publishing booklets of Suffolk interest — local poetry, history and topography — priced at less than £1. Medium-size general stock. Six days.

It is the ambition of many people to visit the White House, home of American presidents, but be warned: there is always a queue and, more important, their books are not for sale. But there is another White House, quite a bit nearer; not so big, but certainly older, where all it takes to gain entry is a phone call. In keeping with the historic setting, **Claude Cox*** at The White House, Kelsale, Saxmundham, Suffolk, IP17 2PQ (0728 2786), sells mostly antiquarian books, which means that you are unlikely to find anything much under £5, but the range of his stock is impressive. The farmhouse is isolated — a mile from Kelsale, in turn 1½ miles from Saxmundham — and hopefully this will discourage the idly curious browser, but collectors will find the extra effort well worthwhile.

Claude Cox and his wife Joan are lifelong book collectors since being taught Latin by Arnold Muirhead, who later became one of the doyens of the trade. They bought the farmhouse in 1970 after Claude left the RAF (as Wing

Commander) and both taught at local schools while they gathered their initial stock. In 1975 the business was launched and the first catalogues issued. Four years later the partnership was joined by their son Tony. By attending book fairs and increasing the flow of catalogues, the turnover was doubled in his first year. Approx 7,000 volumes are divided between about 2,000 19th-century books (lit, travel and topography, science, illus books/bindings, private press and signed copies) in the main bookroom; the same number of 18th-century and earlier, including a section on education, are in an annexe. More recent miscellaneous books are found in a corridor leading to a Suffolk backhouse where, in an upstairs room, there are volumes on history and modern firsts. Architectural buffs would find the house fascinating because it was built in at least three stages from 1600 to about 1780 (Washington's White House was started in 1792). *Strictly by appointment.*

Music teacher Joy Rohan exchanged school classes for a bookshop in 1976 when she opened the **Blackboro' Bookshop**, Blackborough End, Norfolk, PE32 1SL, in a small building of local stone which used to be the village stores, 5 miles from King's Lynn. Although the books are confined to one room many are double banked — which means that Mrs Rohan has about 5,000 s/h and antiquarian volumes, strong on local topography. She also has local maps and prints of the area and sheet music. Only open regularly on Sat and pm Sun but available during the week (home no 0553 5230) *by appointment.*

History buffs will be intrigued to learn that the Wayland Woods at Watton in Norfolk are reputedly the site of the Babes in the Woods murder and subsequent legend. There is nothing as dramatic about the town today — but there *is* a bookshop, the **Watton Bookworm**, Middle Street, Watton (0953 882625), which is run by another former schoolteacher, Len Hoggart. While still teaching in 1973 Mr Hoggart opened a shop for new books but four years later he found larger premises, a 100-year-old building of charm and character, which enabled him to stock s/h and antiquarian books on the first floor. This department consists of one large room and displays approx 3,000 vols with no speciality, plus another

5,000 paperbacks. Although small, the stock sometimes includes items of good quality (the shop has no postal trade which cuts out the chance of choice items being hived off; everything goes on to the shelves). Cl Th pm.

The Saxon Bookshop, 12a St Nicholas Street, Diss, Norfolk (0379 2441), housed in a 400-year-old listed building, is deceptively large because the frontage was once merely the preparation room for the flower shop next door. When Jack and Mary Renwick moved here in 1978 they extended that room by knocking down a wall so that they could display books in two rooms on the ground floor and two more above. Apart from an art and print room, the stock of 12–14,000 s/h and antiquarian vols are designed to offer something attractive to almost everyone, with no specialisation. Jack Renwick was a career diplomat and the couple spent many years abroad, including several (until 1973) in San Francisco. A keen bibliophile, Mr Renwick had always wanted to work with books and eventually gave up his career to open this shop. Unfortunately he died within a year but Mary Renwick, who continues the business, regards it as a testament to his memory. A pleasant and friendly shop. Cl T.

The Compton Bookshop moved from London to 13 Castle Street, Eye, Suffolk (0379 870199) in 1981. Cl M and T.

Norwich, Norfolk, offers an interesting contrast in bookselling styles between the old-established bookseller with a modern philosophy and a relative newcomer with an 'old-fashioned' shop. Both are delightful in their own ways, and complementary.

Thomas Crowe, 77 Upper St Giles Street (0603 21962), a schedule A building dating from 1680 in a quiet cul-de-sac, was founded by the present owner in 1935, although he had previously been trading for five years at Wrexham. Indeed, the Crowes are very much a bookselling family, his grandfather Charles starting in Wrexham in the 1870s and his son Frank continuing under his own name. When Thomas eventually broke away from the business run by his brothers, he took over the present premises which had been a bookshop since the early 1900s. A double fronted building of three storeys and a basement houses about 20,000 better s/h and antiquarian books. In addition to a healthy shop trade, the

Crowes (Mr Crowe's son Nicholas has joined the firm) issue four quality catalogues a year and exhibit at a number of trade fairs in this country and abroad. In fact Thomas Crowe, a past president of the ABA, was one of the pioneers of the London Book Fair, and was later honoured by being made host chairman of the International Fair in the early 1970s. Six days.

Russell Crowe, another son, now has the shop next door at no 75 in friendly competition.

The **Scientific Anglian** was started in 1964 by chemical engineer Norman Peake in what used to be a public house at 30 Benedict's Street, Norwich, NR2 4AQ (0603 24079). If ever a shop bulged at the seams with books, it is here, where Mr Peake has converted several small rooms into four large 'library' areas with floor to ceiling shelving to accommodate 60,000 mainly cheaper s/h books, carefully classified with a code index to 340 subjects (eg 15 sections on chemistry alone). The top floor has a display of about 10,000 fiction titles, which must be one of the largest in the country, and in addition Mr Peake has a reserve of 250,000 books in two warehouses. Should you lose your way, just ask for the bookshop with the rhino's head. Having used up every cubic inch of space, Mr Peake thought it might be dangerous to put books in a landing area on the way down to the basement, so he decided on a shop's mascot, although ever since he has been plagued with offers to buy it — or just the horn! Cl M and Th am.

The **SPCK Bookshop** (see 'Rich Pastures' and 'North London') is well represented in Norwich at 19 Pottergate, NR2 1DS (0603 27332) where Miss E. Birkett looks after a good range of s/h material in theology, history, topography and lit. Six days.

There seems to be something about old bakers' shops that attracts booksellers, and **C. B. & C. Scurfield** occupy another at 1 Wells Road, Fakenham, Norfolk (0328 2450), a pleasant corner site a couple of minutes' walk from the centre of Fakenham, which is only fifteen or so miles by road west of Itteringham in the north of the county. The Scurfields, who came here in 1969, have deliberately opted for s/h rather than antiquarian stock with 10–15,000 vols housed in three rooms.

The accent is on fiction, poetry, children's and local interest. Also new paperbacks (mainly lit and children's) and cheap pictures. Cl lunch and W.

The days when young men were apprenticed into bookselling are gone and the trend is for people to come into the trade having made their mark elsewhere. But **David Ferrow**, 77 Howard Street South, Great Yarmouth, Norfolk (0493 3800), actually opened his first shop in 1940 at the age of 15! Mr Ferrow's very large premises in a back street of the town, where he has been since 1951, carry a stock of some 20–30,000 s/h and antiquarian books in all fields. 'I like everything', he says, which should be good enough for any browser. Cl lunch (except Sat) and Th.

The Manor Bookshop, 109 Langer Road, Felixstowe, Suffolk IP11 8EA (039 42 77832), is a shop for which one has to look, being a bus ride from the town centre and run by a retired schoolmaster who by his own admission is not seeking customers. However, those who take the trouble are welcome and Mr Taylor carries a medium-size general s/h stock (about 12,000) in two rooms — nothing wildly exciting but in many cases books one might not find elsewhere. The business, formerly a fish and chip shop, was started in 1972 when Mr Taylor was 60 and the site was chosen because he did not want a busy shopping area. Cl M, and possibly at other times during the winter, so phone call advisable.

Ipswich used to boast two of the best-looking bookshops in the country, with personalities to match, but the beautiful Ancient House no longer sells s/h or antiquarian books. **The College Gateway Bookshop**, 3/5 Silent Street, Ipswich, Suffolk, IP1 1TF (0473 54776), a timber framed and beamed building dating back to the late 15th century is so named because it stands near the College Gate of the ill-fated Wolsey's college. Indeed certain picture postcards popular with tourists have incorrectly described the shop as Cardinal Wolsey's birthplace.

When Thomas and Myfanwy Cook took over the shop 36 years ago, it sold antiques, paintings and a few books. They got rid of the former and built up the stock of books — mostly antiquarian and good s/h — to well over 15,000. An ideal browsing shop, with a mass of books in something of a muddle, it ranges over two rooms, a passageway and odd alcoves. The contents of these shelves are of general interest, although the Cooks do specialise to some extent in various aspects of East Anglian history, culture and industry, with some new books too in this category. The stock is selective, and Mr Cook will not put anything on the shelves that he cannot imagine someone wanting, which means that turnover is reasonably constant. Cl lunch, W and sometimes M also, but open all Sat.

Caroline Burt*, of the Old Swan House, Swan Lane, Cretingham, Woodbridge, Suffolk, IP13 7AZ (072 882 633), specialises exclusively in books on horses and has about 2,000 vols on the subject, fluctuating according to the demands of four catalogues a year. This means that the general bibliophile is deprived of the 'bonus' of an interesting Mrs Burt and a lovely setting. The house is a genuine early 18th-century Suffolk long house (ie 1,000 feet long), the type in which occupancy was once divided between cattle at one end and the farmer and his family at the other. Caroline Burt, who began bookselling by post in 1978, is a well known writer (as Caroline Akrill) on her specialist subject. *Appointment necessary.*

While in the Woodbridge area, it might be worth popping in to see **Mrs Ann Kent**, Victoria Mill House (there was once a windmill on the site), Victoria Mill Road, Framlingham, Suffolk IP13 9EG (0728 723985), which is a shop in a house — or to be strictly accurate, a private house with the front door left open so that customers just ring the bell and walk in. Mrs Kent started the 'shop' in 1974 in one room but soon added another, so that now approx 4,000 vols are on display and quite a few more are dotted around the rest of the house. The stock is predominently s/h and very general, although there are larger sections on East Anglia and detective fiction. Sheet music is also sold. Open Th–Sat, plus T in summer, but other days *by appointment.*

In an historic town like Colchester, Essex, somewhat over shadowed by the spectacular remains of the Roman and Norman invasions, the shops have a high standard to live up to, and **The Castle Bookshop**, 37 North Hill (0206 77520), does not disappoint us. The proprietor, Anthony Doncaster, came to Colchester in 1948 and took his first shop in Museum Street near the castle (which dates from 1070 and has the largest Norman keep in the country); hence the name. After several moves to premises in other parts of the town, he settled in his present site at the bottom of North Hill about 18 years ago, since when the business has spread into various buildings and annexes on both sides of a small yard. The main part of the shop is a rambling 16th-century building, a ground floor and two storeys above with low ceilings and steps in unexpected places. At one time the place was an inn called the Beehive. Mr Doncaster, who was partnered in 1980 by ex-librarian David Dawson, carries a large general s/h and antiquarian stock with some new books, although there is a degree of specialisation in history, Essex topography and archaeology. Open Sat, but cl Th.

Smaller but not without considerable character in its own right is **Trinity Street Bookshop**, 13 Trinity Street, Colchester, CO1 1JN (0206 72751), run by Chris and Sue Briggs since 1975. The shop encompasses a large ground-floor room and two above in premises that were once the Fleur-de-lys beerhouse (c1550). The largely medieval street runs between the Saxon tower of Holy Trinity church and Sheregate steps, a medieval breach in Colchester's Roman wall. The Briggs, former college librarians who had a shop in Southend before moving to Colchester, have a stock of approx 5,000 s/h and antiquarian books which they endeavour to keep to a reasonably high standard. Cl M and Th.

Smaller still but with a very select stock, almost entirely antiquarian, is **John Drury (Rare Books) Ltd***, 11 East Stockwell Street, Colchester, CO1 1SS (0206 46755), a 17th-century building in the Dutch quarter of the town, ie to the north of the High Street where refugee weavers from the Netherlands once lived from the 16th century. The business is predominantly postal and John Drury's has built up a considerable reputation for the quality of its books, which cover all subjects but with an emphasis on economics, (the name is really an anagram of the christian names of the original owners). David Edmunds, a council adviser on the training of social workers, started selling old and interesting books from this address in 1970 and has more recently been joined by a literature graduate from Oxford, Linda Miller, who now does the cataloguing. Normal shop hours maintained *but phone call advisable especially for Sat.*

Please believe me when I say that I do not have an obsession with size, and the fact that I have listed the Colchester shops in 'descending' order is quite coincidental. However, I am duty-bound to inform you that the smallest bookshop in Colchester — possibly the smallest in the country — is **Michael Barber Books**, Culver Street West (0206 66663), in the centre of town, introduced by the local newspaper thus: 'If you blink you'll miss it'. The shop, a plate-glass 'box' just 4 feet wide (by 18 feet deep) was opened by Mr Barber in 1978 after bookselling by post for several years. Despite its size he tries to stock items that have a wide interest, although naturally the accent is on quality and condition. The whole of one and a half walls are full of books from floor to ceiling, often double banked so that about 2,000 books are on view with many in reserve. Because of the expanse of glass many customers can do their browsing through the window! Cl M and Th.

Ironically, the oldest of the bookshops in the town, **The Colchester Bookshop** at 47 Head Street, where there has been a bookshop for around 100 years, only sells new books.

Quite a number of booksellers are housed in former inns but **The Bridge Bookshop**, Bridge House, Coggeshall, Colchester (0376 61408), was formerly a brewery and the showroom is the old ground-floor cellar area. The brewery had belonged to the Gardner family for over 125 years, being converted by Hilda Gardner in 1939 when she and her husband returned from London, where they had started a print shop in Buckingham Gate in 1925 and a second in Lower Grosvenor Place (now a bookshop) five years later. The main part of Bridge House was built in the 15th or early 16th century, but additions include a Georgian front and a Victorian back! The stock of approx 10,000 very general s/h and antiquarian books includes some local history, and Hilda Gardner also has a large trade in prints and maps. Six days.

Just off the B1027 to Clacton is the village of St Osyth, which has a medieval priory and a deer park. Should you be in the vicinity you might consider a visit to **St Osyth Books***, run by Mrs Judith Butler from her home at 52 Clacton Road, CO16 8PA (0255 820904). Mrs Butler, wife of a university sub-librarian, has been a postal bookseller for some years, opening the bookroom in 1979 to display a tiny stock — around 500 books — with a slight emphasis on art and country life. *Strictly by appointment.*

One of the largest solely antiquarian collections is carried by **Beeleigh Abbey Books*** (W. & G. Foyle), Maldon, Essex (0621 56308), in an unrivalled historic setting. The books were transferred from London, and the stock expanded, as part of the Foyles reorganisation of the late 1960s.

The abbey was founded in 1170 by Sir Robert de Mantel for the Premonstratensian Order, or White Canons as they were known to distinguish them from the black-clad Augustinians. It was used by the order — Edward I and Queen Eleanor visiting the abbey on separate occasions in 1289 — until the 15th century.

The remains of the original abbey, together with the Tudor portion, were bought by William Foyle over 30 years ago as a residence and it is still used as such occasionally by the Foyle family. It also houses the Foyles' private library, which is a museum in its own right. At one time the abbey was opened to the public, but this is no longer done and even the book business is aimed principally at the trade. Collectors are welcome *by appointment only.*

Frank Eddelin is a throwback to the early days of book-selling — a master printer who in 1974 opened his own bookshop, **Atticus Books**, at Kickshaws, 20 Alexandra Street, Southend-on-Sea, Essex (0702 353630). The premises, just off the High Street and opposite a municipal car park, are shared with an antique business (hence the name 'kicksaws' — first used in the 16th century as a corruption of the French 'quelques choses') run by his wife. The stock — a few thousand out-of-print and antiquarian volumes, including some very old books — is quite small but general and interesting.

Frank Eddelin has been involved in books all his life, beginning as a collector. His speciality, although he is reluctant to sell certain books from his collection, is the history of printing, type, binding, etc, and as a member of the Printing Historical Society and London Chapel of Private Press Printers he is an expert on the subject, lecturing to technical colleges on various aspects of the trade, including graphic design. He is also working on a museum of printing presses and ephemera in his spare time. Hours slightly unusual, 11−1 and 2.30−6 five days (cl W).

The speciality of **Laurie Gage Books,** 100 The Broadway, Leigh-on-Sea, Essex, SS9 1AB (0702 710474), is theology but the stock is so large that visitors might assume it was very general. Situated in the main shopping street in Leigh, the shop opened in 1971 and is well known along this stretch of coast, carrying well over 20,000 vols, the majority displayed in a spacious basement area while the ground floor is devoted to bindings, illustrated books and some antiquarian, as well as pictures. Cl M but open Sat.

Collectors' Corner, 5 Highcliffe Drive, Leigh-on-Sea, Essex (0702 79548), carries a fascinating range of antiquarian *objets d'art* as well as books, although the proprietor Lawrence Beer has been a bookseller all his working life and books are his main interest. His double fronted shop (not on a corner, incidentally) has been open 17 years, and a stock of 25,000 general s/h books, with a few new ones related to collecting, attracts bibliophiles from all parts. Five minutes' walk from Chalkwell station. 11−5, ½ day W.

Margaret Pole: Books, 2 Newbiggen Street, Thaxted, Essex (0371 830 320), is a shop in a very small Georgian house facing the famous village church. Miss Pole is one of the trade's old-timers, working in bookshops in the 1930s, before owning her first in Chelsea just before the war. When the blitz started she moved to Cirencester (Glos), where she had another shop until 1951 before returning to her home county, and she has been in Thaxted ever since. Apart from local customers collected over the past 20 years or so, Miss Pole's trade comes largely from visitors to the village (not far from Saffron Walden) and the shop consists of one room and the hall of her home. Small but selective stock of antiquarian and s/h books, some prints, and a few new books on Essex and East Anglia. Cl lunch and W, F.

After 32 years in the air force John Walentowicz retired in

1967 to run a bookshop with his wife. With their combined talents the shop was successful, but it only sold new books — which worried Mr Walentowicz, a keen bibliophile. Although he introduced antiquarian books into the stock, they did not become a separate entity until 1978 when he opened **The Billericay Antiquarian Bookshop**, Sheredays House, 22 High Street, Billericay, Essex (02774 59078). Sheredays House is an antiques centre and Mr Walentowicz has two rooms displaying 8–10,000 vols, mainly specialising in the history and topography of Essex, British topography, foreign travel and natural history. There is also a large selection of prints and maps. Cl Th.

Norman Lord is one of those postal booksellers who realised an ambition in 1980 by opening premises at The City Antique Centre, 98 Wood Street, Walthamstow, London E17, on his retirement from the post office. Although covering a wide range of subjects, the stock is very small (approx 1,500 vols), but in his dealings by post since 1975 he has amassed another 5,000 which are in store. Cl W and Th.

SOUTH EAST

The tiny village of Brasted, near Westerham, Kent, with a shopping 'centre' less than a quarter of a mile long, can claim shops devoted to antiques, art and prints. Representing the book world is **The Attic (Sevenoaks) Ltd***, The Village House, Brasted, TN16 1HU (0959 63507). Don't look for a shop or an attic because the business is run by James and Rosamund Brydon from their 18th-century house, described in one guide book as the most interesting building in the village. The Brydons have been selling books here for 25 years, after being in partnership in a shop at Sevenoaks called The Attic. Current stock is general s/h and antiquarian with leanings towards military, children's, cookery and the arts; and books are displayed in two rooms in the house and a 'studio' in the garden where a mass of cheaper items — from Penguins to classics — are kept. Shop hours, but preferably *by appointment.*

Another very popular bookshop, to which customers make regular pilgrimages from all parts of the country, is **Hall's Bookshop**, 20–22 Chapel Place, Tunbridge Wells, Kent, TN1 1YQ (0892 27842), established in 1898 by a Reuben Hall who continued living in Maidstone and is reputed to have cycled to Tunbridge Wells every day.

The present owner, Elizabeth Bateman, who took over in 1967 after working for the previous owner Harry Pratley for a number of years, is proud of the fact that she runs an 'old-fashioned' bookshop — and rightly so, because it is the combination of a wide ranging and interesting stock and the character of a premises that lifts one shop above its competitors. Talking of 'old-fashioned' in these days of 'instant bookselling', one is reminded that men like Harry Pratley had to serve a full apprenticeship before they were allowed to impose their own influence on a shop, and this is why little has changed; why change a successful formula?

Today the large stock, housed on two floors — the upper a gallery — covers most subjects but has an emphasis on lit (because of the demands on space, the fiction section is rather more selective than it may have been previously), history, art, travel and topography, and prices range from 50p (although there is a 10p box outside) to several hundred pounds. Cl lunch and W.

In common with other old-established businesses, Hall's offers a wealth of anecdotes — such as the occasion about 20 years ago, vividly remembered by Elizabeth Bateman, when an American customer bought a beautiful old map of Dublin as a present for friends in the United States. The usual way of despatching valuable items is to pack them inside a thick cardboard tube, but Mr Pratley conscientiously wrapped the tube in several layers of prints from John Boydell's famous Shakespeare Gallery series which, despite their charm, were quite unfashionable and virtually valueless at the time. Months later the customer was in contact again, puzzled that her friends had been ecstatic about the beautiful prints (about which she knew nothing) without mentioning the valuable map. Hall's wrote to the recipients anxiously asking if they had looked *inside* the tube. Needless to say they had not; and fortunately it had not been thrown away!

Readers interested in biography might try **The Biography Bookroom***, 41 Mill Street, East Malling, Kent, ME19 6DA (0732 844392), a detached private house with a specially built bookroom carrying 3,000 vols, all in this category. The business is run by Alec R. Mills, an architectural designer who turned to bookselling in 1970 and started to specialise almost immediately, and his partner Margaret Lomas, who joined the firm in 1978. The premises, located in the old village of East Malling, 5 miles west of Maidstone and close to the A20, are only a few minutes' walk from the railway station. *By appointment*, including weekends and evenings.

Antiquarian bookseller Alfred King launched **Wealdon Books***, 39 Adisham Drive, Maidstone, Kent, ME16 0NP (0622 62581) in 1980, to specialise in old and out-of-print books on Kent and fiction by local authors. He came to a novel and interesting arrangement to display part of his stock at Goblins Bookshop, which, although a period building of charm, sells *new* books in the High Street at Staplehurst, a village 10 miles to the south. In the fiction section are works by Vita Sackville-West, Harold Nicolson, Richard Church and H. E. Bates. However, what cannot be seen at the shop (0580 891362) from Th−Sat may be found at Mr King's home *by appointment*.

Vita Sackville-West and Harold Nicolson are, of course, associated with Sissinghurst Castle and less than 10 minutes' drive away a comprehensive range of their titles can be seen at **Bridge Conachar**, St David's Bridge, Cranbrook, Kent (05804 713683), an 18th-century building next to the well known windmill. The shop, which has five rooms of good s/h material covering a wide area but specialising in English and American lit, was opened in 1976 by Ian and Rosemary Bell, who had previously been postal booksellers for 10 years. The name was coined when husband and wife became business partners — Conachar being Rosemary's maiden name. Cl lunch and Wed.

Rochester Rare Books, 174 High Street, Rochester, Kent (0634 407086) has made a considerable impact on the town since it opened in 1976 — the first bookshop there for over 30 years. It has also come a long way, while moving a short distance along the High Street. Originally (at no 294) it was a tiny shop of two rooms (8 × 10 feet) so that, inevitably, when it expanded other premises had to be found, near the cathedral. Meanwhile, an outlet for new books, **The Rochester Bookshop**, was opened at no 172, and finally in December 1979 the s/h and antiquarian operation was able to move in next door. Now 25,000 vols of general interest (the only specialisation being the history and topography of Kent, and the British Isles) fill the large ground floor (35 × 20 feet) and two rooms upstairs, with rare books spilling over into the intercommunicating new shop. Managing director of the two businesses is Malcolm John Wright, a former schoolteacher who now also writes and runs a publishing company, John Hallewill, which produced books on local history and transport. Six days. Cl lunch 2−2.30pm. In summer open Sun.

Between the various moves Mr Wright also opened **The Chatham Book Centre**, 38 High Street, Chatham, Kent (0634

43884), where although 10,000 square feet is mainly occupied by new books and remainders there is a large stock of s/h paperbacks, and a range of hardbacks priced at around £1. Six days.

Faversham is one of the most historic places in Kent, parts of the town dating from the 13th century. Just off the attractive market square in a pedestrian shopping area is **The Bookshop,** 119 West Street (079 582 2873), a relatively new building built in the 17th century, with an elegant Edwardian curved glass front. In 1978 the shop was taken over by Max Ardley who now has approx 5,000 books in two rooms. He maintains the nautical books specialisation of Eileen Perryman, who opened the shop in 1975 with Adrian Walmsley, but has developed interests of his own, eg illustrated books and the works of Rudyard Kipling. Cl lunch and Th.

The Chaucer Bookshop, 6 Beer Cart Lane, Canterbury, Kent, CT1 2NY (0227 53912), five minutes' walk from the cathedral, is an attractive double fronted shop built in 1750 as a small town-cottage. Needless to say, it has changed its appearance several times since — on the last occasion when Robert Leach took over in 1976 from Charles Jervis and converted three ground-floor rooms into one large area with the staircase in the middle. Approx 10,000 books are spread around this 'open plan' arrangement and another large room upstairs. The stock is varied and includes a large selection of bindings, English lit and criticism and fairly modern theology. Mr Leach had been in the hotel business for a number of years before deciding he wanted to sell books, and learned the ropes by spending a couple of years with Charles Sawyer in London. Six days. Occasionally cl lunch.

Bell Harry Books, 110 Northgate (by the traffic lights), Canterbury, Kent (0227 53481), which often gets letters addressed to 'Harry Bell, Manager', is in fact owned by retired head teacher Jack Hubbard who named the shop after the cathedral's most dominant tower. A former collector, in 1976 he took over a bric-a-brac shop in an 18th-century listed building. Approx 5,000 selective s/h books are displayed in two rooms, the emphasis being on English lit and Kentish material. Cl T and Th.

J. J. Rigden (Books)* 17 Beverley Road, Canterbury, Kent (0227 69911), specialising in juvenile fiction, has a bookroom in a private house but is happy to see bibliophiles interested in the subject at any time *by appointment.* Eric and Juanita Rigden's stock has a broad appeal — not just the narrow area of over-priced Victorian illustrated books that has been so 'fashionable' in the trade over the past 10 years. They cover all the popular children's writers and all aspects of fiction from adventure to fairy tales, but also cater for the collector interested in scarcer first editions or better illustrated books. The Rigdens began to specialise only five years ago, previously having also sold early detective/fantasy fiction. The size of stock on display varies according to the date of the latest catalogue (six are issued every year and read more like gossipy communications between friends than the usual lists) and turnover is quite fast.

The **SPCK Bookshop,** 2 The Precincts, Canterbury, Kent CT1 2EE (0227 62881), managed by Mr M. Leverton, carries only a small stock of s/h material but in addition to theology it covers lit, history and topography. Six days.

Since the last edition, **Lloyd's Bookshop** has moved from south London to 27 High Street, Wingham, near Canterbury, Kent, CT3 1AW (022 772 774), where Jane Morrison, a specialist in Victorian children's books, has a wide general stock starting from 5p and catering for all tastes. Mrs Morrison is one of the old school (in the nicest sense) who believes that a bookshop should offer something for every customer and not just collectors. As well as books she also sells music. After many years in the capital, Jane Morrison has obviously found her niche in this pleasant little village six miles out of Canterbury. The shop, opposite the Red Lion, which claims to be the oldest pub in Kent, is cl M, T and W pm.

When shops have fan clubs, they have to be rather special. One such place is **The Albion Bookshop,** Old St Mary's Chapel, 46 Albion Street, Broadstairs, Kent (0843 62876), run by Alan and Sheila Kemp, who also have new bookshops run by their son Paul a few doors away in the same road, and at Canterbury, Ramsgate and Margate. Alan Kemp bought his other bookshop in Albion Road in a very run-down state

139

in 1956 and, because of the limitations of space, concentrated on new books. Three years later he bought the chapel as a store but gradually built up a stock of antiquarian and s/h books which interested customers were allowed to inspect. Although the chapel was open for a number of years by invitation, Mr Kemp opened its doors formally in January 1980. It carries a general s/h stock of more than 10,000 vols in one huge room, with a high gallery. The stock is interesting and varied but undoubtedly one of the attractions is the building itself. The oldest in Broadstairs, bearing the date 1601 on the wall facing the street, it is on the site of much earlier buildings — one known as the Shrine of Our Lady of Bradstowe (the early name for Broadstairs) and sometimes as Our Lady Star of the Sea, and another as early as 1070 dedicated to the Virgin Mary. At one time the building, near the harbour with its ancient jetty, displayed a blue lantern visible to passing ships and warning them of their closeness to the North Foreland and the Goodwin Sands. Cl lunch. Six days.

At Easter 1980 Iona Bown, who owns the **Sandwich Bookshop***, Sandwich, Kent (0304 613 192), moved only a few yards, from an attractive 16th-century building, to one even older, Weaver's Building, at no 13 Strand Street — which is probably one of the most beautiful in a town of fascinating half-timbered buildings. The street, incidentally, used to be on the sea front before the sea receded in late Elizabethan times. The shop — a narrow, 30 foot long, oak beamed room, with another, smaller, upstairs — carries a good general stock of about 10,000 vols. Mrs Bown's interests include natural history, poetry, drama and music while her husband, who teaches at the Royal Naval College, Greenwich, advises on naval and military books. Mrs Bown opened her first shop in Sandwich in 1973 after gaining experience as an assistant at the Blackheath Bookshop in south London. *By appointment only.*

D. S. Gunyon, Books & Pictures, 49–51 High Street, Sandwich, Kent (0304 612457), is a bookshop and picture gallery. It was opened in 1970 by Dorothy Gunyon, who has spent 50 years in the s/h book trade, as an assistant in various London bookshops and running a postal service from

Gloucestershire and Kent. Mrs Gunyon keeps some 5,000 books on display — part general, which have a quick turnover, and part Kent books and illustrated works of all kinds and periods. The premises consist of a well lit shop connected by a small picture gallery with a larger bookroom. Six days. Cl lunch.

Deal is one of the relatively unspoilt seaside resorts on the coast of Kent and right on the seafront is **The Golden Hind Bookshop**, 85 Beach Street (03045 5086), opposite the Royal Hotel, a regular haunt of Nelson and Lady Hamilton in the days when ships from all over the world used to shelter by the Downs opposite. Also not far away is Walmer Castle, with its interesting collection of Wellingtonia, and the official residence of the Lord Warden of the Cinque Ports (currently the Queen Mother). The owner, Michael Hosking, was formerly in publishing and a postal bookseller before coming here in 1974. The stock, displayed in four rooms on ground and first floor, consists of about 10,000 s/h and antiquarian vols, mainly in the humanities although his speciality is modern firsts of lit, poetry and drama. Cl W and Th but available on those days *by appointment*.

G. & D. I. Marrin & Sons, Victoria House Galleries, 149 Sandgate Road, Folkestone, Kent (0303 53016), is in an attractive late Victorian building, the last house/shop of its style and character left in the area. The business, run by George Marrin and his son John, was opened in 1967 after 30 years of bookselling in the town and in Hythe and Canterbury — gaining many customers from the Continent. The stock of general literature, rare and antiquarian, and prints and maps (with emphasis on Kent) is housed in five showrooms on the ground floor, with the family living in the house above. Paintings are also sold. Six days, but cl lunch and W pm.

In December 1979 the Marrin family opened **Cinque Ports Books And Prints**, 152 High Street, Hythe, Kent (0303 69669), a 14th-century building of great character, managed by son Patrick. Between 5–10,000 s/h and antiquarian books are housed in one large room on the ground floor, behind a large window display. The style is similar to their other shop, with contents ranging from postcards and printed ephemera to old maps and books, which include sections on natural history, travel, trade and industry. Cl lunch and ½ day W.

James Bateman is another of that very exclusive set who have walked innocently into a bookshop and come out having agreed to buy the place! For the past 15 years he has run **The Rye Bookshop Ltd**, 28 High Street, Rye, Sussex (079 73 2146), established over 40 years ago by the late Gilbert Fabes. Initially Mr Bateman, formerly a chartered accountant, had to call on his newly retired predecessor for advice but he was soon injecting an element of his own personality. Today he has a medium-size s/h stock, general but with leanings towards literature and biography, and a few new books on Sussex. Early cl T.

Ask most people what they know about Hastings, and they will venture '1066?'. It is ironic that the resort should be identified with a battle which did not even take place there, when it has an interesting history by any standards. But this is characteristic of a rather unprepossessing town, over-shadowed by its more vigorous neighbour, Brighton. Those who know and appreciate the aesthetic qualities and tranquillity of Hastings would not be surprised to learn that its bookshops are among the best.

In terms of quality and quantity combined the **Howes Bookshop**, Trinity Hall, Braybrooke Terrace, Hastings, E. Sussex, TN34 1HQ (0424 423437), dominates the South Coast although since the books are almost entirely scholarly this probably limits the appeal. A shop with an impressive tradition, Howes' moved to its present premises — a former parish school of St Trinity Church built in 1870 — in 1977. Only a few minutes' walk from the railway station and the shops, this Gothic red-brick structure has enormous character, consisting primarily of two 50 foot long halls in parallel, each with its own impressive open timber roof, appealing to the student of architecture as well as the browser. The extensive stock, approaching 100,000 carefully classified s/h and antiquarian vols, is highly selective; general but with leanings towards literature and history, and important sections including Kent and Sussex local history, bibliography, arts, 17th to 19th-century calf bindings, fine printing and 1st edns.

Howes Bookshop was established well over 60 years ago by Charles Howes, who had served his apprenticeship in Oxford then temporarily abandoned the trade to be an actor and stage manager but reverted to bookselling after his successes in visits to junk shops while on tour. He left Hastings during the war but returned later to join up with a new partner, F. T. Bowyer. Over the next 15 years the shop and catalogue trade went from success to success — culminating with the election of Mr Howes to the presidency of the ABA. Phase II of the company's history began in 1959 when, shortly after the death of Charles Howes, Mr Bowyer took in another partner, Raymond Kilgarriff, with bookselling experience gained in Brighton, London and Cambridge. The stock expanded and a programme of producing three large (2,000 + titles) scholarly catalogues a year was initiated, spreading the good name of the shop further afield. In 1967 Tim Bowyer was also elected president of the ABA.

After nearly 50 years of bookselling Mr Bowyer retired in 1974 and control of the business passed to Mr Kilgarriff, who also became president of the ABA in 1978 (holding that office in the following year) as well as being its long-term librarian. Very conscious of the decline in the number of bookshops in recent years, the company sees one of its main functions as the rescue of books from loss or destruction as owners die or move to smaller homes. 'The absence of a general bookshop in the locality and vendors' despair of finding a buyer now so often leads to good books being lost for ever', is the company's comment on the current situation. Cl lunch and 12.30 Sat.

The impressive Howes operation is complemented by two very different but interesting businesses, both of whom changed names fairly recently. **Stephen Samuelson, Bookseller**, 20 Claremont, Hastings, E. Susex (0424 421149), occupies premises that are reputed to have been a bookshop since 1915, although when Mr Samuelson from Los Angeles took over in 1972 he retained the existing name of Wilson & Franklin — not bothering to change to his own name for another five years. Near the centre of Hastings, in a quiet street only two minutes' walk from the beach, the shop is opposite the library and art school. Emphasis in a general stock of about 6,000 new, s/h and antiquarian books is on lit, art and natural history. Frequent catalogues. Cl lunch and W, but open Sat.

The **Old Hastings Bookshop**, 14 & 15 George Street, Hastings, E. Sussex (0424 425989), was actually only inaugurated in 1976 although there had been a bookshop on the site for over 30 years. The new owner, John Brooman, a writer, who brought with him the goodwill and contents of the shop he had opened six years earlier in Queen's Road, Spearman Books, and amalgamated it with what had been the Powys Bookshop, owned by Francis Powys, son of Theodore. Soon after, he extended the premises by acquiring the shop next door (no 14) and today the stock is of medium size, with a broad appeal. Cl W.

Few people realise that Phyllis Hastings, the popular and prolific author actually dabbled in bookselling by post for a few years before she and her husband Philip opened **The Antiquarian Bookshop**, Battle, E. Sussex, TN33 0AN (042 46 3729), a few minutes from the railway station. As one might have imagined with a woman identified with historical romance, she chose a 13th-century listed property, the home of John Hammond, the last abbot of Battle Abbey, after the dissolution of the monasteries. (It is situated almost opposite the spot where King Harold fell in the misnamed Battle of Hastings.) The shop was a tailor's for many years, making livery and ceremonial dress for many of the country's stately homes. It is really one room into which a general s/h and antiquarian stock of approx 5,000 vols is squeezed, with a reserve, often in boxes, spilling over into the rest of the house. Open Th–Sat.

Only a stone's throw from Hastings is **Freda Fardoe**, 19 Gensing Road, St Leonards-on-Sea, E. Sussex TN38 0HE (0424 429490), situated in a quiet back street in an area which retains something of the charm of a village. Freda Fardoe, disenchanted with commercial life in London, opened the shop in 1966 and enjoys not only bookselling but meeting a local community need. There is no local public library, for example, and shelves outside, displaying paperbacks and cheap hardbacks, provide a useful facility. Inside, the shop carries a general stock of s/h books, including good sections of illustrated books and modern firsts. Apart from local schools, who use the shop to replenish their libraries, the place is a draw to schoolchildren who are made especially welcome and encouraged to browse. Miss Fardoe also sells a few prints and a good range of handmade pottery in the basement. Hours 10–2 and 3–6 or 6.30. Cl W.

Bookman's Halt, 127 Bohemia Road, St Leonards-on-Sea, E. Sussex (0424 421 413), has been a bookshop for over 20 years but it was given a new lease of life in May 1980 when Clive Linklater, a postal bookseller who had also worked for bookshops in Hastings, decided to run his own shop. At that time it sold only occult books and traded under a different name but presumably the spirits or stars were against the idea and its fortunes slumped — until Mr Linklater came on the scene and promptly reverted to the original shop's name. At one stage in its history the premises had housed two shops, because the double frontage has *two* doors with what amounts to a partition dividing two rooms. Mr Linklater capitalises on this structural feature by housing approx 3,000 vols of general interest (including a sprinkling of antiquarian) in one room, and approx 5,000 paperbacks in the other. Cl W.

In the same road at no 116 is the **Bohemia Bookshop** (0424 432 186), run by Frank Letchford and specialising in aviation, but unfortunately most of the out-of-print material has been replaced by new books.

Raymond Smith, 30 South Street, Eastbourne, E. Sussex (0323 34128), is a 'good looking' shop with an elegant air reminiscent of Bredon's antiquarian department at Brighton, particularly its previous shop in Prince Albert Street — which is hardly surprising since Raymond Smith was the inspiration behind it. Having entered bookselling in 1946 after leaving the RAF, he soon went to the Brighton shop and stayed until 1963 when he moved to his present premises. The shop, a large ground floor and basement, has been a bookshop since 1907, well known along the South Coast as 'Glover & Daughter'. A large general s/h and antiquarian stock, particularly strong in foreign books (Mrs Smith is a linguist) and railways. Six days.

Alfriston, another of the charming villages typical of old

Sussex, acquired its first outlet for antiquarian books, the **Alfriston Bookshop**, 12 North Street (0323 870307), in the spring of 1980. In comparison with some of the buildings in the village the shop, owned by Elizabeth and Graham Alcock, is not especially old, having been built in the late 16th century and being the village bakehouse for over 200 years. According to legend there is a mysterious underground passage leading to the river Cuckmere, dating back to smuggling days. The Alcocks, who had been selling books by post, took over what had been an antique shop and the atmosphere of 'treasures' tucked away in nooks and crannies has been retained, with s/h and antiquarian books in a wide range of subjects replacing the antiques and *objets d'art*. The very small stock is supplemented by greetings cards and ephemera. Cl M and W, but visitors seen *by appointment*.

Shirley Deubert, a postal bookseller for several years before deciding to meet the public, opened her first shop in Seaford in 1980. In June of the following year she moved to 31 High Street (0323 891390) to become **Findan Books & Antiques**. Her stock of 3–4,000 s/h vols is general, mainly non-fiction.

One would be naive to judge a bookshop on its appearance, because even in bookselling terms beauty can be only skin deep, but Eric Blundell, at the **15th Century Bookshop**, 99 High Street, Lewes (079 16 4160), is a bookseller of considerable experience and his contribution makes any visit to Lewes a delight. The building itself is half timbered and dates, according to the Sussex Archaeological Society, from about 1450; it is believed to have been the first house to be built outside the town walls. It became a bookshop in 1946 and nine years later was taken over by Mr Blundell, who had his first bookshop in Bloomsbury just before the war.

The stock, consisting of about 10,000 vols of a general nature, three-quarters s/h and one-quarter antiquarian, is housed in two shops made into one at street level but a display of some hundreds of books in cases outside, at the top of a steep lane, is a special attraction. ½ day W — although sometimes Cl all day in winter and out-of-season months.

Just along the hill in a more 'modern' (Georgian) part of

the town is **Bow Windows Bookshop**, 128 High Street, Lewes, E. Sussex (079 16 2839), opened in 1963 as a branch of Wm Dawson & Sons. A former public house and tea shop, the building is 18th century. A good s/h and antiquarian stock is strong in English lit (including firsts and press books), natural history, science, travel, topography, bibliography, art and collecting. Frequent catalogues. Cl Sat except *by appointment*.

Farther along the High Street at no 159 (previously the premises of Kokoro, now at Brighton) is **A. J. Cumming** (079 16 2319), a small double-fronted shop opened in 1976 by Andrew Cumming. Bookselling was his first job. The stock, in one room, consists of over 5,000 volumes of fairly general interest, with a leaning towards natural history, books of local interest and foreign travel. Six days, cl lunch.

People associating Brighton with the Regency period tend to assume it has a long history when in fact as a town it is less than 200 years old. Yet, already the largest in Sussex and still bubbling over with the freshness of youth, it has achieved a satisfying blend of commercial and cultural interests. There have always been a number of bookshops and a strong nucleus holds its own against the general national erosion. Costs here are just as high, but the general attraction of the town as a place to live and the stimulation of healthy competition has infused fresh blood, so that new shops replace those which fall by the wayside. In the main, the town's s/h bookshops are functional, without frills, and good value for money.

George Sexton (Books) Ltd, established in 1886, has now gone, and K. J. Bredon's Bookshop, which opened before World War II, sells only new books. Fortunately **Holleyman & Treacher Ltd**, 21a & 22 Duke Street, BN1 1AH (0273 28007), is still one of the largest booksellers on the South Coast, with 100,000 vols in two adjoining shops, basement and first floor. The business — started just before World War II, closed for the duration and reopened in 1945 — has been run from the earliest days by George Holleyman. The stock is general s/h and antiquarian and the only special subjects are archaeology (following Mr Holleyman's original training) and music (run by the shop's manager Michael

Kadwell). The building, near the town's famous clock-tower, is about 100 years old and when the two shops were 'joined' it was discovered that one had been a temperance hotel. Six days.

Since the last edition **Kokoro** (a rough translation is 'heart and soul') has moved from Lewes to 36 Duke Street, Brighton (0273 25954), where there is a lower gallery of fine Japanese works of art, especially block printing. Colin and Brian Page started the business in 1970 and, apart from Japanese Art and books, the emphasis in a medium-size general stock is on antiquarian material. Six days.

The most elegant setting for a bookshop in this most attractive part of the town could be claimed by the **Theatre Bookshop**, 26 New Road, BN1 1UG (0273 681405) — building and road being constructed in 1805 by order of the Prince Regent to form a new western boundary to the Royal Pavilion Estate. The shop itself, structurally unaltered since erection, could hardly be called 'elegant' because its four floors are rather cramped by the mass of books — but a squeeze I for one find pleasant. The business has been established over 19 years, but was taken over a few years ago by Mr Ryman Atkinson after the death of the founder Miss J. E. Tee. A good general stock of antiquarian and s/h books, constantly changing, includes a 'bargain basement' and 'arts attic'. The shop, strong in theatre, also carries prints, old postcards and ephemera. Open noon–5.30 M–F, all day Sat.

Several shops are clustered around the station to the north of the pier. Three minutes away in the main road leading to the town and sea is **Barry's Books**, 12a Queens Road (0273 23105), which has been in existence for many years but was taken over in 1976 by Desmond Fenwick, who had been an assistant there for the previous 10 years. A single fronted shop, the exterior is quite misleading because inside books are displayed on a ground floor with half landing as well as on two floors above — enough space to house approx 20,000 vols, although a large section is made up of remainders. The s/h stock is general but strong on theology. Six days, but also Sun in summer.

Mr Fenwick also runs the **Collectors' Bookshop**, 32 Gloucester Road (0273 695003), just off the main road, which he opened in 1979 partly as an 'overflow' outlet but mainly to offer a more select s/h stock. The small shop (one deep room on the ground floor) has on display approx 6,000 vols, strong in art and architecture, lit and history, with special sections on Irish and Scottish books. Six days.

Trafalgar Street, by the station, has traditionally been a mecca for bookshops but currently there are only two. First to arrive (in 1972) was **Bioscope Books Ltd**, at no 27 (0273 684754), well known as a specialist in books on the cinema, although surprisingly this only represents 15% of the stock. The proprietor, Ross Mackinnon, started in the trade at the age of 16, serving his 'apprenticeship' with the local Holleyman & Treacher and then the Theatre Bookshop before setting up on his own at the ripe old age of 20. The single fronted shop is on two floors, with the cinema books (including new titles) and film stills near the entrance and the rest of the space displaying approx 8,000 s/h books of general interest. Six days.

David Boland took over an antiques shop at no 44 to open **The Trafalgar Bookshop** (0273 684300), in December 1980. A corner shop, the stock is currently confined to one room and consists of approx 6,000 s/h and antiquarian vols of a general interest with leanings towards sporting books, colour-plate books and steel engravings. Mr. Boland, who has been interested in books for most of his life and once ran a stall in Portobello Road, raised the capital for this venture by working in Holland for a period as a technical author. Six days.

In terms of quality and turnover, one of the most popular shops in the town is **The Odd Volume**, 53 Upper Gloucester Road, Brighton (0273 27845), off Queen's Road and a 100 yards from the station, where the speciality is modern firsts and there is a large selection of 19th and 20th-century literature. Opened in 1979 by Jonathon Dodds (ex-publishing), Dave Brewer and Tony Miller (whose backgrounds were academic), the partners made an immediate impact — compensating for their lack of experience with enthusiasm and intelligence, ensuring that they had the right sort of stock at the right prices. A single fronted shop with 5–6,000 s/h vols, another speciality is

149

politics (which takes in economics and history). Between the shelves prints and paintings are displayed. Six days. (The shop is represented in a novel 'commune' type bookshop in London's Portobello Road market — see 'West London'.)

Renaissance Books, 52a North Road, also off Queen's Road and about five minutes' walk from the station, is a small shop opened in January 1980 by Catherine J. Walton and her mother. Initially, shortage of shelf space limited the size of stock to around 1,000 vols of general s/h interest, but the intention was to specialise in lit and poetry.

Picture Books, 88 St James Street, Brighton (0273 697 381), is compared by its proprietor Camilla Francombe to a lighthouse. Obviously that description is more symbolic than physical, despite the fact that the building is tall and narrow — in fact six floors, three of which belong to the shop. The stock of approx 20,000 s/h and antiquarian books occupies not only extensive shelving on each of the three floors but every nook and cranny, and even parts of the narrow spiral staircase. A reserve stock clutters up the living accommodation above the shop. Camilla, daughter of Kim Francombe of Worthing, was raised among books, had a spell with Foyles, and opened her first shop in partnership with Stuart Broad, a lecturer, in 1976 before moving to the present, larger and more central site in 1978. Initially, the emphasis was very much on illustrated books, particularly of the 1920s and 30s, but gradually the stock became more general so that today the shop has a very wide appeal (content as well as atmosphere). Six days. Open some evenings in summer, but by inclination and not habit.

Public House Books, 21 Little Preston Street, BN1 2HQ (0273 28357), is what might be termed an 'alternative' bookshop and of fringe interest to most readers as almost 90% of the stock is new paperbacks. Good s/h books are only carried in the specialist areas of contemporary English and American lit, mythology and legends, occult and Eastern religions — a range which comes somewhere between that of Watkins of Cecil Court and Indica, which had such a meteoric but short life in Bloomsbury some years ago. The shop is also unconventional in that the aim of the owner, Richard Cupidi, is to offer more than just a place to buy books: the shop offers what he calls an 'experience' and has a somewhat eccentric but warm and friendly atmosphere in an offbeat setting — a small mid-Victorian public house, probably the last in Brighton with its original characteristic façade. Coffee available.

Kemp Town Books, 91 St George's Road, Brighton (0273 682110), a bow fronted shop in the Kemp Town district, carries both new and s/h stock to meet local demand. However the proprietors Vernon and Gisela Hendy, who came here in December 1973, have a special affection for the s/h side and carry around 2,000 items of general interest, with leanings towards photography, art and illustrated, modern lit and (in the basement) politics. Vernon, a former teacher, still teaches foreign students English in the mornings and takes over the afternoon 'shift' while his wife runs the shop in the morning. ½ day W.

K. Lane Bookshop, 52 Blatchington Road, Hove, BN3 3YH (0273 731386), run by Mr and Mrs Kenneth Lane since 1959, and has a medium-size s/h stock covering fiction, poetry, history, biography and natural history, together with Mr Lane's own speciality, circus. Three minutes' walk from Hove station. Early cl W, open Sat.

The Wilbury Bookshop, 69a Church Road (by Wilbury Road), Hove, BN3 2BB (0273 772115), changed ownership in the summer of 1980 when Philip Pegler, former nurse and journalist (latterly with *The Bookdealer*), moved into bookselling for the first time. It is a tiny shop with a stock of approx 3,000 s/h items of general interest apart from Philip's specialities, oriental philosophy, India and natural medicine. The mood is one of careful disarray, ie books everywhere, but no dust and one cannot help noticing that the floor is carpeted. Six days.

A proprietor's personal contribution to his bookshop varies considerably, but when a good business is old enough it seems to develop an identity of its own, so ownership can change hands without greatly influencing the shop's character. **James Bain Ltd**, 18 Market Square, Horsham, W Sussex (0403 2187), was established in the year after the Battle of Waterloo and has a fascinating history (related in *Bain, a bookseller looks back*, 1940, with preface by Hugh

Walpole) as a distinguished London bookseller. Today it is a simple (but very good) country bookshop, yet to bibliophiles who remember both addresses it is much the same.

In the early days, the business sold new as well as old books and also, in the bookselling tradition, published. When the last member of the Bain family died in 1936, it was passed to a long-serving member of the staff who was joined by a former librarian at Chatsworth, and kept the shop going during the war. In 1946 it was bought by Rodney Drake who had spent a few months in publishing. The site was scheduled for rebuilding and, when James Bain eventually had to leave William IV Street in 1966, Mr Drake had to decide whether to find alternative premises in the West End or move out of town. He wanted to concentrate on antiquarian books, so while a decision on location was being taken he sold from his home by catalogue and when the present premises — a bookshop for 25 years — became available in 1971 the business moved to Horsham. The catalogue business was now discontinued and everything channelled through the shop, an old building in the Market Square with a stock of some 10,000 books housed in a small ground floor showroom with two rooms upstairs. Coverage is very general, the ratio of s/h to antiquarian being 60:40, the more expensive books being available only on application. The business, run by Mr and Mrs Drake and a part-time staff, seems very different on the surface from the West End days with a team of 9–11 people, yet the books are much the same and the customers are remarkably similar. Cl Th, open all Sat.

The Drakes also run **The Merlin Gallery**, High Street, Petworth, W Sussex (0798 42235), with a small but select stock of books and prints. Cl W and lunch.

Another specialist postal bookseller worth a visit for those interested in the subject is **Post Mortem Books***, 45 Wilmington Close, Hassocks, W Sussex, BN6 8QB (07918 2612), run by Ralph and Elaine Spurrier. This business deals only in detective fiction and 2,000 s/h vols are displayed in one room and the hall at the house in the centre of the village, which is itself 10 minutes by train or 15 by car from Brighton. *Strictly by appointment.*

Another of the large rambling bookshops ('dusty but well

organised', volunteers one of the partners) which have a wide appeal is **The Old Bookshop,** 52 North Street, Worthing, W Sussex, BN11 1DU (0903 202066). Opened in 1951 by Raymond Blossett, who was joined four years later by Colin Chiswell, the shop has 40—45,000 s/h and antiquarian vols of general interest on the ground floor and in three rooms above, the only speciality being sheet music. C1 W (except in high summer).

Worthing has two other interesting bookshops — both founded and inspired by women booksellers, although their enthusiasm spread to other members of the family. **Frances Books**, 3 Crescent Road (0903 31169), near the town centre, has been established slightly longer — the shop was opened in 1970, although Mrs M. F. Lee had already been trading as a postal bookseller for four years, persuading her husband to give up his architectural practice to become her partner in 1968.

Apart from building his own business, Michael Lee became treasurer of the Provincial Bookseller's Fairs Association (PBFA) and took over as secretary when Gerald Mosdell retired in February 1980. In the same year he instituted a marked change in the policy of the shop — utilising his skills in design and lay-out in the process. The bulk of the books were cleared and in place of fiction, biography and the usual bookshop 'standard' texts, came a much smaller, very select, mainly antiquarian stock, displayed to advantage in a purpose built showroom with fitted carpet, glass showcases and books picked out by spotlights. Subjects now include travel and topography, natural history, colour-plate books and fine bindings. Mr Lee felt that too many booksellers kept their better books under lock and key (for security reasons in the main), whereas he takes a pride in showing them off. Six days, cl W pm.

Kim Francombe opened **Kim's Bookshop** in 1972, at 17 West Buildings (0903 206282), by the sea front, after gaining her experience in antiques markets and postal bookselling. The initial impetus was provided when a dealer friend visited her home, was impressed by the number of books and suggested the Francombes take a stall in a local market. It was never their intention to run a full-time shop, but trade snowballed and the inevitable happened. The shop has two rooms above open to the public and a selective stock, Mrs Francombe's special interest being natural history and illustrated books, especially birds, orchids and fungi. Her daughter Camilla, who came into the firm in 1973, 'graduated' to running her own shop in Brighton but her place was soon filled by another daughter, Linda. Mr Francombe, although a fervent bibliophile, has not yet been 'engulfed' by the business although he helps out at weekends and spends his holidays going to auctions. Six days, but cl lunch and early W.

A newcomer, **Colin Mears Bookshop**, 17 Station Parade, Tarring Road, West Worthing, W Sussex (0903 503530), almost opposite the railway station, is only a tiny shop; but, since the stock of 2,500 is divided between children's illustrated books (early Victorian to 1950) and non-fiction, the selection in each speciality is quite impressive. The shop, with its relatively large window display, was taken over in October 1979 by Colin Mears who had been dealing by post for the previous five years. Cl lunch and W.

Doris Rayment Books actually has two retail outlets, at the Petworth antiques market in East Street, Petworth, W Sussex (0798 42073), and a smaller shop **Books & Antiques** at the original Petworth antiques market in Angel Street, established in 1967. At both there are a variety of stalls which could interest wives/husbands of the browser while he/she concentrates on books. At East Street the bookroom displays 3–4,000 s/h and antiquarian items of general interest, while at Angel Street the stock is even smaller but more select. Six days, cl lunch.

Ephemera, 12b High Street, Arundel, W Sussex (0903 883120), is an offshoot of a printing and stationery shop which has been established on this site, in the shadow of Arundel Castle, for the past 110 years. As Harry Mitchell Jacob approached retirement he concentrated his attentions on books, an interest that began over 50 years ago when a tramp walked into the shop and sold him a book for 6d which he later sold for £1. Small general stock but constantly growing. Six days.

The Bookshop in Norfolk Road, 13 Norfolk Road,

Littlehampton, W Sussex BN17 5PW (090 64 3638), established in 1969 by E. & W. H. Gillespie, is probably the only shop in the country specialising in books on the police service. Situated in Beach, the older and more attractive part of the town, in a cluster of interesting businesses including three selling antiques, the shop also has a small general stock, some new, a little bric-a-brac and some prints. Cl ½ day or all W (depending on season).

Anthony D. Lilley*, 1 North Place, Western Road, Littlehampton, W Sussex (090 64 4028), is actually a shop officially open from T−Sat, but since the proprietor is primarily concerned with mail order he is sometimes away on buying trips and an *appointment* is therefore advisable. However, more often than not the shop is manned and, as Mr and Mrs Lilly live above, anyone calling on the offchance can ring the bell. Mr Lilly, a bookseller for 30 years and initially manager of Hatchard's antiquarian department, has only a small stock on display but is probably worth a visit for those interested in natural history.

The **Bognor Regis Bookshop**, 39 West Street, Bognor Regis, W Sussex (024 38 22030), was established in the 1950s but taken over by George Thompson in 1967 soon after he opened a shop (in partnership) in nearby Chichester — although the two operations are run quite separately. A short walk from the town centre, near the sea front, this rather large shop has a big general s/h stock with some antiquarian items. Cl lunch and W.

George Thompson had been a bookseller in London and in the trade for 16 years when he opened the **Chichester Bookshop Ltd**, 39 Southgate (0243 785473), in partnership with John Dent in 1966. Expansion resulted in taking over the shop a few doors away at no 33 where the more expensive items are concentrated. The shop, near the station and opposite a free car park, carries a large general s/h selection including some antiquarian. Cl Th pm but open all Sat.

Vivian Meynell has been a bookseller in Chichester since 1946 but for most of that time he was part of Offord and Meynell Ltd, and the shop was only renamed **Meynell's Bookshop** when he moved from his popular shop in East Street to 11 The Hornet, Eastgate Square (0243 782018), 30 years later. The name-change came about because the 'new' premises are approached through an unrelated art gallery, up some stairs into a large, light and pleasant room with floor to ceiling windows. A stock of approx 10,000 s/h and antiquarian vols is very general but strong in fiction, biography, natural history, topography and the arts. Cl M and lunch.

SOUTH AND SOUTH WEST

The traditional Cinderella image endured by the booktrade in Devon and Cornwall must inevitably change with the extension of motorways and the generally improved links (eg the Avon Bridge at Bristol) with the region. Devon particularly has also benefited from the influx of fresh blood as booksellers search for lower overheads in pleasanter surroundings. The position of Hampshire and Dorset remains reasonably healthy, with a number of delightful bookshops.

The Farnborough Gallery and Bookshop, Selbourne House, 26 Guildford Road West, Farnborough, Hants (0252 518033), must be the only bookshop in the country also stocking saddlery and horse riding gear. The premises, opened in 1979 by former postal bookseller Peter Taylor, carry a select stock of approx 5,000 s/h and antiquarian books specialising in military history and modern firsts, as well as paintings and original prints. At the moment the books occupy two rooms but at the time of going to press there were plans for further expansion. Cl W.

From the outside, the attractive double fronted red-and-white brick Georgian building that houses the **Liss Bookshop and Gallery**, 73 Station Road, Liss, Hants (073 082 2406), looks more like an art gallery than bookshop but inside the illusion is quickly dispelled. Opened at the beginning of 1978 by Olive Butler, who had been a postal bookseller and now runs the book operation, and Ellis Gabie, who looks after the gallery, the shop (3 miles to the north of Petersfield) carries a stock of approx 40,000 books, one-third of which are antiquarian — predominantly natural history. The bulk of the stock, which Mrs Butler describes as 'good browsing material', is displayed in the main shop alongside paintings and art materials. Most subjects are covered and constant efforts are made to upgrade weaker areas. An upstairs room carries the antiquarian stock and there are separate areas for paperbacks, pocket-size books and theology and cheaper fiction, although this includes modern firsts and often provides some good buys. Six days.

Frank Westwood, proprietor of **The Petersfield Bookshop**, 16a Chapel Street, Petersfield, Hants (0730 3438), is one of the better known names in bookselling — yet the business was founded by Dr Harry Roberts, well known East End doctor and one of the instigators of the Panel scheme which preceded the National Health scheme. Mr Westwood, who had previously run the book side of a combined antiques and books business, decided to concentrate on books and took over the Petersfield Bookshop in 1958. The shop trade prospered and the premises next door (once a slaughterhouse) were purchased in 1973, so that the shop area is quite extensive now. The front door opens onto a new book and art materials department which leads into a print and picture gallery, while behind are fine bindings in glass cases and a large s/h and antiquarian dept. The general stock is large, but with specialities in travel and topography. A picture framing workshop is housed upstairs. Six days.

The Bookshop, The Square, Emsworth, Hants (024 34 2617), is a converted Georgian house which sells mostly new books, although there are usually a few thousand s/h items of general interest. The proprietor, Miss D. M. Way, opened her first bookshop in 1946 after leaving the WRNS, simply because she liked books and thought she would give it a try. She moved to the present site — a pleasant part of the village between the square and the harbour — in 1962. Cl lunch and W pm.

Theology, Puritan and Reformed books are the speciality of **Academy Books**, 13 Marmion Road, Southsea, Hants (0705 816632), and with a stock well in excess of 20,000 books the subject is obviously covered pretty comprehensively. However the double fronted, six roomed shop is worth a visit from those with much wider interests because another 15,000 s/h vols come into the category of general stock, with most subjects covered. The proprietor William H. Robinson began dealing by post in 1970, opening his first shop two years later before moving to the centre of Southsea in 1974. Six days.

Some specialist subjects are so narrow that 1,000 titles represents a very comprehensive coverage. This is the number of books on humanism that **Donald E. W. Howells*** has in stock at his home at 24 Pitreavie Road, Cosham, Portsmouth, Hants, PO6 2ST (0705 374476) where he operates a postal service. A former civil servant, Mr Howells retired in 1980 having arranged to take over the specialist stock of bookseller Kit Mouart of Cuckfield (Sussex), installing the books in a print shop in his garden from which he has also started a private press. *Strictly by appointment.*

A number of booksellers have come into the trade by chance, but few more accidentally than Alan Obin who runs the **Warsash Nautical Bookstore**, 31 Newton Road, Warsash, Southampton, Hants SO3 6FY (048 95 2384). A marine engineer by profession, he decided to opt out of the industrial rat race at 40. It was while studying the possibility of hiring out cruisers and lecturing that he came across a bookshop for sale in this lovely South Coast yachting village — then owned by yachting writer Philip Bristow and specialising in nautical books! The combination of site and subject seemed too much of a coincidence, and the Obins took it over in 1973. Situated in a pleasant country lane, the shop is very near the Southampton School of Navigation and supplies the college library as well as students who come to browse. The stock of new as well as s/h books covers all aspects of the sea and nautical interests. Six days, but cl lunch.

People go into bookselling from all walks of life but **T. A. Cherrington**, 67 Bedford Place, Southampton, Hants SO1 2DS (0703 24265), is one of the very few farmers — if not the only one. Tom actually began by selling antique agricultural implements together with books, before the books took over and even farming as a subject had disappeared by the time he opened his first shop in 1976. He moved to the present premises, a shop with attractive leaded-light windows on the northern edge of the town centre, four years later. The ground floor and basement, covering over 800sq ft, house 10–20,000 volumes which range from paperbacks to rare items, although the stock is mainly in the £1–£10 bracket. Six days.

In 1959 **H. M. Gilbert & Son**, 2½ Portland Street,

Southampton, Hants SO1 0EB (0703 26420), celebrated the centenary of the firm, which was founded by Henry Gilbert, a printer and bookseller from Halstead in Essex who came to the town as a refugee from religious harassment. Henry March Gilbert spent some time at Sotheran's in London to gain experience, returning home in 1869 to take over the business on the death of his father. 'H.M.', as he was known, was not only a bookseller but a writer and publisher and as the business thrived the shop was moved to an address in Above Bar where it remained until destroyed by the blitz in World War II. Fortunately, the transfer of books to the present premises had been almost complete and, although Portland Street was damaged by bombing, the shop survived.

Among the literary names who frequented the shops (particularly the older one in Above Bar) and became friendly was T. E. Lawrence, when he lodged nearby, and who came incognito. Today the shop is run by Bruce Gilbert who joined the firm in 1946 after war service and has since become a member of the Council of the Booksellers Association and was recently chairman of the Hampshire branch. Perhaps because of the character of the town, the Southampton shop is more noticeably commercial than the Winchester branch, with such regular activities as author 'signings'. Apart from a busy passing trade, it also has a substantial business with local schools, libraries and — as one might expect — a shipping line. Although visitors might be amused at the address — and correspondents certainly prefer to 'correct' 2½ to 2a or 21* — people in Southampton would not bat an eyelid; after all, the bookshop's back door is in Regent Street, and the number is 1½. Six days.

*The shop has preserved a letter addressed to: 2½d Postcard Street.

The history of **H. M. Gilbert & Son**, 18/19 The Square, Winchester, Hants (0962 2832), is necessarily shorter, dating back to 1904 when it was transferred from the High Street, where a branch had been established nine years earlier by H.M.'s younger son, Owen. Meanwhile he had returned to Southampton in 1889 to run that business for the next 50 years and H.M., who lived in Winchester, continued with the 'new' shop until his death in 1930. The newer flourishing

160

business was bequeathed to his second wife, who ran it with a manager, but when she died it was bought by her step-grandson Bruce Gilbert, who now controls the two shops from Southampton. His son Richard Charles Gilbert (the fifth generation) is now also a partner, based mainly at Winchester. There is a large and first-class stock of s/h and antiquarian (and new) books, covering the broadest range of subjects. In 1978 the beautiful part-timbered Elizabethan building was completely restored revealing a 14th-century wood-panelled banqueting hall, concealed by ceilings and partitions. This made a perfect home for the antiquarian books on what is now an extended ground floor.

The SPCK Bookshop just around the corner at 24 The Square, Winchester, Hants (0962 66617), is typical of the group's positive policy with regard to s/h and antiquarian books. Housed in a Queen Anne building next door to a public house which used to be the rectory of St Lawrence's Church, one of the oldest in Winchester, and run by Geoffrey Fair, an enthusiast for s/h books, the stock of well over 5,000 vols covers lit, history and topography as well as theology. Six days.

The Printed Page, 2 Bridge Street (a continuation of the High Street), Winchester, Hants (0962 4072), has a fairly offbeat specialisation — books on canals. It was opened in 1977 by Christopher Wright, formerly an international management consultant who had collected books and prints on the subject for some years and eventually decided to put his expertise to some commercial use. Books on canals were extended to local topography but the stock remains very small although there is a bigger selection of prints and maps housed in the two rooms of this interesting building — once two busy shops with an ominous connection, a barbers and a pie shop! The location is just outside the old city walls by Eastergate. Cl M.

The Hampshire Bookshop, Kingsgate Arch, Winchester, Hants (0962 64710), is a modest business dealing exclusively in regional material, but it remains a must for readers interested in architectural history. The shop is actually contained within the famous Kingsgate, one of Winchester's surviving medieval gates built into the south wall of the city.

161

The gate is mentioned in the Winchester Survey of 1148, although the present structure belongs to the 14th century. The pedestrian entrances to the gate are 18th century and the shop's pretty bow window, in character, came from the George Hotel which once stood in the High Street. Run by Margaret Green, a specialist in Hampshire history and a local writer, it carries new as well as out-of-print material on the county and the Isle of Wight. It also has an interesting display of original engraved prints, lithographs and antiquarian maps. Cl lunch, M and Th.

Laurence Oxley, of The Studio Bookshop and Gallery, Alresford, Hants (096 273 2188), is a bookseller who is reluctant to wait for people to come to him. Although this is very much a small family business, it exhibits regularly at book fairs, and at one or two international ones every year (eg Los Angeles and Tokyo). Mr Oxley also lectures to further education classes on the general subject of books. Near Winchester and housed in a protected early 18th-century building, the business — opened by Mr Oxley in the early 1950s — has four rooms converted into what has become a very long showroom with a gallery for prints and maps. A large general stock of approx 20,000 vols includes sections on India and the Far East, leather bindings and Hampshire topography. A workshop at the rear carries out restoration work on books and paintings and prints. ½ day W.

There are a number of bookshops on sites so valuable that the proprietors could realise a small fortune by selling up and working from home. **D. M. Beach**, 52–54 High Street, Salisbury, Wilts, SP1 2PG (0722 3801), probably comes into this category. While property prices in Wiltshire cannot compare with (say) London, this marvellous corner site in the High Street is an enormous overhead for any bookshop, although fortunately it has established such a thriving trade that the proprietor Anthony Pearce is able to resist the temptation to sell by catalogue.

The building must be the second oldest in the country occupied by a bookshop — having been dated pretty accurately to 1380–90 by two pairs of scissor beams in the roof. Little is known of its subsequent history except that in the late 19th century it was an antiques shop. The business was established by Dorothy Margaret Beach, who had started bookselling in the town in 1930 and moved to the present site four years later, retaining the name although her married name became Pearce. Mr Pearce, whose background had been in art and picture framing, came into the shop and the s/h and antiquarian stock began to specialise in colour-plate books, topography, atlases, bindings and children's books. He died a few years ago at the age of 89, having worked until the end. Their son Anthony, who joined the business at the age of 17 and returned immediately after national service, continued the special interest in maps and atlases. Between 40–50,000 vols have a wide general interest, but the rarer books tend to be in the specialities. They are displayed in the main shop, which is approx 100 × 90 feet, and the showroom upstairs where there is usually something for everyone. Not to be missed. Six days.

At the **Everyman Bookshop**, 5 Bridge Street, Salisbury, Wilts SP1 2ND (0722 3531), just off the High Street, only 20–25% of the stock is s/h, but the owner's policy is to be very selective and not to waste shelf space with nondescript material. Tony Martin opened the shop in 1976 and obviously found the policy paid because after the first four years the turnover had risen by *seven* times. The Everyman is another of the shops that plays classical music (in this case Mozart) as an entertainment and not merely as mindless background music; and in my view shops that take the trouble to 'package' their wares intelligently deserve to succeed. The shop actually occupies four floors but the 5,000 s/h items are divided between the basement, where they share space with remainders, and the new Penguin floor. A few rare or particularly attractive books can be seen on request. Six days.

If you happen to be in Lymington, Hants, take a look at **King's of Lymington Ltd**, 105/6 High Street, SO4 9ZD (059 0 72137), although it barely qualifies for this book as it sells only new books. However the shop, a double fronted and bow windowed building, was established in 1735 and has remained in the King family ever since — probably the longest period a bookselling business has been operated by one family. The present owner, Edward King, is the author of *A*

Walk Through Lymington, 1972, and his daughter is unfortunately last in the family line. The very few s/h books in stock are concerned with local history. Open 8.30 (the shop is also a newsagents), early cl W.

The fact that the town had supported *any* bookshop for so many years was one of the reasons that persuaded Peter Hughes and Sandra Smeeth to open the town's first s/h and antiquarian bookshop — **Hughes & Smeeth Ltd**, 26 St Thomas Street, Lymington, Hants (0590 76324), in 1976. The shop, on the ground floor of a double fronted 17th-century building, is at the top (entrance) of the town (St Thomas Street being an extension of the High Street). The stock of approx 10–15,000 books is of general interest but strong in natural history, travel and topography and maps and prints. Both partners gained much of their experience with Beach of Salisbury; Mr Hughes for 14 years, and Miss Smeeth as manager of their maps and prints department. Six days.

Although most of its business is done by post and at book fairs, **Tara Books Ltd***, South End House, Church Lane, Lymington, Hants SO4 9RA (0590 76848), can still display around 4,000 vols in what must be one of the country's only bookrooms housed in a stable block. Tara Books was started by Peter and Elizabeth Watson at Winchester in 1973, moving to their present premises, a beautiful Queen Anne house with walled garden, four years later. The stock, in the main between 1750 and 1920, covers social and economic history, fashion and travel. Peter was an industrialist before becoming a full-time bookseller and Elizabeth's academic training was to prove useful in dealing with library requirements. *Strictly by appointment.*

Derrick H. Nearn of **Heritage Books,** 7 Cross Street, Ryde, Isle of Wight (0983 62933), must be the only bookseller in the UK who could speak to a customer in Kikongo — as well as French, Portuguese and his native English. Derrick, a Fellow of the Royal Geographical Society and a Batchelor of Divinity, spent several years as a missionary in Angola, where he spoke Portuguese, and latterly in Zaire (until 1977). Having retired and determined to open a bookshop on the Isle of Wight, he spent a year in preparation, buying and converting a little teashop. The shop is uncharacteristically modern with bright coloured furnishings and white shelving shown off to advantage by clever use of spotlights. Approx 7–8,000 vols encompass new, s/h and antiquarian and in an upstairs print room he also displays old Isle of Wight prints. Cl Th (and W in Jan and Feb).

New Milton, Hampshire has the advantage of being on the road between Lymington and Christchurch and it extends into Barton-on-Sea which is right on the coast. It is pleasant to find a relatively large stock of s/h books (between 20–30,000 vols) at **Books & Things**, 99 Old Milton Road, BH25 6DN (0425 617521), opened in 1977 by former schoolteacher Tony Keith. A large shop with a 20ft frontage, and 40ft deep, displays its stock in one room with library shelving down the middle. The books are of general interest and 'Things' refers to comics, magazines and paper ephemera. ½ day W.

Bournemouth's oldest bookselling business, **Commin's Antiquarian Bookshop**, 100 Old Christchurch Road, Bournemouth, Hants BH1 1LR (0202 27504), established by Horace Commin in 1892, has its early days chronicled in a privately printed *History of Commin's*, 1956, which listed some of the distinguished customers, eg Aubrey Beardsley. When Mr Commin died in 1911 the business passed into other hands and since 1956 has been owned by John Ruston. The shop occupies an enormous building and when Mr Ruston decided to concentrate on the s/h and antiquarian side in 1968, he let off the bottom two floors — now rented by Hatchards — and retained the top three. Very large general stock (the only speciality being archaeology) occupying six rooms, the largest of which is devoted entirely to antiquarian.

Mr Ruston has made some spectacular acquisitions in his time — although none more accidentally than the occasion a few years ago when he inspected a private library in which the fine bindings were rather more impressive than the contents. On leaving he asked whether there were any other books in the house. Someone vaguely recalled having seen a few books in the attic — cast-offs which turned out to be the considerable personal collection of the 1st Earl of Eldon — one of the nation's most famous Lord Chancellors — overlooked since his death in 1838! Six days.

Another old-established business, **Sidney Wright (Booksellers) Ltd,** 12 & 13 Royal Arcade, Boscombe, Bournemouth, BH1 4BT (0202 37153), was established in 1905 and eventually taken over by Mr Wright's former assistant, Peter Shore, who has been here now for 44 years. The business consists of two adjoining shops in a Victorian arcade, carrying a general s/h stock of several thousand vols. Cl W, but open all Sat.

A letter of the alphabet after a street number usually conjures up visions of poky little half-properties but the **Ashley Bookshop,** at 30B Ashley Road, Boscombe, Bournemouth, has enough room to display 40,000 s/h books because the premises were once The Boscombe Tabernacle Church. Mr and Mrs E. W. Horne, who took over in 1975, decided to move to the present building, keeping such features as the stained glass windows, the high pitch pine ceiling and first floor gallery while greatly increasing the display areas. The stock is very general, but specialises in English topography and natural history. Six days.

One of the country's largest stocks of books on food, wine and cookery can be found at **Culmus Books,** 23 St Leonard's Road, Bournemouth, BH8 8QL (0202 519683). In a room on the first floor some 4–5,000 books, together with prints and related ephemera, are the speciality of Ron Kaufmann, who recently retired from a career in lecturing on cookery and food studies (he has also written books on the subject, and was co-translator of the highly regarded *Le Guide Culinaire* by Auguste Escoffier). The shop was opened in 1975 by Ron and his wife Dorothy who looks after a stock of approx 7–8,000 s/h vols in two rooms downstairs, together with a sprinkling of cheap items in the entrance hall. Cl M and lunch, although the Kaufmanns live on the premises and will see visitors *by appointment at other times.*

Christopher Williams*, 178 Old Christchurch Road, Bournemouth, Hants BH1 1NU (0202 23130), gained his initial experience at a London bookshop before starting his own business on the South Coast in 1967, with his wife Pauline in partnership. He did have a bookshop in the same road (at no 214) for 18 months but to get the sort of books he wanted felt he could not be 'tied' and moved to his present office premises, on the second floor above the Woolwich Building Society, where he sees customers *by appointment* between buying and attending book fairs. Although the stock of 2,000 s/h and antiquarian items is small, it is very select and worth a visit from those interested in the arts, bibliography and West Country topography.

A mutual interest in sailing brought Sarah Vose and Bob Davis together to launch **The Parkstone Bookshop**, 443 Ashley Road, Parkstone, Poole, Hants (0202 743432), in 1980, although their stock of 10,000 s/h vols is very general. Trained as a dancer, Sarah spent 15 years working in s/h shops in Richmond and Blackheath, meanwhile helping her mother start a new bookshop in Midhurst. Bob Davis worked on computer technology before moving to Poole. The wide forecourt is a display area for 'bargains'. Hours initially uncertain so phone call advisable.

Bill Hoade managed pop groups for a number of years before going into bookselling, initially with Commin's of Bournemouth, and opening the **Wimborne Bookshop**, 10 miles away at 26 West Street, Wimborne, Dorset (0202 887320), in 1977. The shop is in a listed building with a huge display window converted from a double fronted Victorian shop, although the building dates back to the 1750s. The stock is small (approx 3,000 s/h and antiquarian vols) but select, with archaeology, the main speciality, housed in one room, and prints and more general books, eg topography and natural history, in the other. The shop also offers a picture framing service. ½ day W.

The **Book in Hand**, 17 Bell Street, Shaftesbury, Dorset has all the qualities to make it a very special bookshop. The present owner is Christopher Driver (editor of the *Good Food Guide*) who inherited the shop from his father, a retired doctor. The atmosphere which Dr Driver created so captivated the American naturalist Edwin Way Teale that in his book *Springtime in Britain*, 1971, he said of the shop: 'Of all the bookstores I encountered, this was the one that left the most enduring impression . . . the elderly man beside the tiny fire amid those thousands and thousands of dusty books.' The shop is housed in a listed late 16th-century building, its ground floor below street level, with original Tudor fireplace.

The stock of some 8,000 books is general and Mr Driver's own buying interests range from instumental music to the social history of food. The shop is now managed by Mrs Gillian Weall. Picture framing is also arranged and an independent potter, Anne Chase, works from a shed in the garden. The character of the place is epitomised by the cast iron shop sign depicting a shelf of books, designed and made in a nearby forge. Cl lunch and by 4.30pm, and W.

Two miles from Tolpuddle is Puddletown, Dorset, interesting in its own right and site of **The Antique Map and Bookshop**, Saddlers, 32 High Street (the main A35 from Bournemouth to Dorchester), DT2 8RU (030 584 633), part of the home of Mrs H. M. Proctor. The entrance is round at the side of the house, built in 1820 and used for many years as a saddlers. A spacious shop maintaining much of its original character, it carries an interesting medium-size stock. Apart from a selection of s/h books in the entrance hall priced at £1 or less, the material is selective and although fairly general is strong on illustrated books, fine bindings, topography, natural history, works on collecting and lit. There is also a good range of 17th/18th-century maps, mainly of Dorset and adjoining counties. Cl lunch and ½ day W; in winter prior phone call advisable.

At the heart of the delightful old Dorset town of Dorchester is **H. V. Day**, The Old Roman Catholic Church, 25 High West Street, DT1 1VW (0305 4904). The business was actually started in London in 1936 by Harvey Day and Mollie Van Noorden, formerly in fine art publishing, moving to Dorchester in 1945 and to these premises in 1977. Despite the size of the fascinating building, the stock is very small but of excellent quality and mainly antiquarian, being fed from a large store not open to the public. On display in one large showroom are early engravings, prints and old maps. The church was built in 1888 — *17 miles away* at Wareham! It was intended as a monastery, but the order did not grow and, in 1906, the monastery was dismantled, the stones numbered and brought by horse and cart to be set up again in the country town. It then served as the parish church for nearly 70 years until the community moved to another church and the redundant building was taken over by Harvey Day to house the present bookshop. Cl lunch and ½ day Th.

One can hardly miss **R. E. Greenland,** 8 Church Street, Dorchester, Dorset (0305 2517), since it is the only shop in the road (just off the Bournemouth–Bridport road). Established 24 years ago, the business was bought in 1972 by Ronald Greenland and his brother Gerald, who left in 1980 to run his own business specialising in trees. About 5,000 s/h and antiquarian vols are housed in one large room, the only speciality being Thomas Hardy and, to a lesser extent, books on Imperial Russia. Cl Th pm.

The Treasure Trove, run by Sheila and Peter Barrett at 28 & 29 East Street, Weymouth, Dorset (030 57 72757), is tailor-made for the 'treasure' seeker. Housed in a delightful 1720 shop and house, protected as a building of special architectural and historical interest, the business has a large collection of antiques and curios on the ground floor and a large stock of s/h and antiquarian books upstairs. The ceiling had to be reinforced to withstand the weight of an estimated 40,000 vols — the contents of two bookshops which had closed — including sections on military affairs (especially the Boer War), education, literature and history. They range in quality from modern firsts to cheap Victorian novels, and with the exception of paperbacks are grouped in subjects. One minute from the sea front and the harbour, cl lunch and W pm.

The **Marine-Workshop Bookshop,** The Cobb, Lyme Regis, Dorset (029 74 2429), occupies the 200-year-old scheduled building used at one time for bonding wine, spirits, tea and coffee arriving at the harbour, known since the 12th century as 'The Cobb'. The books are protected by stone walls 3ft 6in deep and massive hardwood beams. On display are about 6,000 classified general interest s/h and antiquarian volumes although Maurice Bishop, who founded the business in 1959, has several thousand more in stock. Six days: in summer open Sunday, in winter most of the time, depending on the weather. Its exposed position means it is hardly worth opening in a full gale because customers cannot get there.) Incidentally, the shop is staffed by seven retired bibliophiles who each put in a day a week and if one looks closely you will be surprised to see one of them writing his sermon for the following Sunday.

Lyme Regis has been the home for many years of John Fowles, which is one of the reasons **Serendip Fine Books**, 11 Broad Street, Lyme Regis, Dorset (02974 2594), is usually able to offer signed copies of his books. Situated in the heart of the town, the present shop — featured in the filming of Fowles' *French Lieutenant's Woman* for which the frontage was strikingly (and indefinitely) victorianised — is the fifth owned by Chris and Marguerite Chapman in the 12 years they have been in the town. The main room is devoted to new books (including Mr Chapman's own publishing imprint which started modestly a few years ago with local history booklets but has developed into an interesting and diverse list) but the back room has around 3–4,000 general s/h and antiquarian volumes. Six days, often open until 10pm in summer.

The **Victoria Book Shop**, 14 Temple Street, Sidmouth, Devon (039 55 4461), was opened in 1974 by Ken Austin of the Victoria Book Shop, Swindon (see West Country section). Stock consists of about 30,000 s/h vols displayed in five rooms. ½ day Th in winter, but occasionally open Sunday pm.

John Lyle*, Harpford, Sidmouth, Devon (0395 68294), is the doyen of booksellers specialising in cookery and wine and his stock ranges from modern paperbacks to 15th-century material in the £5,000 bracket. In fact, because the business he started in 1952 is mainly mail order, the bulk of his stock is new — most of the s/h and antiquarian being sold as soon as he gets it. However, since Mr Lyle manages to buy complete libraries, the stock of old and out-of-print material obviously fluctuates. His other, more recent but just as impressive, speciality is books on the Surrealist movement, art and literature, in English and French, in which he claims to have the world's largest stock. Again, many of these are new. One catalogue on the subject issued in 1980 contained over 2,300 items, which indicates why they are often regarded as standard bibliographies. The growth of books on Surrealism coincided with his mounting of the biggest ever exhibition/symposium on the subject which ran at Exeter for a month in 1967. Harpford is a hamlet between Sidmouth and Exeter. *Strictly by appointment.*

Bampton Books, 23 Newport Street, Tiverton, Devon (08842 57412), is a leading specialist in books on broadcasting. The name comes from the town of Bampton in north Devon where the proprietor L. V. Kelly settled on his return from Canada in 1972. After three years he moved to Tiverton, where he concentrated on mail order and book fairs (in 1976 he issued a catalogue on broadcasting listing some 2,100 titles). The shop, a Class I listed Georgian building in the centre of the town, opposite the hospital, was opened in 1977. Naturally, the specialist subject is maintained principally by post, and for day-to-day trade there is a general stock of approx 8,000 vols, some antiquarian. Prices are reasonable, but there is also a room displaying paperbacks and hardbacks with a maximum price of £1. The broadcasting stock is usually more than 1,000 books plus magazines, which include massive runs of journals such as *Radio Times* and *The Listener*. A recent development has been the extension of broadcasting into journalism. There is also a collection of vintage radio sets on display — although not for sale. Cl Th and lunch.

Lympstone, just outside Exmouth, in south Devon is one of my favourite villages. **The Strand Bookshop** (039 52 3924) in the heart of the village is run by Robert and Rosemary Burton who moved here in 1976 from a 17th-century former cheese factory in Cirencester, Glos. The present building was built (in part) in 1740 and has been an inn and a dairy. Now the two front rooms knocked into one offer between 5–10,000 s/h books, carefully selected to provide what the Burtons regard as books people want to read — as opposed to 'decoration' or collectors' items. Mrs Burton's involvement with books began in a library before she started bookselling in 1967. The combination of an interesting stock at reasonable prices and a delightful setting by the River Exe should encourage browsers to call when in the vicinity. Six days, cl lunch.

In 1974, Royston and Marianne Parry took over the old-established **Dickens Centenary Bookshop**, 13 City Arcade, Fore Street, Exeter, Devon EX4 3JE (0392 31587), so named because it was founded while the city was celebrating its association with Charles Dickens. The Parrys, with very little conventional bookselling experience, reckoned that enough energy, friendliness and application would attract people into the shop — and the tiny premises are usually full of students or local residents. Mr Parry (now succeeded here by his son Roy) turned the limited shelf space to advantage by ensuring rapid turnover on the s/h stock and 8–9,000 vols. Some shops keep better books for special customers, but here everything goes onto the shelves and 'old' stock is constantly pruned to make way for fresher material — which means that people have an incentive to drop in more frequently. The Parrys' helpful advice to visitors touring the West Country is: 'In the city of Exeter, the cathedral is only 300 yards from the secondhand bookshop!' Six days.

The success of their shop in the City Arcade inspired the Parrys to open **Exeter Rare Books**, at 14A Guildhall Shopping Centre, a modern pedestrianised precinct (0392 36021), leaving Roy Parry Jnr in charge. Their second shop, situated in the gallery of this attractive development, carries a stock of several thousand s/h and antiquarian titles with a number of very interesting or finely illustrated older books. It is difficult to pinpoint specialities with the high turnover that is Mr Parry's policy, although West County topography, particularly of Devon, is one of the stronger features. Six days, cl lunch.

The **SPCK Bookshop**, 1–2 Catherine Street, Cathedral Yard, Exeter, Devon, EX1 1EX (0392 73640), managed by Mr R. Davidson, is another in the group that offers a more general s/h stock taking in history, lit and topography as well as theology. Six days.

The precinct opposite the cathedral is the traditional home of old bookshops in the city, being the site of (among others) James Commin — best-known of them all for more than half-a-century, until the 1960s. In 1981 **Mike Nott** moved to 17 Cathedral Yard, EX1 1HB (0392 35086) from nearby Gandy Street, where he had run Castles of Exeter for six years. The two-room shop houses approx 5,000 general s/h items, strong in English lit and local topography. Six days.

The 200-year-old building which houses **The Brunswick Bookshop**, Brunswick Place, Dawlish, Devon (062 686 3318), has an exceptional view overlooking the waterfalled River

Daw with its black swans and ducks. The only bookshop for some distance, it carries new as well as general s/h and antiquarian stock of some 7,000 vols and a good range of prints and maps. It is owned by Gordon Wright who came here 26 years ago after running bookshops at Godalming and Farnham in Surrey, and whose special interests are Devon and Victoriana, including scrapbooks, peepshows and Valentines. His customers include book enthusiasts who come from all parts of the county. Cl Th, although as Mr Wright is semi-retired hours can be unpredictable so a phone call is advisable.

At the **Last Bastion Bookshop**, 75 Fore Street, Bovey Tracey, Devon, TQ13 9AB (0626 833438), Cindy and Alan Huxley make a point of providing entertainment for children. Toys are available while parents browse, or if the weather is suitable they can go into the garden with the Huxley children to be occupied with guinea pigs, rabbits, cats and even a hen. However the Huxleys, who took over the shop in 1979 when it sold only new books, try to be as helpful to their adult customers. The Old Bookroom houses a general s/h stock with no speciality apart from West Country books and Alan Huxley, a professional translator who spent some years in Russia, runs a binding and restoration service. Cl lunch and ½ day W, although since the Huxleys live on the premises they will always see visitors out of shop hours by appointment.

From now on, most of the better shops more or less hug the South Coast to Cornwall, but there is a small cluster of shops that justify a detour across country. The first two are just across the border into Somerset (the rest of this county is included in the West Country section).

Mr N. V. Allen, who runs **Alcombe Books**, 26 Alcombe Road, Minehead, Somerset (0643 3425), is chairman of the Exmoor Natural History Society. His stock of around 5,000 is general but with the emphasis on travel, topography, evangelical theology and (of course) natural history. In fact visitors who may have searched in vain in remote corners of the moor for certain birds or red deer can usually settle for a book on the subject, and Mr Allen's answer to gaps on his shelves is to write the book himself (his publications include

173

Birds of Exmoor, Waters of Exmoor, Exmoor's Wildlife and *Churches and Chapels of Exmoor*). In addition to running the shop — opened in 1969 after a spell as a postal bookseller — writing and publishing, Mr Allen also lectures on his specialist subject and on book collecting.

In a tough economic climate, more and more bookshops have been tempted to diversify — in fact, 'fringe' activities such as the sale of greetings cards are no longer unusual. But there can be few stranger sights than a bookshop which also stocks wood burning *stoves*, as does **Watkins**, Bridge Street, Dulverton, Somerset (0398 23395). Although associated with the shop of the same name in London's Cecil Court, it is a general shop selling new, s/h and antiquarian books. The stoves appeared because of the firm's traditional links with ecology. Richard Robinson, the managing director, had been impressed with their efficiency and, surprised that no one seemed to sell them, decided to market them himself! ½ day Sat.

Torridge Books of Langtree*, Great Torrington, Devon, EX38 8NR (080 55 200), started operations in 1959. Mary Heath had been to a lecture by Henry Williamson in Bideford, where she and her husband George lived at the time. Inspired, she started to collect his books until eventually she was able to sell off extra copies. The postal business — subjects extended to country matters generally, including West Country topography — moved to its present location about seven miles south of Bideford in 1968. Stock, which now also includes modern firsts, varies in size according to the frequency of catalogues issued but an average of 3,500 volumes are usually available for inspection. The Heaths travel extensively to replenish their shelves with books that are of the same high standard. *Strictly by appointment*, for the visitor's sake as well as Torridge Books', since the site is not easy to find, although rewarding once there for the moorland views.

Eve Lowell runs **The Dartmoor Bookshop**, 6 North Street, Ashburton, Devon (0364 52585), which opened in 1973, as an adjunct to her husband's long established newsagents. It began with the conversion of an unused room at the back of the shop, with another room upstairs for stock, but such was the success of the operation — largely because of Mrs Lowell's choice of stock, in terms of selection and quality — that two years later they had to restore another room. In addition to the two rooms books spill over to the staircase and landing.

To get to the bookshop, customers have to go through the newsagents (the only one, and situated in the town centre, known as the Bull Ring), but this has the advantage of extending the opening hours from 9am to late afternoon throughout the week. The stock is very general; and there is always something unusual and offbeat to be found. There is, for example, a section on book production; and, because of her own developed interest in the subject, and binding in particular, she does her own repairs and restoration. Ashburton, one of the original tin mining towns, is halfway between Exeter and Plymouth.

The **Castle Lane Book Corner**, Market Square, Torquay, Devon (0803 28991), is housed in a huge stone building that was once a local police headquarters. The shop, opened by Ivy Earl-Smith in 1977, is one of several businesses in the huge building, situated on the corner and containing a warren-like interior complete with cells. Here you can browse in the cell once occupied by the infamous man they could not hang, John (Babbacombe) Lee (who was reprieved after the third attempt to hang him had failed).

Ivy Earl-Smith, a booklover all her life, was working as a secretary when she decided to open a shop. Apart from the necessary redecoration and fitments, she deliberately retained the essential character (iron bars over the cell doors and one of the windows overlooking the street). Well over 50,000 volumes are spread through the rambling shop — the biggest display in the large room at the front, with others in the winding corridors, part of the courtyard and the cells at the back. Apart from the relative absence of fiction, the stock is general, ranging from paperbacks to fine bindings. Cl. W.

With one shop a former police station, it is a strange coincidence that the only other shop in Torquay (indeed for quite a large area), **Period Pieces**, 286 High Union Street, Torquay, Devon (0803 24124), is run by a former detective-inspector and his wife who was a secretary in the police force. Ernie

175

and Audrey Wickstead are booklovers who had toyed for some time with the idea of opening a bookshop, and in 1980 compromised with a double fronted antiques and bric-a-brac shop. But almost overnight the nearby Torre Bookshop closed down and they were able to take over that stock. At that stage only a third of the shop was taken up with books but the figure soon became a half, and eventually they dominated the premises; with the inevitable improvement in quality. Today there are approx 10,000 s/h volumes covering a broad area of interest. Six days.

At **Collards Bookshop**, 4 Castle Street, Totnes, Devon, books are crammed into four rooms on three floors. The shop started in 1972, growing out of Collards Wholefood Restaurant launched two years earlier, and for a time refreshments were still served. The stock is obviously extensive, with modern firsts, fine bindings and illustrated books on the ground floor, general s/h material on the first floor, and Beryl Collard's speciality, crime fiction, on the third. If you should turn up on a Tuesday in summer don't be surprised to see an assistant dressed in Elizabethan clothes, because this is part of a town tradition. Six days in summer; ½ day Th in winter.

The Bookshop, 72 Fore Street, Totnes, Devon (0803 864088), situated between the Arch and the museum, is a small shop — but bigger than it first seems, having a frontage of only 11 feet but going back about 60 feet. It was opened in 1970 by Ken Parnell, a carpenter, who came into bookselling after running a market stall for 18 months. Today he has around 7,000 s/h and antiquarian volumes on display but more than twice that number in reserve; the interest is very general. Cl Th.

Friday is market day in Totnes and there are two bookstalls in the marketplace; a third, run by Barry Higgs, is upstairs in the vestibule of the Civic Hall.

Before Eric Bucknall opened **The Old Bookshop (Brixham) Ltd**, 9 Bolton Street, Brixham, Devon (080 45 2402), in 1971, he lectured in engineering at universities all over the world. For much of that time was a one-man travelling library with 3,000 technical books in his baggage for the benefit of his students. He moved to Brixham straight from a teaching post in Bangladesh (having earlier been a professor at the University of Texas), with no bookselling experience, but quickly built up a large stock. In 1978 he retired and the shop was taken over by Margaret Hartshorn who, apart from local topography and interesting sea items, has a large general stock (approx 35,000 volumes) filling seven rooms. She also stocks early magazines on aeronautics and model engineering.

Fritz Merkel of **The Chantry Book Shop**, 11 Higher Street, Dartmouth, Devon, TQ6 9RB (08043 2796), is a fascinating bookseller — knowledgeable, dynamic and helpful. Known locally as the 'Viking Hippie' because he endured a total hip replacement several years ago which means that he can only carry things in a rucksack (usually heavy enough for any two men) Mr Merkel is a former POW of the Americans who came to this country after marrying an Englishwoman. In 1968 he took over a shop which had been developed over the years by the well respected Eric Hooper. Befitting his expertise, Mr Merkel's stock is always interesting and of good quality, with around 5,000 s/h and antiquarian items covering most areas housed on ground floor and basement. Old maps and prints are another feature. Hours 10am–4pm, cl lunch, W and ½ day Sat.

James A. Mitchell* had been selling books from his home at 1 The Manor, North Huish, South Brent, Devon (03647 2288), when the stock began to overflow and in March 1979 he opened a separate shop, the **Ivybridge Bookshop**, 20 Fore Street, Ivybridge (07554 3666). Now he commutes between the two, devoting rather more of his time to the shop, although he will always see browsers at home, *by appointment*. The stock in both places is very similar and of general interest (10,000 vols at North Huish and approx 4,000 at the shop) although there are stocks of old sheet music and Ordnance Survey maps, new and old. Shop cl W and ½ day Sat.

St Nicholas Books, 36 New Street, The Barbican, Plymouth, Devon (0752 663079), was taken over in 1978 by Wally and Deon Foster, bibliophiles who had run an antiques business for the previous four years. The shop is housed in an attractive property built for a merchant in 1580, with many

Elizabethan and Jacobean features. The stock is small but select, and vies for attention with a selection of English and oriental pottery and porcelain. Six days, cl lunch.

The three-floor New Street Antiques Centre, 27 New Street, Barbican, Plymouth, near Plymouth Hoe and the Mayflower Steps, which houses **Pandora** (0752 61165) is a converted warehouse dating back to Napoleonic times. Pandora, run by Bill and Shirley Musgrove, used to be at the Barbican Antiques Market and has only a small stock of a few hundred books on local history, natural history, and fine bindings, but a reserve 'back-up' is kept at home. It also sells picture postcards and printed ephemera. Six days.

The Bookcase, 28 King Street, Tavistock, Devon (0822 2410), on the edge of Dartmoor, was opened in 1970 by Jerry Harden when he retired from the United States Air Force. The shop, with two storerooms above, carries about 10,000 s/h and antiquarian books of a general nature, as well as maps and prints. Six days, early cl W.

Richard Gilbertson, who has been in the trade since 1948 when he was in Cecil Court and who moved to Cornwall seven years ago, has come up with an interesting new dimension in bookselling, from a new shop (opened end of 1974), the **Angel Hill Bookshop**, Launceston, Cornwall (0566 3533). The shop carries a small exclusive antiquarian stock, but in addition will sell volumes of poetry containing a manuscript poem alongside the printed word. Mr Gilbertson has published works by such poets as Ted Hughes, Thom Gunn and Kathleen Raine and in the 'Manuscript Series', as the new venture is called, he offers a book of poems by a famous writer with a manuscript of one (usually a good copy of the original). His stock speciality is children's books and books on Cornwall and north Devon.

When the shop is shut there is often a notice in the window suggesting that visitors call at 'the white cottage at the bottom of the hill'. However *appointment advisable*. (Incidentally Angel Hill derives its name from an incident in 1440 when Bishop Lacey was visiting the town. He is reported to have dozed off and when awakened by the greeting of local minstrels interpreted the sound as angels singing.)

Having reached the age of 70 Edward Brown, the country's

178

leading specialist in books on cricket has given up his office (**E. K. Brown***) in the town centre to operate from Bevois Mount, Church Street, Liskeard, Cornwall (0579 45128). He can still show 20,000 books, two-thirds s/h, although this does include a section on rugby. In fact, after purchasing the John Arlott collection (including 10,000 signed postcards) in 1980, it took him four months to move all of his stock from his previous premises. A retired schoolmaster, Mr Brown opened to the public in 1968 although he had started bookselling 20 years before. Now the books are displayed in a garden storeroom, with the intention of gradually reducing the numbers slightly in order to concentrate on better and scarcer titles. *Strictly by appointment.*

The **Chapel Court Bookshop**, Shutta Road, East Looe, Cornwall (05036 3700) was opened in 1977, in what used to be the Methodist Sunday School. The proprietor Louise Ross, a bibliophile from London learned much of the business from regular visits to Fisher & Sperr of Highgate (see 'North London'). When the converted schoolroom began to bulge at the seams in 1980 the first floor of the chapel was also converted. Now the second bookroom houses approx 3,000 better s/h and antiquarian books, with a gallery displaying maps and prints. She has the ambitious target of trying to have one example of every map of Cornwall ever printed. The antiquarian stock includes rare books of Cornwall, colour-plate flower and bird books, while downstairs a slightly larger range of s/h and out-of-print books is more general. Cl lunch, normal hours except in winter which can be unpredictable, so phone call is advisable.

There are few enough bookshops in the region, so it is pleasant to report a postal bookseller, **Kenneth Langmaid***, Glencairn House, Grampound Road, Truro, Cornwall, TR2 4EE (0726 882280), who has a large enough stock and sufficient room to welcome members of the public. The business is run from the house, and a general stock of about 12,000 books is kept in a large warehouse. Grampound Road is not a road but a village, and Mr Langmaid's house, which he bought in 1964, was once the post office. Although the stock is general, Mr Langmaid has strong leanings towards lit, politics, history and theology, and is also interested in regional novels. Visitors need their own transport, but a visit should be interesting. *By appointment*, particularly so since October 1980 when his wife opened a separate shop premises.

Elisabeth Antiques, 57a Little Castle Street, Truro, Cornwall (0872 713 45), is a single fronted shop near the museum. Elisabeth Langmaid's main business is antiques and ephemera for collectors, such as stamps, pictures and postcards, but she also has a display of some 1,500 s/h books of a general nature. Moreover, when customers express an interest in a particular subject, Mr Langmaid is able to bring in a further selection from his larger stock at home. Cl Th.

The Quay Book Shop, Quay Street, Truro, Cornwall TR1 2HE (0872 76817), opened in 1969 by Bruce Burley, has several thousand volumes of mixed quality, the only speciality being the topography of Devon and Cornwall and the Isles of Scilly. Mr Burley began his bookselling career with a spell at Francis Edwards' in London, but then went into the hotel business before returning to his first love. Having started in Quay Street near the Great Gothic cathedral, he moved two years later to larger premises in the same street. Part of a complex of buildings erected in 1860 as public rooms, the shop has stock in four rooms. Six days, cl lunch (early Th in winter).

The business of **Derek Godfrey** is split into two parts — an office and stockroom at his home, 'Wellesley', Mitchell, nr Newquay, Cornwall (087 251 425), and a stall in Truro's Pannier Market, open W, F and Sat in winter and every day in summer. There are about 2,000 books at Truro, backed up by several thousand in a barn at home although he no longer sees people there — a pity because his home/office was the local manor house, named after the family of the Duke of Wellington who was once Member of Parliament for Mitchell.

P. R. Rainsford*, Market Place, St Ives, Cornwall, is an office in two rooms above a chemist, but the public is welcome, although an *appointment by letter* is advisable, as Peter Rainsford is not always available. A painter (a member of the Penwith Society of Arts) as well as a bookseller, he specialises in books on fine and applied arts, out-of-print and rare, being particularly strong in art reference, modern

French illustrated and bibliography. The business carries a stock of about 6,000 selected vols.

Peter Dalwood moved to 44 Causewayhead (near the centre of town) only recently from the very distinctive Egyptian house to which he moved in 1970. He had previously run a shop in Bristol for 21 years. About one-third of a stock of some 10,000 vols is new, and Mr Dalwood has also reprinted in paper-back three books on the history of Cornwall. The s/h and antiquarian material is general, although there is a strong leaning towards English lit, history, archaeology, art, ships and the sea and Cornwall. Cl lunch and W.

WEST OF ENGLAND

Some of the most important names in English literature — Coleridge, Southey, Wordsworth and Lamb — owe their initial impetus to the good taste of a young man called Joseph Cottle, who opened a bookshop in Bristol in 1791 when he was just 21. Told by a despondent Coleridge that he had been the round of London booksellers with a collection of poems, that all but one had refused even to look at the manuscript and that the only offer was 6 guineas for the copyright, Cottle paid him 30 guineas in advance of completion (1796). Southey was paid 50 guineas plus 50 copies for his first works, and the poet wrote in praise of him: 'One rarely meets a bookseller as inexperienced and ardent as himself.' Wordsworth was similarly given his start with the publication of his *Lyrical Ballads*, in which Coleridge's 'Ancient Mariner' first appeared — although the book sold so slowly that Cottle was compelled to part with nearly 500 copies to a London bookseller. Wordsworth remaindered!

Bristol has continued to inspire booksellers, and men of the calibre of William George. **George's**, 89 Park Street, Bristol, Avon BS1 5PW (0272 276602), is situated on a large corner site, and the entrance to the impressive s/h department is in a third road at the back, intriguingly called There and Back Again Lane. The stock is very comprehensive and includes local topography, genealogy and archaeology and a special interest in Americana dating back to the founder, who issued a catalogue of old American literature as early as 1876. The director in charge of the department is Tom Prigg, who joined the firm in 1938 — in fact none of the present board have any links with the George family, except the senior director, Fred Catley, who was taken on by Charles George in 1928.

William George started in Bath Street (at a rental of 3s 6d a week) in 1847 and his first accounts were written in copperplate writing at the other end of the exercise book in which he was adding French grammar to his hitherto neglected education. In 1884 he moved to the present premises, at one time occupied by Dr William Budd, pioneer of preventive medicine and the study of infectious diseases. With this last move, Mr George's two sons Charles and Frank took over as partners and in 1892 they opened a branch in Oxford (other branches were also opened in Newport and Plymouth, but did not last). Mr George died in 1900, his son Frank five years later, and Charles carried on alone despite poor health until in 1929 Basil Blackwell was asked if he would assume responsibility for the running of the business. Frank's son F. C. George stayed on, with a special interest in the antiquarian side, until the late 1930s.

Having dramatically expanded over the years, the need for additional space became pressing until, in 1963, excavations were carried out at the back of the building and a new semi-basement and two floors were built. Six years later two more floors were added, the whole building having been strengthened with steel to support the tremendous weight of books. Six days.

John Roberts Bookshop has a trail of books to lure people to a first-floor shop above another shop at 43 Triangle West, Bristol, Avon BS8 1ES (0272 28568). A bookcase in the street leads to shelves in the passageway with very cheap items, so that few book hunters can resist going upstairs to the large 'gallery' showroom where a general s/h stock of some 10,000 vols covers all subjects with the accent on topography, travel, sociology and lit including 1st edns. Mr Roberts opened the shop in 1960 in new premises in the suburb of Clifton, after selling books by post for about 10 years during his days as a professional musician. A well known saxophonist in the 'big band' era, he became musical director of the Grand Spa Hotel overlooking the Clifton Gorge and began bookselling in his spare time. The shop also publishes books on Mr Roberts' special-interest subjects, natural history (eg local floras) and local topography, under the imprint Chatsford House Press. Six days.

R. A. Gilbert*, the specialist in occult, folklore and theology had a shop in the town for 10 years until 1977 when he reverted to mail order from home, 17 Quarrington Road, Horfield, Bristol, Avon BS7 9PJ (0272 514759), but welcomes visitors *by appointment*. In addition to bookselling, Robert Gilbert writes on the occult — his bibliography of A. E. Waite is the standard work, and he is currently working on a biography of the mystic and occultist. The stock of about 4,000 vols is kept in a warehouse nearby.

Mr Gilbert's wife Patricia, whom he met when they were in friendly competition, still runs **The Wise Owl Bookshop**, which has moved since the last edition to 189 Whiteladies Road, Blackboy Hill, Clifton, Bristol, Avon (0272 311806). The shop carries a general s/h stock, but strong on music (including sheet music) and entertainment.

Browsers have come to expect unusual opening hours but Philip Brownsey, who opened the **Mangotsfield Book Shop**, 4 Cossham Street, Mangotsfield, Bristol, Avon BS17 3EN (0272 563367) in the centre of a village 6 miles from Bristol in April 1980, is unique. During the week he only opens from 6–8pm, although on Sat he keeps normal hours. Mr Brownsey is only a part-time bookseller, working during the day in the probate department of a local solicitors, and if this restricts his time for buying the medium-size s/h stock is supplemented by new books and remainders.

David and Diana Clarke, who had found the quick turnover formula successful with their first shop in Reading, launched **Haymarket Bargain Books**, Haymarket Walk, St James Barton, Bristol, Avon (0272 20939) in 1978. Having the same system and layout, buying is that much easier — here again there are approx 5,000 s/h vols sharing shelf space with a similar number of remainders. Situated in a basement precinct by the sunken roundabout, the shop cannot easily be seen from the road. Six days. (Expansion is still their intention, so watch out for further Clarke shops in the West Country.)

One of the country's most distinguished bookselling families is represented by **George Bayntun**, Manvers Street, Bath, Avon BA1 1JW (0225 66000), bookbinders of international reputation as well as booksellers, and sister company **George Gregory**, 8 Green Street, Bath, Avon, BA1 2JY (0225 66055). Gregory's has the longer history and indeed is the oldest-established bookshop in the town, founded in 1845, but the guiding force in the growth of the two companies was George Bayntun, an outstanding personality.

Mr Bayntun started his own bookbinding business in Bath in 1894, initially only binding books and magazines for private or trade customers. He soon realised it was profitable to buy and sell, after re-covering or restoring. Establishing a reputation for good work at low prices, he began to take over small binderies on the retirement of their owners. In 1920 he bought the bookselling business of George Gregory, with its vast stock, but the biggest leap forward was the acquisition of the Robert Riviere bindery, in 1939, with the Riviere collection of tools and plant. So, the Manvers Street premises house probably the finest craft bindery in the world, a feature of which is the vast collection of tools for finishing, many of which follow the designs of important binders of earlier centuries. There are also many sets of type and hand letters so that old bindings can be copied accurately.

The book side of the business, not surprisingly, specialises in bindings, and carries a very large stock bound in new leather, consisting mainly of first or fine editions of English lit, standard sets, illustrated and sporting works; also a large selection of antiquarian books in old bindings. Apart from bookselling, Mr Bayntun also published sets of Surtees' sporting novels, hand-coloured by local women, Ingpen's edition of Boswell's Johnson, lavishly illustrated, and other major works. George Bayntun died at the beginning of World War II, his last few months crowned by the frequent patronage of Queen Mary, who granted him the appointment of Bookseller to Her Majesty. After his death, Gregory's was sold, most of the staff joined the services and nearly half the premises were commandeered by the Admiralty.

In 1963 the founder's grandson, Hylton Bayntun-Coward, regained ownership of George Gregory and expanded that business, under the management of W. J. Stanton, to encompass a broad s/h and antiquarian trade, thus allowing Bayntun's to concentrate on fine bindings and rare books. In 1977 he opened a Museum of Bookbinding in an annexe, and his work for the ABA culminated in his appointment as president in 1980. Gregory's, which also carries engravings, prints and maps and has a gallery for exhibitions, is open six days; Bayntun's five days; cl lunch, but available by appointment Sat and other times.

The Kingsley Book Shop, 16 Margaret's Buildings, Brock Street, Bath, Avon, BA1 2LP (0225 24315), owned by Alec and Joan Dakin, got its name in an offbeat manner. The previous owner had been a fan of Charles Kingsley and for a time a bronze bust of the author occupied pride of place, but the point was rather lost when an over-zealous assistant sold the statue by mistake. When the present owners took over in the late 1970s, the pleasant 'confusion' was replaced by a more orderly system which included not only upgrading the stock but even basic requirements such as classifying the books. Although the intention was to keep the interest very general, (several thousand books are priced at £1 and under) there are now good sections on theatre and drama and book production. With the books displayed more attractively the problems of space became more acute, and the Dakins (Alec is an Egyptologist and retired classics teacher) had to resort to structural alterations to extend the browsing area. The shop is housed in a 1767 building believed to have been a chapel for the exclusive use of residents of the crescent and surrounding area 200 years ago. The shop is officially closed on M but on that day it is occupied by a stamp dealer who can also sell books; the Dakins also 'cover' themselves at lunchtime by eating at a restaurant opposite, from which they can see the shop and attend to visitors if necessary.

Derek and Glenda Wallis, who opened at 6 Chapel Row, Queen Square, Bath, Avon (0225 24677) in September 1980, are avid book collectors who met and married when Derek was working in Canada. On his return to England, he decided to give up his career as a chemist and do something in books. Without waiting to learn the ropes they jumped in at the deep end in 1971 by opening Bibliotique, a two room shop in an attractive Georgian terrace about half a mile north of the city centre. They closed this popular shop in May 1981 to concentrate on the second shop, in the centre of the city and much larger with three rooms and a basement, which has a bigger, slightly more 'upmarket' stock, mostly non-fiction. Founder members of the PBFA, they still exhibit at a number of fairs.

Peter Goodden, a postal bookseller for a number of years, now has premises on the first floor, 7a Bridge Street, Bath, Avon BA2 4AS (0225 60867), above The Bridge Bookshop which sells new books, although he has a separate entrance. Apart from a medium-size stock of s/h books in modern lit and art, Mr Godden is one of relatively few booksellers who takes a serious interest in out-of-print s/h music. Six days.

Bath is another of the cities where the local **SPCK Bookshop** carries a reasonable stock of s/h material in addition to theology. Situated at 5 Bladud Buildings, BA1 5LS (0225 65402), the stock covers history, lit and topography. ½ day Th.

Rothwell & Dunworth, 15 Paul Street, Taunton, Somerset (0823 82476) used to be a Chinese restaurant. In fact, only the size of the place gives any clue to its origins; in every other respect, inside and out, it looks like a distinguished s/h and antiquarian bookshop. Partners in the business are Caryl Rothwell, who had a shop in a private house at Tiverton (Devon) for five years, and Michael Dunworth who gained his trading experience at book fairs. The stock of over 10,000 vols in two large rooms is selective, with a good proportion of it antiquarian. A third room displays material priced at £1 and under. The shop's main leaning is towards academic books, although it is also strong on natural history and field sports. Cricket books are another feature. Six days, but not open until 11am.

The stock of **Ciderpress Books*,** The Cottage, Church Street, Kingsbury Episcopi, Martock, Somerset (0935 823326), is limited to approx 2,000 s/h vols but since these are confined to three main areas, Africa, gardening and natural history and Eastern Europe and Asia, coverage is quite comprehensive. The proprietors Peter and Naomi Bickford started bookselling in 1972; Peter spent many years in Africa, while Naomi is a horticulturist by profession. Their home is 'famous' for its unusual sloping chimney, believed to be unique in the British Isles, although no one knows the reason for its peculiar construction. Although the leaning chimney is only 100 years old, part of the cottage dates to the 14th century when it was used as a lodging house for priests and apprentices when the village was an 'outpost' for the diocese of Glastonbury (hence 'Episcopi'). Ciderpress Books can be found literally next door to the parish church with its tall tower, but *strictly by appointment*.

Jacquemine Charrott-Lodwidge, Underwall, Langport, Somerset (0458 250543) runs **Pelekas Books***, from the cottage to which she moved in 1980. Jacquemine is an art director for films and TV, who decided to supplement her income between assignments by selling part of her collection of children's and illustrated books, used mainly for reference. The stock is therefore small but selective and the cottage — named after the famous wall built in 1340 — is situated in a lovely part of the country, near the top of Langport Hill, by the foot of Whatley Steps. There are herons at the bottom of the terraced garden, and a river from which excellent rough fishing can be had; accompanying husbands or wives not interested in books are invited to bring fishing rods. The building has been redesigned, with film-set type features such as a spiral staircase and a gazebo, where the books are now housed.

Jacquemine Charrott-Lodwidge (the surname comes from a husband with Huguenot origins, and a Cornish father) has a fascinating background. She served in the Free-French army during the war and was sent to spend two years in the deserts of Syria working with the Bedouins. Studying the history of architecture and antiques inevitably took her to Greece for several years, and Pelekas is named after a village in Corfu. Normal hours, when Jacquemine is not on location, so *strictly by appointment*.

So much has been written about Glastonbury and the Arthurian legend that it might justify a specialisation in its own right but the 6,000 or so s/h and antiquarian books at **Haddan's Bookshop**, 30 Benedict Street, Glastonbury, Somerset (0458 31753), represent a good, general cross-section of interest. The small shop, on the ground floor of an old red-brick house near the ruins of the famous abbey, was opened in 1977 by Diana Thomas and her husband, a retired architect. Six days.

Somerton in Somerset is the ancient capital of Wessex, just 6 miles from Glastonbury, and attracts a number of visitors.

But there was no bookshop until December 1979 when Mr and Mrs B. Ives, who had been the local grocers for the previous five years, decided to open **Simon's Books**, naming the business after their son. A medium-size s/h stock is very general, with no specialities. Cl M but open Bank Holidays.

Having already mentioned strange village names, I doubt whether many readers have heard of Queen Camel, nr Yeovil, Somerset. Apparently in pre-Saxon times it was known as East Camel, but King Harold's mother lived there for a while and it was renamed in her honour. The origins of the Camel part are more obscure; there are romantic associations with Camelot because of the proximity of Cadbury Castle, but Queen Camel and West Camel were already in existence when King Arthur is supposed to have ridden through and spotted the castle he was to call Camelot. A more likely explanation is that it was named after the local river Cam. Our interest today is with **Steven Ferdinando***, at The Old Vicarage, (0935 850210), a postal bookseller who has three rooms (two large) set aside for browsers, but *by appointment only*. The house is a Georgian vicarage with an interesting history, and Steven is likely to offer visitors tea on the lawn once they have found the books they want. The medium-size general stock has a bias towards English lit and all aspects of country life, although the only speciality is Somerset and Dorset history and topography, and books by Thomas Hardy, William Barnes and members of the Powys family. Steven became involved with bookselling in 1973 and started the Out of Print bookshop in Liverpool before coming south.

Michael Lewis & the Ashley Bindery opened a shop at 17 High Street, Bruton, Somerset (0749 3557), towards the end of 1980 after many years of postal bookselling. I have not seen the premises or stock, but Mr Lewis describes it as 'large'. The firm is known for the quality of its antiquarian and scholarly books in lit, history and economics, illustrated books and typography, as well as original and old bindings. It also sells maps and prints. Six days, ½ day Th.

When the **Old Curiosity Shop**, 15 Catherine Hill, Frome, Somerset, BA11 1BZ (0373 4482), was opened in 1970 the name referred to the bulk of its stock, antiques and bric-a-brac. But by the time Ron and Betty Hackett took over six

189

years later books had pushed everything else out. Mr Hackett, formerly in computers, had no experience of selling books, but the previous owner, Barry Moores, stayed to help out in the shop for six months. An 18th-century building, part of the original St Catherine's convent, it faces on to the road with one large window in which general s/h material is displayed and a lockable bow window at the side for antiquarian books. Inside, a large single room contains the bulk of the s/h stock, with a circular staircase leading to a room displaying better books, although access is by invitation only. Cl lunch and Th.

It took **Ronald Lees** 25 years to get into the book trade, so when he opened his first shop at 32 St John's Street, Devizes, Wilts, SN10 5LT (0380 2774), in 1972 there was no question that he had made the right decision. Mr Lees' earlier career had been in journalism, although he was able to keep in touch with his first love through collecting and writing about books. Apart from new titles, almost entirely concerned with collecting or hobbies, he stocks about 5–6,000 general s/h and antiquarian items with a slight emphasis on modern firsts and illustrators. Maps and prints also in stock. Browsers are obviously welcome. Six days, early cl W.

Only a few yards away in a late 18th-century square building, once a public bath house, is **d'Arcy Books**, The Chequers, High Street, Devizes, Wilts, (0380 6922). Owned by Colin and Jennifer MacGregor (d'Arcy is her maiden name), the shop opened in 1981 after a spell in Marlborough, and has a broad-ranging stock of some 25,000 books. Early cl W.

The **Victoria Book Shop**, 30 Wood Street, Old Town, Swindon, Wilts, SN1 4AB (0793 27364), was established in 1966 by Ken Austin. At present, a stock of over 50,000 books (including new and remainders) is spread over seven rooms on three floors, a basement and in odd passages and stairways. The range is broad but the rooms are numbered to assist browsers in finding their areas of particular interest. The only specialities are local history and regional authors, eg Richard Jefferies, Alfred Williams and A. G. Street, and because Swindon is a railway town the shop keeps a good selection of books on this subject, particularly the Great Western railway.

Mr Austin was joined in partnership in 1972 by his son Stephen who had gained his bookselling experience with W. H. Smith. Six days.

Lechlade is a typically pretty Cotswold village, best known for the 15th-century church of St Lawrence. Tiny though it is, the village has a bookshop with a stock of 14,000 s/h and antiquarian items. Run by Norman and Peggy Leaver, the **Lechlade Bookshop,** 5 Oak Street, Lechlade, Glos, GL7 3AX, is housed in a 17th-century oak beamed building on which there is a preservation order. Cl M.

Paul Weller Ltd, 1 Dollar Street, Cirencester, Glos, GL7 2AJ (0285 2764), is one of the largest bookshops in the West Country. Only one-sixth of the turnover comes from s/h and antiquarian stock, but that department was only launched in 1977 and growth has been steady. The shop with its 70ft frontage has dignity and style as well as spaciousness. Built in the 1680s, it is really two buildings, with over 20 rooms full of books. The wide ranging s/h and antiquarian material is found on the first floor. Apart from a room for paperbacks, and another of hardbacks with a ceiling price of 25p, the bulk of the stock is displayed in two large rooms (each 30 feet long) lined with dark mahogany shelves and centre units; one room has the original 17th-century wood panelling. The number of vols on show — the antiquarian behind glass — is not much more than 10,000, with another 15,000 in reserve, and the quality of the antiquarian side is rising all the time. Paul Weller came into bookselling relatively late, having been a professional soldier for 20 years and leaving with the rank of major to enter law. He exchanged wig and gown for books in 1970. Catalogues issued. Six days, cl lunch.

Thompson's Book Shop at Dunstall House, Park Street, Cirencester, Glos, GL7 2BX (0285 5239), which opened in October 1980, specialises in books on architecture and allied subjects. James Thompson is applying his expertise as an architect to Dunstall House, a former nurses' home with 16 bedrooms, which he and his wife Susan bought along with a large nonconformist chapel. From this huge property they have carved out a combined shop and homes for themselves and family, and separate accommodation for others. Mr Thompson worked for the Royal Commission on Historical

Monuments before becoming a lecturer, and he and his wife spent 18 months as postal booksellers before opening the shop. Although architecture will remain their speciality, the stock has gradually become more diversified. Cl M.

Alan and Joan Tucker, Station Road, Stroud, Glos, GL5 3AP (04536 4738), is just outside the station courtyard. The Tuckers lead a hectic life running two new-book shops, as well as an antiquarian and s/h business. The latter is housed in several small rooms on the first floor above their children's bookshop, and the large and varied stock based on English lit is very reasonably priced. The Tuckers started as s/h booksellers in the town 20 years ago in two weavers' cottages on the site of the new magistrates court and police headquarters. When the expiration of their lease meant a move and more expensive premises, they were obliged to expand the business into new books and paperbacks. In 1977 they took a suite of offices over one of the shops so that the out-of-print and antiquarian material could be kept separate.

Joan Tucker has written a picture book, *Stroud As It Was*, and with Alan compiled a 'Reading for Enjoyment' list of books for six to eight-year-olds which is used by the National Book League for travelling exhibitions, together with Alan's 'Signal' list of poetry books for children. He also writes occasionally for private presses such as Brewhouse and Poet & Printer, and has his own small press, the Stilt Press, although the demands of bookselling leave little time for this pastime. They love Stroud or else they might be based in a much larger town running a considerably larger operation. Well worth a visit. Cl Th and lunch.

Another well known bookseller who opted out of the London 'rat race' to trade from a house in the country is **Ian Hodgkins***, Mount Vernon, Butterow, Rodborough, Stroud, Glos (04536 4270). In fact, one might get the impression that Ian had gone to the other extreme to avoid casual browsers by finding himself a castle stronghold. Mount Vernon, the name of the house (complete with turretted tower) from which he operates, is aptly named. It was built in stages between 1790 and 1824, on the crown of a steep hill just outside Stroud, by a wealthy dyer who (rumour has it) wanted to keep an eye on his workers, who lived in cottages at the foot of the hill. The

192

huge house, set in six acres, had been allowed to run down and when Ian took it over in 1979 he was obliged to undertake an extensive renovation programme.

Mr Hodgkins, who ran Sebastian d'Orsai until starting his own specialist business in London in 1973, probably has the largest stock on the pre-Raphaelites in the country and has extended his specialisation to 19th-century illustrated books, with an emphasis on colour printing and an extensive collection on the Brontes, from first editions to biographical material. An average of four catalogues a year is issued, but there is always a large stock, now housed in the entrance hall and various rooms on the ground floor. A 'must' for bibliophiles interested in these specialist subjects, but no general stock. *By appointment.*

In the guide's first edition I somehow managed to overlook **Alan Hancox**, 101 Montpelier Street, Cheltenham, Glos (0242 513204), next door to the famous Ladies College, and I received a number of letters. His reputation for one of the best antiquarian and secondhand bookshops in the West Country is justified. Behind the shop window is a tiny reception area crowded with books, but no staff, so that one has to embark on a journey through a narrow tunnel (with books on either side) to look for signs of human life. The reward is a huge cavern-like bookroom at the end of the tunnel, reminding me of the caves at Wookey Hole or Cheddar, except that this one is exceptionally cosy. This area, which Alan Hancox created himself from five separate rooms, has books arranged in an open plan effect, with seats in the middle of one section. It is well but soothingly lit and, since Alan provides a continuous recital of classical music very much in the mood of the place (Elgar, Vivaldi, Brahms etc), customers can spend several hours browsing in a pleasantly relaxed atmosphere.

Alan started bookselling in 1949 after working as a youth hostel warden — which might explain why a large number of children come in on their own, particularly on Saturdays. He took over the present shop in 1966 and is so well known in Cheltenham that he manages to keep his shelves replenished by buying locally. His selling philosophy is enlightened; everything very reasonably priced so that stock does not remain on the shelves for long. Nothing is more irritating than to walk into a shop and see the same books on show as six months before.

Alan only produces one catalogue in a year, but those which do appear are often works of scholarship, such as one on the works of Edward Thomas several years ago which may have had something to do with the revival of interest in the poet. He happens to be an admirer of Thomas, and as programme director of the Cheltenham Literary Festival in 1980 he featured the poet as one of the festival's three main themes (along with Henry Williamson and Auden). The large stock is very comprehensive, ranging from cheap novels to modern firsts and antiquarian. ½ day W, and lunch hours 12.45–2.15pm, longer than usual because this is when he does some of his buying.

Abbey Antiquarian Books* at Winchcombe (the ancient capital of Mercia), near Cheltenham, Glos are postal booksellers who do *not* invite visitors to their home, which stands in the grounds of what used to be Winchcombe Abbey. I have included them, however, because of their diverse and interesting stock and their friendly working relationship with Major and Mrs Tom Hancock who run the local Phoenix Bookshop on North Street, which sells new books but has a special display of their antiquarian items. Abbey Antiquarian Books, run by Christopher John Aeschlimann, a retired American lawyer, and his sister Anne Adye, developed from their shared collecting hobby. One speciality is illustrated books of fable and books of emblems, mainly of the 18th and 19th centuries (partly arising from Mrs Adye's expertise in early childrens's books and chapbooks). Other areas of interest include early post-incunabula; fine books with woodcuts (herbals, early medical books and zoological works) and 18th-century copperplate travel and natural history books. They do have a stock of inexpensive books but visitors to the area must take pot-luck with the current display, changed every few weeks at the Phoenix, although a selection of items of particular interest can be despatched to the shop if a call to 0242 602589 is made in advance.

Philip and Jean Syed are another couple attracted to fine

old buildings in need of restoration. At the end of 1976 they had to move from their **Aurora Bookshop*** in Tewkesbury, Glos housed in a row of terraced dwellings under the longest medieval roof in England, and came two miles out of town to another fascinating building, The Bothy, Puckrup, Tewkesbury, Glos (0684 294001). The property — part dating from the 14th century, although the bookroom is only 18th and 19th century — was once two cottages known as The Old Farmhouse of Puckrup. The restoration work needed was extensive, but Philip has done everything himself over a four-year period. Because of their limited space, the Syeds had to cut down the size of the stock but upgraded the quality, and today they can display some 5,000 s/h and antiquarian vols with strong sections on English lit, sets, topography and natural history. *By appointment.*

The Church Street Gallery, 39 Church Street, Tewkesbury, Glos (0684 295990), opened in December 1977 by Fred and Margaret Taylor, is basically an antiques shop on three floors but with a few hundred out-of-print books on various aspects of collecting. The Taylors, specialists in pottery, porcelain and furniture, started selling books when they got tired of lending people their own reference books and now have a reasonably comprehensive collection on the ground floor. Six days.

The delightful Cotswold town of Chipping Campden, Glos was the headquarters of the Guild of Handicraft, founded in 1888 by Charles Robert Ashbee (not to be confused with Henry Spencer Ashbee the collector of erotica!), which produced fine books through the Essex House Press. Alcuin Press, another famous source of fine books in the 1920s and 30s, also operated from nearby.

Today the tradition ie the *sale* of good books, is being maintained by **Serif Books**, Harrow House, Lower High Street, Chipping Campden, Glos, GL55 6DY, whose proprietor Seumas Stewart is an authority on the world of books. His *Book Collecting, a Beginner's Guide* (David & Charles) is indicative of his empathy with the bibliophile who genuinely cares for books, rather than the collector primarily interested in investment. The garden of Harrow House, an interesting mixture of building styles of the 16th, 17th and

18th centuries and once an inn, actually backs onto the former silk mill taken over by Ashbee in 1902. When Seumas Stewart moved here in 1960 it had reverted to being a private house, and the converted shop with its tiny display window is very small. However, whether it is the personality of the proprietor, or the profusion of books — there are 15,000 vols although not all on display — the shop's reputation extends far beyond the county. The stock is fairly general, but includes specialities in natural history, gardening and subjects relating to the country. Six days, although occasionally ½ day Th.

Coffeebooks was launched in 1970 by ex-schoolmaster Louis Bailey to display the widest possible range of books and to serve coffee and light refreshments. Within a couple of years, Mr Bailey had three shops and storage rooms overflowing with volumes of every description, and the idea of serving light refreshments became impractical because of the space taken up by the books. These days he reckons he has over 250,000 volumes, many contained in 12 rooms at his home. The first large shop was demolished in 1975 to make room for a new police station and law courts but Mr Bailey still operates from a small, crowded 16th-century shop at 15 Meer Street, Stratford-upon-Avon, Warks, (0789 66204), specialising in Shakespeariana, but with no room for serving coffee. Six days, plus Sun pm.

In 1975 Mr Bailey moved even closer to Shakespeare's birthplace, opening another shop a few yards away at 29 Henley Street where the manager Roy Pierce is a well known local bibliophile. Large enough to enable light refreshments to be served, it carries a comprehensive stock of s/h and remainders; not the highest quality but a varied range. A third shop at Fountain Way in the new shopping precinct carries mainly paperbacks and remainders.

Robert Vaughan, 20 Chapel Street, Stratford-upon-Avon, Warks (0789 5312), was previously in theatre administration. Mr Vaughan opened his first bookselling business in London in 1953 before moving to Stratford 10 years later, and in 1975 to the present premises — a three-storey timber framed building dating back to the reign of Henry VIII. About 20,000 books are housed in the spacious ground floor; about half of general interest, but including fine bindings, English topography, sets, and three specialities: first and fine editions in English lit, books on theatre and associated fields, and Shakespeariana. The latter might be expected in view of Mr Vaughan's background, which covered every type of show from Shakespeare to the Folies-Bergère, during a period in which he was in charge of productions in more than 20 West End theatres. Six days.

Next door is Dorothy Withey's **Chaucer Head Bookshop**, at 21 Chapel Street (0789 293136) — once the home of Julius Shaw, a friend of Shakespeare and an executor of his will — but the stock is predominently new, although there is a section of s/h material strong in Shakespeare on the ground floor. Cl lunch and ½ day M.

The village of Broadway (Heref/Worcs) is a tourist haunt, and at one end of the mile-long main street is **Stratford Trevers**, 45 High Street (0386 853668). Regrettably, soon after the last edition, Mr Trevers had to move from Picton House, first to a shop on The Green, 'returning' in 1979 to an interesting 17th-century building, one of the oldest in the High Street. The shop consists of one very large room, big enough to house around 20,000 s/h and antiquarian vols and prints. The books have a general appeal, ranging from fine bindings to modern firsts — everything of a standard one would expect of someone who has been selling books and prints since just after World War II. Six days plus Sun afternoons.

Bookworms, 81 Port Street, Evesham, Heref/Worcs (0386 45509), very conscious of the agricultural heritage of the Vale of Evesham, carries a good selection of books dealing with the country, among its general stock of 7–10,000 vols. Opened in 1971 by former journalist Christopher Garrett, and June Slaughter, who had been in advertising, the shop occupies two rooms in a Victorian building on the main Evesham–Oxford road, enjoying a good passing trade and that of tourists in summer. Cl M.

The Malvern Bookshop, 7 Abbey Road, Great Malvern, Heref/Worcs (06845 5915), is in the centre of the town, overlooking the historic Priory Church. The shop itself is small and has insufficient room for anything more than the window display, a few 'bargain' shelves and the staircase, but several thousand general vols can be seen in three rooms on the first floor. Interest is broad, the only speciality being local history and collectors' books, which include some new titles. It was opened in 1955 by Reginald Lechmere, who had been in publishing and graduated to bookselling. Early cl W and cl lunch.

Richard I granted Worcester its first Royal Charter in 1189 and buildings survive from the early medieval period. **Andrew Boyle (Booksellers) Ltd,** 21 Friar Street (0905 23893), occupies a building dated by its cruck arches to the 13th century. Walking down Friar Street one needs to look out for an overhead sign 'Books', because there is no shop front, the ground floor being occupied by a firm of insurance brokers. Bibliophiles have to walk through the shop to get to the books upstairs, housed in a cluster of rooms on two floors. The business, recognised as one of the most distinguished of the ABA's provincial members, is run by Patricia Leeming, daughter of Andrew Boyle. Her own daughter, currently working for a leading London antiquarian bookseller, makes a third generation in the trade.

It all began in Birmingham in the 1880s, when Edward Baker opened a shop which retained his name when Greville Worthington took it over for a period in the 1920s. It was run for him by Andrew Boyle, who in turn bought the business in 1930. A few years before the war Mr Boyle moved to London, changing to the present name. His daughter Patricia took over the business shortly after his death in 1956, moving to the present premises a year later. At Friar Street the floors are so warped and sloped that some of the old bookshelves have been replaced by more functional metal shelving, yet the overall picture is so captivating that one scarcely notices the anomaly.

The stock of many thousands of volumes consists predominantly of older books (as opposed to modern firsts) but is very general in appeal, although two of the larger specialities are juvenalia and the history of education, which must rate among the best in the country. The children's books, including games, feature a large number from the 18th century and pre-1800 chapbooks. Because of Mrs

Leeming's interest and knowledge of the subject, one is less likely to find the 'popular' illustrators (such as Kate Greenaway) than truly novel material of historical interest. When I was there, for example, I found an 18th-century leather bound schoolboy's work book for £50 which I found much more fascinating than fashionable 'pretty' pictures. However, the stock is so comprehensive there is something for every taste, including many hundreds of inexpensive boys' books of the 19th and early 20th century. A good idea of the quality of the stock can be obtained from the catalogues issued six times a year. Normal hours but closed T pm and Sat; if making a special visit to Worcester, a phone call is advisable.

New Street is a continuation of Friar Street and at no 44, another listed building, one finds **Books & Ephemera**, opened by postal bookseller Norman Low in 1980 largely because his house was bursting at the seams. Mr Low became involved in books 10 years earlier when he was selling stamps and coins, and someone offered him a library! As a postal bookseller he specialised in items of Scottish interest, and this portion of his stock of approx 10,000 vols is displayed on the upper of two floors. The remainder of the books, s/h and antiquarian, have a wide interest. Six days, occasionally cl lunch (stock may be viewed outside hours by phoning 0905 352191).

Shropshire is one of the country's most beautiful counties, and arguably its most delightful town is Ludlow. Like so many medieval towns it relies heavily on the tourist trade, which is a pity because interesting local shops, such as **The King's Bookshop**, 139 Corve Street (0584 3761), merit a healthier local trade. John King, an ex-librarian with King's College, London, came to Ludlow when he and his wife decided to open a bookshop in 1976. Housed in two rooms on the ground floor, the stock consists of about 7,000 vols of a general s/h and antiquarian nature with a slight emphasis on English lit and military history. By comparison with the town's high standard, the outside of the shop is fairly undistinguished, yet the building pre-dates 1450; look for it just down the hill from the eye-catching Feathers Inn (1605). Six days, cl lunch and ½ day Th.

Liz Anderton's **Bookstack** operates from a National Trust property near Wolverhampton, but she does keep a stock of books at her home, 15 Castle Street, Bridgnorth, Shropshire (074 62 3896) which may be inspected *by appointment* (see 'West Midlands' section).

Nigel Collins (Fine Books), established in 1975, is housed at the Southgate Gallery (which sells fine 19th and 20th-century watercolours and paintings), 20 Market Place, Shifnal, Shropshire (0952 460351), a late 18th-century shop in the centre of the town. Mr. Collins' stock is small but select in his main speciality — antiquarian and modern illustrated books on British art and pre-Raphaelite literature. Another speciality is lit on all aspects of the life and work of George Orwell. Cl M and Th.

John Thornhill started collecting books on ornithology and natural history when he was eight, but although he has been a bookseller for a number of years he has no intention of selling his collection, and the subjects are not particularly in evidence at his two shops. **John Thornhill (Nevill Antiques)**, 9 & 10 Milk Street, Shrewsbury, Shropshire (0743 51013), was the first to open, in 1973, and a good medium stock is mainly antiquarian but with an emphasis on books on the topography of Shropshire and on collecting. At **Candle Lane Books**, 28 Princess Street, Shrewsbury (0743 65301), the stock of antiquarian and s/h material is very general. The shop is named after the original street which, in the late 14th century, housed candlemakers. The premises are early 17th century. Both shops six days, cl lunch.

No prizes for guessing the subject specialisation of **The Parish Church Bookshop**, 47 High Street, Whitchurch, Shropshire (home no: 0948 3559), opened in 1980 by R. G. Cooper, whose last spell in bookshops was at the outset of World War II. As well as theology Mr Hooper has some 2,000 general titles, supported by his personal library. Cl lunch (two hours) and ½ day W.

The Pierpoint Gallery, 10 Church Street, Hereford, HR1 2LR (0432 67002), a bookshop for many years, was taken over in 1970 by Alexander Beaver, an industrial photographer from the Midlands, and his wife Hazel. Although the front windows and door are Victorian vintage, the rest of the building was erected in the early part of the 18th century and the oak beamed rooms provide a pleasant setting for a good medium-size stock of s/h and antiquarian books ranging from 5p to £50. Two rooms on the ground floor display antiques, maps and prints, while three upstairs include sections on theology and local history. Cl Th but open all Sat.

Although the *guide* has a good cross-section of country booksellers, few can match the setting **John Bevan** has chosen for himself at St Francis, Great Doward, Ross-on-Wye, Heref/Worcs (0600 890878), where in 1979 he opened a little shop attached to his home. His bookselling experience was gained working for the highly respected G. V. M. Heap of Wells for nine years before taking over in 1974 when Mr Heap retired. The shop's catalogues were regarded as a model of scholarship and, indeed, remain the mainstay of the business, now that Mr Bevan mixes bookselling with a little farming from the top of the Great Doward, with its spectacular views of the ravine and countryside below. The Doward is a designated Area of Outstanding Natural Beauty and contains the site of the earliest Palaeolithic habitation in this part of the country. Because of its flora and fauna several acres are reserved by the Hereford & Radnor Nature Trust. The shop carries a stock of approx 2,000 miscellaneous books, although primarily classics, Greek and Latin texts, history and (a recent development) Roman Catholic literature. The Doward is signposted off the A40 about three miles outside Monmouth, but a *phone call is advisable.*

Landsman's Bookshop Ltd, Buckenhill, Bromyard, Heref/Worcs (088 52 3420), is concerned mainly with new books on agriculture and horticulture but does carry a number of out-of-print titles on the subject and is unusual in operating a mobile unit, touring agricultural fairs and colleges. The business, started in 1958 by Mrs Kathleen Young, was moved five years later to the present address, an old manor house dating from 1620. When she died in 1979 the business — an office and bookstore, a long room lined with shelves, open to the public *by appointment* — was continued by Kenneth Stewart who was joined by his son Peter. The caravan-bookshop travels over a large section of the English and Welsh countryside.

WALES

Where else to begin but at the very heart, with **Richard Booth Books,** Frank Lewis House, Hay-on-Wye, Powys (0497 820322), arguably the largest secondhand 'shop' in the world. One cannot move far without bumping into one or other of the showcases for Richard Booth Books — quite apart from other bookshops drawn to the town by the success of this trailblazer. There is not a category of book, or subject, that cannot be found somewhere in this bibliophiles' boom town. A fire at the Castle, Mr Booth's headquarters for so many years, has meant a reshuffling of stock — now divided between Frank Lewis House, otherwise known as Book City, particularly strong on American books (in the topography department each state has its own section), and The Cinema, regarded as the biggest single shop. Other Booth sites include The Print Shop, which has illustrated books, watercolours, postcards and maps, as well as prints; a shop ostensibly mis-named 'The Limited' in view of its very large general stock, plus a good coverage of the sciences; and a 30p bookshop. Booth also sells a huge number of paperbacks, bought mainly in the US and classified under subjects, eg English philosophy. Most departments are open six days, some until late Sat, and some also open Sun, so a prior phone call is sensible.

Although Mr Booth established the business in Hay-on-Wye in 1962, mainly because he liked the town, he was very conscious ot its position in relation to south Wales and Bristol, where there are perhaps 10 million people; and to the Midlands, with probably another 10 million. The drive from these heavily populated areas via Hereford, Leominster or Brecon is pleasant; the nearest railway station is Hereford (20 miles), from which there is a bus service. Of course some of the most regular visitors are people involved in the bookworld, dealers or librarians whom Mr Booth entertains in groups. Parties from the College of Librarians at Aberystwyth, for example, come here for what might be termed a mini-symposium, and Mr Booth has overnight accommodation for people who take their book buying seriously.

Although one would imagine Richard Booth has a monopoly in Hay-on-Wye, in practice there are opportunities for competition. In developing his own business he has created a mecca for booklovers and deliberately encouraged smaller shops to share the bonanza. The turnover of book-shops in Hay-on-Wye in recent years has been quite high, but since the massive Richard Booth operation is the obvious attraction I have been selective. Some of them open on Sundays during the summer.

Largest operation is **River Wye Booksellers**, 14 High Town (0497 820875), opened in 1978 by Nia Bullock and her husband Michael in what was a cobblers and now has approaching 30,000 books on two floors. Nia gained her bookselling experience with Richard Booth and specialises in illustrated and plate books, although the bulk of her stock is general. Seven days.

Near the clocktower is **The Clocktower Bookshop**, The Pavement (0497 820 539), a double fronted premises bought by Kemeys Forwood from Richard Booth in April 1978 which carries a stock of approx 8,000 general s/h books. Strong in lit, natural history and travel. Mr Forwood was a postal bookseller for three years before moving to the town. Six days.

The Hay Music Shop, 2 Lion Street (0497 820870), is one of the relatively few shops specialising in music, with not only sheet music and books on the subject but records and ephemera (old cylinders, phonograms etc). The coverage in these areas is extensive — from Palaestrina to Punk — filling two rooms. From Easter to October normal hours, six days; winter *by appointment* only.

The Merlin Bookshop, St Mary Street, Chepstow, Gwent, NP6 5EW (029 12 2354), was opened in 1971 by Stanley Seaman after spending 18 years with George's of Bristol, latterly as senior cataloguer. In 1974 he moved two doors away to larger premises — the two rooms have a depth of about 50 feet — in which there are 10–12,000 new and s/h books, very varied, with probably something for every taste. Mr Seaman died in 1981 and, although the shop was expected to stay open under new ownership, it would be wise to check first by telephone.

Although **Albany Books**, 113 Albany Road, Cardiff, CF2 3NS (0222 498802), is basically a general s/h and antiquarian bookshop with a large and interesting stock, chess — books about, and the game itself — is very much the preoccupation of the proprietor John Barrett. Although the section is limited to modern books on the subject, he does occasionally have the rarer chess volumes on his shelves, although anyone asking for them is likely to be challenged to a game on the spot. The shop, opened in 1975, consists of three large rooms on the ground floor displaying 20,000 general books, with several thousand more upstairs in reserve. Although he sells anything from paperpacks to old manuscripts, Mr Barrett does try to be reasonably selective. Stronger sections include (in addition to chess) Welsh topography, natural history and books on firearms. Six days, occasional ½ day W.

Although it actually has a shop front, **L. Foulkes***, 17 Fairwater Grove East, Fairwater, Cardiff (0222 569488), is basically a mail order business. A full-time bookseller for the past nine years, Len Foulkes has a stock of approx 10,000 s/h vols and is prepared to see people *by appointment*.

Mrs Doreen Budge, 61 Waterloo Road, Penylan, Cardiff (0222 485 369), has been in these double fronted premises since 1975, having established the business in Bristol 15 years earlier. Approx 5,000 s/h vols are displayed in one large room on the ground floor, of general interest apart from one specialisation in art and antiques. Cl M and T and for lunch.

Dylan Thomas was the inspiration behind **Dylan's Bookshop**, launched in 1970, and over the years the shop seems to have increased its affinity with the poet — particularly since it moved to its present site in Salubrious Passage, a tiny Georgian alleyway in one of the oldest parts of Swansea. The premises taken over here by Jeff and Liz Towns were frequented by Thomas because of his close friendship with the jeweller who had occupied it for many years. The business was started because Mr and Mrs Towns believe that Thomas has been neglected by his home town, of which he wrote 'an ugly, lovely town . . . crawling, sprawling, slummed, unplanned, jerry villa'd and smug suburbed by the side of a long and curving shore'. Because of the size of the present shop, the stock in two rooms is limited to approx 7,000 s/h vols of a general nature, although naturally strong in Welsh lit (including Dylan Thomas), history and topography. However, the Towns have a larger, antiquarian and generally better quality collection at their home nearby which can be seen in the evenings, or during the day if there is someone to take you. ½ day Th.

There are many Dickensian-style bookshops around, but I knew of none without electricity and depending on bottle-gas for its lighting, that is, until 1978, when Maureen Yaffey opened **Cratchit's**, 22a Lammas Street, Carmarthen, Dyfed, SA31 3AL, and found that the dedicated browser takes everything in his stride. The shop — once a vet's surgery — is tucked away inside an old courtyard, and is first spotted by the boxes of books on the kerb. The stock of approx 4,000 s/h and antiquarian books is of general appeal. Open only on W, F and S.

Many bookshops in Wales are not on any direct route. This means that the bibliophile has to be more adventurous, but at least he has the consolation of knowing that the cream is unlikely to have been skimmed off by those before him. **Leslie and Patricia Parris**, have a shop at 1 Craig Road, Llandrindod Wells, Powys, LD1 5HS (0597 3484), and have been in this old spa town since 1976. The bulk of their business is done by post with frequent catalogues on such specialist subjects as bridge and other indoor games and Royalty, but the small shop has some 4,000 s/h vols on most subjects. Leslie, an ex-librarian, and Patricia, an ex-teacher, know their books, and intrepid browsers are unlikely to come away empty handed — nor do I mean from the box of cheap or free books outside. Cl M but out of shop hours by appointment.

Aberystwyth, like most university towns, has character, and **Ystwyth Books**, 7 Princess Street, Aberystwyth, Dyfed (0970 617511), manages to capture the air of scholarship. It has one of the half-dozen best frontages in the town and when Terry Hinde, former civil servant and university lecturer, opened the shop in 1976 he was careful to retain its character. Here the ground floor is occupied with new books and remainders, but the first floor carries a good quality stock of 8–10,000 s/h, plus a section of 3,000 books on Mr Hinde's speciality, the history of science and technology, which is not on display but can be seen on request. Cl W.

The Bridge Bookshop, 15 Vicarage Hill, Wrexham, Clwyd (0978 59968), was taken over in 1980 by schoolteacher Alister Williams and his wife Susan, who runs the shop during the week. An end-of-terrace building with plate glass window, near the railway station, it carries remainders and s/h paperbacks on the ground floor and about 3,000 general s/h vols in one room above. Six days, ½ day W.

In cultural terms, north Wales has been revitalised by the establishment of a purpose built theatre complex, Theatr Clwyd, at Mold, to which audiences come from as far afield as Liverpool, Manchester, Chester, Cardiff and Swansea. Bibliophiles have another reason for visiting Mold and its environs because **Tom Lloyd-Roberts**, currently the only member of the ABA in Wales, is based at the Old Court House, Caerwys, Mold, Clwyd, CH7 5BB (035 282 276). Not only is his stock of 20,000 antiquarian books of top quality, but the shop is probably the oldest inhabited house (as opposed to castle) in Wales. Dating from the 15th century, at one time it contained three types of court — the early manorial court, the Assizes for Flintshire (until 1672) and the magistrates court, which sat until 1882. Today, books — the specialist areas being Wales and Welsh history, general history from archaeology to modern times, travel and topography, and fine arts — are displayed in the judicial wing and additional rooms in the annexe.

Mr Lloyd-Roberts, an accountant by profession and bibliophile by inclination, bought the premises merely as a place to live but in the 1960s he became a bookseller, initially trading only by catalogue. Cl lunch and open Sat only between April–October. Caerwys is actually 9 miles outside Mold, and a half hour's drive from Chester.

Acting as wardens in the local youth hostel for 15 years and selling books by post in their spare time gave Ray Morley and his wife, also called Ray, an appetite for a busy life. Since 1973 they have run the **Bay Bookshop**, 14 Seaview Road, Colwyn Bay, Clwyd, LL29 8DG (0492 31642), and for some of that time stalls in three towns — although with the shop's development this is now restricted to one at Llangefni on Th. The shop carries a large general stock of about 20,000 vols in one large ground-floor display area, carefully classified. No specialisation except for books on Wales. There is also a postcard corner. Early cl W for most of year, but open W and Sun pm from mid-July to mid-Sept.

The possibility of finding the unexpected is one of the attractions of the 'old fashioned' bookshop, and at **David E. Hughes**, 21 Madoc Street, Llandudno, Gwynedd (0492 77700), the policy is not to classify the large range of about 40,000 books, so browsing is an interesting experience: one can find items for 25p alongside a £20 volume. The business was opened in 1968 by Mr Hughes, who is very modest about his stock and his own relatively short experience in bookselling but has built a good reputation; few people are disappointed with a visit. The entirely s/h stock, displayed in five rooms on two floors, has no speciality. Early cl W; open all Sat.

When Vivien Candlish had to give up social work to have a child, she was determined to start a career that could not be interrupted; she became a bookseller. Starting with a market stall in Bangor, North Wales, she 'graduated' in January 1980 to **Wordgames**, 38 High Street, Bethesda, four miles from Bangor on the A5. Because the shop is small, the stock is limited but as Vivien specialises in two main areas — books by women writers and feminist books, feminism and children's books — her coverage is quite extensive. In common with most specialists, the stock, on ground and first floor, includes some new books. Six days, but ½ day W.

MIDLANDS

Since there is no clear 'route' to follow in this region, I have divided it between West Midlands and East Midlands. However, shops are listed for the convenience of readers, and not always to conform with Post Office demarcations.

One of the great bibliophiles, Arnold Bennett, did his browsing during his constant travels. The **Antiquarian Book Centre**, 104–110 Hope Street, Hanley, Stoke-on-Trent, Staffs (0782 261352), is less than 20 yards from where he was born. The position is just a coincidence: the proprietor, Keith Wainright-Fisher, had an office in the street before he opened his first bookshop there in 1970. He later expanded into the adjoining shop and subsequently the third and fourth, and now has a stock of many thousands of vols over the four buildings. At no 100 he also opened the **Arnold Bennett Bookstore**, but this sells only remainders. He might have restricted his bookselling activities to a postal service but felt there was a need for a shop in Hanley, which had had no bookshop for several years. Apart from an obvious speciality in Arnold Bennett material, his stock is very varied, with local interests such as Keele University, the Potteries and mining. Everything is carefully classified although sometimes Keith's sense of humour (or judgement) can confuse the browser. You'll find 'sex' alongside 'cookery' because he reckons both are part of domestic science! Six days.

 Robert A. Picken is located opposite a prison — in this case Stafford Gaol — the address being 11 Gaol Road, Stafford (0785 53425). I mention the fact only because a prison is such an unmistakable landmark; I can assure you that very few people can direct a visitor to their local book-shop! When Mr Picken came here in 1979, he was the first bookseller in the town for over 30 years, so perhaps the novelty alone will spread the good news. At the outset Mr Picken stocked only paperbacks, but he quickly acquired the taste for quality books and now has a stock of some 8,000 vols crammed into his one room. Although the stock is general, there is a large section of books related to engineering — Mr Picken was previously a director in industry. Cl W and Th, but viewing possible on these days by appointment.

Because of the paucity of bookshops in the area, you might think it worth a visit to what is principally a mail order business — **Hutton Books***, Barnfield, The Pavement, Brewood, Stafford (0902 850229), run by Patrick and Felicity Hutton. They have approx 5,000 s/h books displayed at their home, which can be inspected *by appointment only*. The Huttons, whose background is in education, began book-selling in London in 1977 when they bought up the stock of a retiring bookseller. They have operated from the present address, about eight miles north of Wolverhampton, since March 1980. Special interests include topography (local, London and foreign); art and natural history.

Britain's only s/h bookshop located in a National Trust property is run by Liz Anderton of **Bookstack**, who lives at 15 East Castle Street, Bridgnorth, Salop (074 62 3896) but who has her bookroom at Wightwick Manor, Wightwick Bank, W Midlands, 3 miles west of Wolverhampton on the A454. The bookroom is accommodated on the ground floor of the Lodge, where there is also a pottery and browsers can visit (and park their cars) without necessarily paying to enter the Trust property itself. The stock on display is limited to about 2,500 vols of general interest, although Liz Anderton can draw on a larger stock from home. In addition, there are small specialised sections on Victorian art and lit, especially the pre-Raphaelites, needlework and gardening. Wightwick Manor is closed in February, but open most Bank Holidays; opening hours (afternoons) somewhat complex so phone call (to Bridgnorth) advisable.

V. J. Bulman, 53 Bath Road, Wolverhampton, W Midlands, WV1 4EL (0902 51247), opened at these premises in 1969 after a gap of five years since the last s/h bookshop in the town closed. The shop, about 10 minutes' walk from the town centre, is a former art gallery and such is the shortage of bookshops that people come to Vincent Bulman from Birmingham and outlying areas. Formerly an employee of Barclays Bank, Mr Bulman had been a collector, specialising in Victorian fiction, and gradually eased his way into the trade via mail order. His current stock of about 8–10,000 s/h vols in four rooms, reasonably well classified, has no speciality and is mainly in the cheaper price range — his better books frequently snapped up by trade visitors. 11–6, cl M.

The concrete-jungle city centre of Birmingham epitomises the trend in so many cities towards 'institutional' trading, with escalating rents forcing out traditional businesses to be replaced by banks and building societies (and in the case of London foreign tourist or airline offices). In Birmingham, however, the division is emphasised by the planners' ring-road, which restricts s/h and antiquarian bookshops to the suburbs.

Stephen Wycherley, 95 Vivian Road, Birmingham, W Midlands, B17 0RD (021 427 7284), has been around long enough for people to seek him out at Harborne, roughly half-way between the centre and the M5. He has been here since 1976 and previously had another shop not too far away. A stock of approx 10,000 s/h and antiquarian vols is housed in one large room on the ground floor and three smaller ones above. The interest is very wide, but stronger categories include lit, travel, illustrated books and antiquarian folklore. Cl W.

The gulf between collecting and bookselling was brought home to Roger Middleton when he opened his first shop at Oakham in 1969, and he was wise enough to cut his losses and go to work for an established shop (Ian Cowley of Nottingham) until he felt he had sufficient experience to try again. In the spring of 1974 he opened **Middleton's Bookshop**, 232 Warwick Road, Greet, Birmingham 11, W Midlands (021 772 3575), on the main A47 road to Warwick, and gradually upgraded his stock until today he can display over 15,000 vols in three rooms, plus an antiquarian room, with prices ranging from £10–£1,000. General. Six days.

The **Birmingham Bookshop**, 567–569 Bristol Road, Selly Oak, Birmingham, W Midlands, B29 6AF (021 472 8556), opened in 1976 and was taken over in 1980 by I. K. and S. C. Watson. Two minutes from the University, the shop carries a general stock of some 10,000 s/h and antiquarian. Six days.

Two miles north of Spaghetti Junction one finds **Bracken Books**, 380 Birmingham Road, Wylde Green, Sutton Coldfield, W Midlands, B72 1YH (021 373 8958), named after a 19th-century local historian who was so modest that most of her books were published anonymously. The name was conferred in 1975 when John and Agnes Hill, collectors for many years, took over what was already a bookshop set in an attractive row of early 18th-century cottages. The size of the shop limits the stock to a few thousand vols (supplemented by a few new books and remainders), but the Hills have many more books in reserve, estimating their total stock at approx 15,000. This is one of the relatively few bookshops where visitors from Europe can relax because, apart from a little French and German, Mrs Hill speaks fluent Dutch. Six days.

L. Roydon Smith, Churchview, Farewell Lane, Burntwood, Walsall, W Midlands, SW7 9DP (054 36 2217), established as a bookshop in 1974, was run as a general store for 15 years by Mr Roydon Smith and the premises had been the site of the village store for over 100 years. However, in 1972 — with Kenneth Hayward who had just retired from the RAF — Mr Roydon Smith began selling, by post, books that had been amassed through buying for his antiques interests. The business snowballed and in less than two years books took over the shop premises, so that currently there is a general stock of over 20,000 books (including 5,000 paperbacks), classified in five rooms. Although the postal district is Walsall, the shop is actually 3 miles from Lichfield. Open W and Sat or *by appointment*.

Burton-on-Trent, Staffs is a town one would associate more with beer and brewing than books and bookhunting, but there are two shops for which visitors should make a beeline. At the time of going to press **The Needwood Bookshop**, 55 New Street (0283 41641), a few minutes' walk from the town centre, consisted of six rooms on two floors, but plans were in hand to convert both cellar and loft to expand the 15,000 s/h items already in stock. Chris Shepard, a former English teacher who opened the shop in January 1975, is determined to keep the stock as broadly interesting as possible, although he happens to have a particularly strong section on theology. Six days.

The Bridge-End Bookshop, 198 Bearwood Hill Road, Burton-on-Trent, Staffs, on the south side of the river immediately over the Trent Bridge, is a very different type of business — dealing in comics and magazines in a big way, apart from hardback books. The shop, housed in a rustic-style single-storey building (once a blacksmith's), was opened in 1971 but taken over six years later by Pete Stancer who used to be a postal bookseller. At any one time he has on display around 2,000 US comics, 3,000 British comics, 5,000 paperbacks and 6,000 hardbacks in addition to magazines and ephemera. Cl T and Th. Weekday hours slightly unusual: 10am−12, 2−7pm, although in the holiday season the shop might be open every day from 9am−7pm.

Lichfield, despite its remarkable cathedral (the only one in England with three stone spires preserved), is hardly one of our major tourist centres, yet many visitors from overseas break a journey especially to pay a visit. The fact that Samuel Johnson was born here is one of the attractions, but the other is the *bookshop* near his house, now a museum. The **Staffs Educational Bookshop**, 4−6 Dam Street, Lichfield, Staffs, WS13 6AA (05432 24093), is frequently recommended to me, and it is not difficult to see why. The misleading name was coined by the proprietor Geoffrey B. Morton when he opened the shop in 1940, because there was a slump in antiquarian books and he decided to specialise in education. When other subjects gradually overshadowed academic books (in numbers) he did not bother to change the name because the business was already well known. The shop is housed in two adjoining buildings: in two ground-floor rooms of City House at no 4 and nine more on two floors at no 6, a rambling 15th-century property which uses old ships' timbers in its structure. It is largely the atmosphere of this building, with many thousands of s/h and antiquarian vols displayed in two huge rooms downstairs, and then in room after room above, that has earned the shop its reputation. Although the coverage is very general there is still an emphasis on out-of-print academic books, which include Greek and Latin classics; another obvious speciality is Samuel Johnson. Six days.

Laura and Ron Crooks make a considerable contribution to their community. In addition to the energy they put into **Laura's Bookshop**, 58 Osmaston Road, Derby, DE1 2HZ (0332 47094), they spend much of their spare time lecturing and broadcasting (Radio Derby) on antiquarian and local books. Because of their extensive knowledge and large personal collections on this subject and local history, they are a useful source of reference for libraries and institutional bodies. Although the two room shop, a corner site with two big display windows near the Eagle Centre Precinct, was only established in 1969, Ron had worked for the Frank Woore shop for 30 years. If one includes Woore's predecessor Frank Murray, there have only been three antiquarian booksellers in Derby for over 100 years. Apart from specialities in Derby and Derbyshire history and topography, and illustrated books, the stock is very general. There are also fine antiquarian maps and prints and old postcards. Cl M and W.

In 1974, Dr. David Mitchell gave up his job in local government to open **Scarthin Books**, The Promenade, Scarthin, Cromford, Derbyshire (062 982 3272). Dr Mitchell had no experience of selling books and bought the property originally as a home. A double fronted shop with new books on one side and s/h and antiquarian on the other, the stock has a very wide appeal — the only specialisation being the works of Derbyshire authors — some 10,000 vols range from SF and Westerns at 20p to plate books worth many hundreds of pounds. The s/h books spill upstairs onto the landing, while another room is often given over to exhibitions. The shop overlooks the millpond in the centre of Cromford, an 18th-century factory village laid out by Richard Arkwright, who established the world's first cotton mill here (now open to visitors). Dr Mitchell is one of those booksellers who tries that little bit harder — a scientist by training, he has even taken the trouble to work out that Frankenstein's monster must have passed within 50 yards of the shop while pursuing

213

the professor to Matlock Bath! Cl lunch and ½ day Th; open Sun pm.

Anyone interested in dogs would have a field day at **Doggie Hubbard's Bookshop**, 10 Victoria Terrace, Buxton, Derbyshire (0298 4604), which only opened in 1973, although the proprietor Clifford Hubbard has spent a lifetime selling dog books. Indeed Mr Hubbard has been involved in dogs since he was a kennelboy in 1927, a career which includes extensive writing. For 33 of these years he has been preparing a gigantic bibliography, at last nearing completion — which should be impressive, since his own collection housed in the two floors above the shop runs into some 22,000 items in 28 languages, of which hundreds are not in the British Museum or even recorded. Many of them are finely bound. The shop area has shelves double banked with old and scarce 'doggiana' and paintings of dogs displayed above.

EAST MIDLANDS

Some booksellers exaggerate the size and quality of their stock but the only claim one might challenge in the case of William H. Carlin, who runs the **Drury Hill Bookshop**, 12 Heathcoate Street, Nottingham, NG1 3AA (0602 53335), is that his assistant is the finest Irish setter in England. There are undoubtedly very few dog bookshop assistants, and readers must judge for themselves. The shop was started in 1967 in Drury Hill, which was the oldest medieval street in the town. When this was demolished two years later by what Mr Carlin ironically describes as an 'enlightened' local council, he moved to the present address on the edge of the historic Nottingham lace market. The stock is reasonably large, mainly s/h and a few antiquarian — all marked in pre-decimal currency. A pleasant and relaxed shop, but customers interested in Parson Woodforde and the Rev Francis Kilvert are assured of a special welcome from Mr Carlin who is a member of both societies. Early cl Th.

Ten minutes' walk from the city centre is **Jermy & Westerman**, 199 Mansfield Road, Nottingham, NG1 3FS (0602 44522), opened in October 1977 by ex-teachers Pete Jermy and Roger Westerman. A small, compact shop built at the turn of the century, it carries a stock of some 5,000 s/h and antiquarian vols, mainly of general interest but with a strong section on local topography. There are also several thousand postcards and picture cards of all types and ages. Six days.

Only a couple of hundred yards away is **Nial Devitt Books** at no 133, opened in November 1980 by a man who had been a postal bookseller for some time and who has now filled two rooms with between 5–10,000 s/h and antiquarian vols. The subjects covered are varied, but Nial Devitt specialises in folklore and history (in which his wife, Margaret, used to lecture) and books on Ireland (an interest generated and developed by the death of his father's headmaster, shot by a British firing squad in 1916). Cl M.

The Bargain Book Centre, 1 Nem House, Bridlesmith Gate, Nottingham (0602 55770), part of the Harvey's of Leicester 'chain', carries approx 10,000 s/h vols (including a few antiquarian items) alongside a similar number of remainders, in an attractively long (74ft) two-tier display area, housed in a modern office block. Although intended for remainders when opened in 1974, it was realised that there was a need for s/h material and this was added a couple of years later. Manager is John Hammond, secretary of the H. G. Wells Society, and author of works on Wells.

Ian H. R. Cowley*, whose shop in the centre of Nottingham was one of the biggest and best sources of s/h and antiquarian material in the Midlands, moved in April 1979 to 96 Derby Road, Sandiacre, Nottingham (0602 393379), a few minutes from junction 25 on the M1. Although the new premises are a conventional shop, Mr Cowley no longer has assistance and tends to close when he has to go out, so a *phone call is advisable*. Much smaller than the 10 room shop he occupied in the city for 16 years, the stock is similarly condensed, but, as you would imagine from a man of his experience, is of good quality and quite diverse.

Although Vance Harvey has been the driving force in bookselling in Leicester since 1968, he has been forced by circumstances (ie redevelopment schemes) to move twice. **Harvey's Bookshop** had to leave 2 King Street and is still looking for new premises. Further information can be obtained from head office (0533 881334). Stock is 30,000 vols of general s/h and antiquarian material which is mainly held at the Nottingham Bargain Book Centre (*see above*). There are two other Bargain Book Centres in Leicester, at Granby Street and Market Place.

Rebecca Dearman, 90 Charles Street, Leicester (0533 21009), in the city's main shopping street, was opened in 1972 by Rebecca (Vance Harvey's sister) and Nigel Dearman. Although single fronted, the shop is large, with approx 40,000 s/h and antiquarian vols displayed in five rooms on three floors. There is no speciality, the appeal being very general. Six days.

The Readers Return, 32 New Buildings, Hinckley, Leics (0455 611017), was established by Pam Williams in 1974 to stock s/h paperbacks. Three years later she was joined by Michael Raftery who introduced the hardbacks to stock. Today there are approx 8,000 s/h books (divided equally between the two) of a general nature and mixed quality, although an effort is made to maintain a good stock of modern firsts. Cl Th.

Horse racing enthusiasts will immediately identify **The Brown Jack Bookshop**, 78 Main Street, Lubenham, Market Harborough, Leics, with a famous gelding of that name which won the Queen Alexandra Stakes six years on the trot from 1929–34, and which was retired to Lubenham. The shop, usually only open on Sat, is run by Reginald L. Leete who has a small general stock of 2–5,000 better s/h and antiquarian items, together with atlases and sporting prints. Mr Leete has three 'hats' — in addition to bookselling he is a framer (working with his wife who does colouring) and a racecourse bookie in his spare-time. The shop, opened in 1967, is 2 miles from Market Harborough on the A427, and when shut Mr Leete may be found working from home, 87 Lubenham Hill (0858 65787) or at The Old Granary, in the centre of Lubenham, which houses the Leicestershire Sporting Gallery.

The only bookshop in Coventry is **Gosford Books**, which opened towards the end of 1977 when the proprietors Robert Gill and Sabina Pugh decided it was time that someone did something for the city's neglected booklovers. The shop is located in a row of Victorian dwellings opposite the art faculty of the polytechnic and carries a stock of around 8–10,000 s/h items in two rooms. Although Mr Gill takes a special interest in philosophy, he tries to keep the interest as wide as possible and the prices range from 15p to £75. Sabina Pugh trained in bookbinding at the London College of Printing, so the shop offers a binding and restoration service. Six days.

Duncan M. Allsop opened his first shop at 26 Smith Street, Warwick (0926 43266), in 1966, after gaining considerable experience with Stechert-Hafner Inc, the American library agents and booksellers, at their London office. Warwick was selected not only because of its tourist attractions and its university, but because of its very central position — one can get to any part of the country easily by train or road, the motorway being less than a mile away. Indeed, Mr Allsop's only miscalculation was to call the business **The Warwick Castle Bookshop**, inviting calls ever since from people enquiring about tours of the castle, teas and refreshments! Housed in a 200-year-old building, the shop carries approx 15,000 vols in three rooms and passageways on the ground floor, although at the time of going to press plans were in hand to convert this into one very long display area. More expensive items upstairs are available on request. The stock is very broadly based, the only specialisation being Warwickshire and illustrated/coloured plate books. Prints are also sold. Six days.

Leamington Spa seems to have been neglected by the arts, but there is at least one good s/h bookshop: **Portland Books**, 11 Spencer Street, Leamington Spa, Warks (0926 38793), two minutes from the station. The business was launched by Jan Wedding in 1974 on leaving university, and this is his third shop in the town. It carries a display of approx 10,000 vols mainly in the 50p–£20 range, although there are some better quality items. The only emphasis in a general stock is on the arts, with around 1,000 vols on lit and criticism. Six days.

The Old Hall Bookshop, 32 Market Place, Brackley, Northants (0280 704146), is housed in four rooms on the ground floor of an imposing 18th-century house in the centre of the town, and because of its position on the A43 attracts custom from a wide area. The career of John Townsend, who runs the business in partnership with his wife Lady Juliet Townsend, seems to have come full circle — he started in bookselling before going into industry. The stock of approx 15,000 s/h and antiquarian vols is general, but strong in natural history and field sports, local history, literature and children's books. Cl lunch and occasional W during winter period.

Oakham is a lovely town that was given a new lease of life by the development of the nearby reservoir and nature reserve. In 1979 Allan Morrison and Tony Marshall opened the **County Bookshop,** 11 Melton road, Oakham, Leics (0572 2403), where approx 15,000 s/h and antiquarian vols are displayed in three rooms (and a warehouse). The shop they took over used to be a popular creamery and even after a year former customers would come in, ignore the books and demand to be served with fresh cream! Allan, who owned the Old Constables Bookshop at Uppingham for 16 years, also dabbled in the county markets before going into partnership with Tony, a former schoolteacher who preferred books, whom he had originally supplied with stock. Stock very general. Six days.

The small town of Uppingham in Leicestershire has two s/h shops and a third due to open. **Old Constables Bookshop,** 2 High Street West (057 282 2212), started by Allan Morrison of the County Bookshop, Oakham, was taken over in 1976 by former marketing executive Mike Goldmark who initially treated the shop as a hobby, opening two days a week, but quickly became 'hooked'. Although only one room, the place is packed from ceiling to floor, and even *on* the floor, so that it can be difficult to move. The stock of about 5,000 vols is general although English lit and criticism is Mike's forte. ½ day Th.

In 1981, after two years of trying, the Goldmarks opened a second shop in much larger premises — the ground floor and basement of what used to be the council offices, 14 Orange Street (057 282 2694), which they purchased earlier as a combined shop and home.

Almost opposite Old Constables in the High Street is the

Rutland Bookshop, run by Edward Baines and housed in a tall, narrow building with a spiral staircase. The stock is general although Mr Baines' speciality is hunting books.

Staniland (Booksellers), 4 St George's Street, Stamford, Lincs (0780 55800), is at the east end of the High Street, now a pedestrian precinct. The shop was opened in June 1979 by Meaburn Staniland, formerly an editor with Penguin Books, and his wife Margaret, having run a bookshop in Henley-on-Thames for four years. A very general stock of approaching 10,000 vols ranging in price from 5p to £200, but mainly from £2–£5, is displayed in five rooms on two floors. Spaces between shelving are decorated with prints, maps and ephemera which are not for sale, although the shop does a healthy trade in old postcards. Cl Th.

Round the corner from the town's outstanding landmark, the historic George Hotel, is **Books, etc**, housed in part of a former railway inn at 3b Wharf Road, Stamford, Lincs (0780 54980). Opened in 1978 by Abe and Becky Schein, the shop consists of one large room carrying a stock of just under 5,000 s/h and antiquarian vols covering most subjects but with special sections on Africa, hunting, local topography, illustrated books and the USA — Abe is a New Yorker. The 'etc' refers to stamps, prints, old children's toys and games, as well as general ephemera and postcards. Six days; also Sun afternoon in summer.

On the edge of the East Midlands **Anthony W. Laywood***, of Knipton, Grantham, Lincs (047 682 224), keeps normal shop hours at his lovely old stone house, approx one mile from the Grantham–Melton Mowbray road (A607) near Belvoir Castle. In this large nine bedroom house with pre-18th-century origins, four rooms are kept quite separate for the display of 12–15,000 solely antiquarian books. The main theme is English lit before 1850, but Mr Laywood also has a range of quality books on most subjects. He came to bookselling in 1968 after running a small hotel but having been trained as a metallurgist. Catalogues issued. *By appointment.*

NORTHERN COUNTIES

In the days of ecclesiastical supremacy, York was for many years capital of the North and has a 'literary' history almost as old as London's. Several distinguished printers and booksellers made their marks here, among them Thomas Gent, the man who abridged *Robinson Crusoe* and who died here in 1778 in his 87th year.

Barbican Bookshops have three shops within a stone's throw of each other in the city, each interesting in its own right and with a combined stock in the region of 120,000 vols. Because of their close proximity it is worth taking a look at them all, although the former Donald Pickering shop, 42 The Shambles, York sells only new books. The Barbican, 24 Fossgate, YO1 2TA (0904 53643), which has been extended, now has a stock of around 70,000 s/h and antiquarian books with a strong section on Yorkshire topography. However, theology is the main speciality, representing nearly half the total stock, probably the largest s/h collection apart from Higham's (SPCK) in London. These even spill over into a small adjoining building known as Collectors' Cottage. The third, the Barbican Bookshop in Walmgate Bar, York — only open on Sat and at other times by appointment — has the most fascinating history. This is the only place in England where one could (if one wished!) still walk round a complete barbican, the outside defences of a city or castle. Erected mainly in the 13th century, Walmgate Bar has played an interesting part in the history of York; during the Civil War, for example, it was bombarded by Cromwell from a nearby hill and still bears the marks of shot. Until a few years ago people still lived in the two-storey Elizabethan dwelling house attached to the Bar. As if the '3½' premises were not enough, managing director R. C. Rollinson even has further stock at his home. All open six days.

Another very large display, this time in one shop, can be found at **Ken Spelman**, 70 Micklegate, York, YO1 1LF (0904 24414), described in Rogers' *York*, 1951, as 'one of the most beautiful streets in Europe'. The premises are medieval in origin but the present structure is 17th century with extensive Regency (c1810) modifications. The business was established in 1948 by Mr K. E. Spelman, although there had previously been a bookshop on the site. Peter Miller, who joined him in 1968, bought the shop when Mr Spelman retired five years later. Approx 40,000 s/h and antiquarian books of general interest, and a big collection of Yorkshire maps and prints, will keep any bibliophile engrossed, in a pleasant atmosphere complete (in winter) with a grand old coal fire. Ask at the counter for information on the antiquarian room upstairs. Six days.

Thomas C. Godfrey Ltd, 21 & 25 Stonegate, York, YO1 2AP (0904 24531), was established in 1906 but after a variety of ownerships was taken over in 1968 by the University Bookshops group, founded by Blackwell's and Oxford University Press to promote the sale of books in university towns. A second shop at the university, run by Managing Director, J. S. Janiurek, who controls a staff of 20, stocks only new titles. Only a small percentage of the company's turnover is from s/h books, although this is not inconsiderable; the quality is good, with interesting sections on topography, local history, archaeology and English literature, including modern firsts. Cheaper books are also displayed.

One could write a book on the adventures of Mr Janiurek who, as a young Polish soldier during World War II, was captured by the Germans and shifted to different POW camps, ending up in occupied France. Throughout this harrowing time his most closely guarded possession was a wooden box containing a few books on Polish history and literature. Jan escaped from France and reached this country via Spain, Gibralter and Scotland. After the war he went to Oxford and then obtained his first job in bookselling, spending the next nine years with Thornton's.

Almost opposite at 42 is the **SPCK Bookshop** (0904 54176), which has a general secondhand stock on the first floor.

At the end of Stonegate is a tiny passage called Minster Gates, once known as Bookbinders Alley because the shops mainly belonged to bookbinders and printers. The corner house features a small statue (1801) of Minerva, Roman goddess of wisdom and drama, seated on a pile of books. Today the only shop still selling books is the **Minster Gates Bookshop,** at no 8 (0904 21812), which actually opened in 1970 as Discovery Books but was taken over five years later by Nigel Wallace. Built in the late 18th century with the typical narrow frontage, the shop has a stock of approx 15,000 books housed on three floors. General interest, but with a leaning towards the arts, illustrated books and lit. Six days.

Almost opposite the Barbican Bookshop and a complete contrast in size is **Michael Cole**, 41 Fossgate (0904 31752), who has a very small but select stock of antiquarian books. Mr Cole, who used to work for N. G. Leslie (Rare Books) of Hull, is only open F and Sat, or *by appointment*.

A few minutes' walk south is a relatively new arrival, Fiona Clewlow at **Yesterday's Paper**, 24 Fishergate (0904 27715), who specialises in detective fiction, collectors' comics and magazines and printed ephemera of all kinds prior to 1960. The shop opened in 1979 as the offshoot of an antiques shop Fiona ran with her husband Allan. Six days, but phone call advisable.

Another newcomer just across the Skeldergate Bridge is **Colin Stillwell (Books),** 16 Bishopsthorpe Road (0904 27467), which opened in December 1979 after Colin and Sue Stillwell had run Libra Books, a catalogue business. Slightly away from the centre of town (not more than 10 minutes), the shop relies to some extent on local custom as opposed to tourists and scholars, and even has a Mills and Boon collection. A general stock of 6–7,000 vols with a slight emphasis on contemporary lit, drama and poetry is found in two quite large rooms, with a third open to the enthusiast. The Stillwells have a constantly fresh supply of material because Colin still works as a freelance publisher's rep. They also exhibit at PBFA fairs. Five days. 1pm–5.30, cl Sat.

At **Gard Books*** of York (0904 52347), the partners, Philip Titcombe and Pamela Morton are only occasionally available, but their stock, predominantly music books and general literature, is of a high standard. The size of the stock also relates to frequency of catalogues issued, but I have frequently found good books here that were not available elsewhere. Philip, a lifelong collector, has a degree in music and sings with the Worcester cathedral choir; Pamela, head of an infants' school, has broader interests. The partners have a subsidiary private press company, Fairfax Press, launched in 1980 by a 400-copy edition of Sacheverell Sitwell's *Valse de Fleurs*, of which 60 were signed by the author and accompanied by signed lithographs by his friend Henry Moore. *By appointment only*.

Headingley, near Leeds, W Yorks, is not only famous for its Test cricket ground but is regarded as an open student campus for the university and a large college of education. **Walker's Bookshop**, 28 Arndale Centre, LS6 2UG (0532 751319), is accordingly one of the largest and most attractive single bookshops in the region. Again, less than 10% of the stock is antiquarian but the shop's three floors, with a selling area of 73,000 square feet, are a model for present demand. The business was established in 1837 but having moved to a modern setting in 1966 endeavoured to maintain a period atmosphere, eg a Dickensian bow-window frontage. The top floor, with access to the very large roof-top car park of the Arndale Centre, has a vast display of every type of new book; the middle floor is a specialist children's bookshop, and the ground floor a general eye-catching mixture, with an annexe housing a good selection of antiquarian books on Yorkshire topography and natural history. The business remained in the Walker family until 1951 when it was taken over by Basil Jackson, who moved it to the centre 15 years later.

Only a stone's throw away, and about three miles from the city centre, is **Almar Books**, 10 Commercial Road, Kirkstall, Leeds, W Yorks, LS5 3AQ (0532 780937), opened by Alan and Marjorie Jones who came into the business in 1974, moving to these premises five years later. The stock of about 10,000 s/h and antiquarian books is general, housed in one large ground-floor room and two above, with a heavy emphasis on local topography and history. The smaller of the upstairs rooms has been converted into a gallery and monthly exhibitions feature the work of local artists. The shop is very near Kirkstall Abbey with its folk museum. Cl W.

James Miles (Leeds) Ltd, 80 Woodhouse Lane, Leeds, W Yorks, LS2 8AB (0532 455327), was started by James Miles in 1870 and in 1890 he moved to a shop in Guildford Street, Leeds; over the next 16 years he moved twice to larger premises. The brothers Archie and Frank, who had taken over the business on the death of their father, moved to the shop's present address in 1930. In 1947 Frank Miles sold the shop — said in the 1940s to be one of the finest in the north of England. In January 1973 the business was bought by Austick's Bookshops, Leeds, who felt that such a long association with the antiquarian trade should not be allowed to die. Through illness the prestige of the firm had begun to slide and the task of restoring it was given to the present manager, Sidney Clark, whose experience covers over 40 years in antiquarian, s/h and new bookselling. The stock has been steadily upgraded and now stands at over 20,000 s/h and antiquarian vols housed on two floors, as well as a very large stock of remainders. Situated a few yards from the Civic Hall, open all day Sat, but cl M.

Archie Miles Ltd, 28 Victoria Road, Richmond, N Yorks, DL10 4AS (0748 3648), is the last remaining link with James Miles, who died in 1924. His business, continued and expanded by his sons Archie and Frank, was eventually sold by the younger brother, Frank. However, Archie's son Raleigh was determined to perpetuate the memory of his father and set up a shop in Harrogate where he traded for 15 years until his death in 1971. His widow, with her new husband, transferred the entire stock to an old protected building in the historic town of Richmond, three or four miles from the A1 at Scotch Corner. So it was that both shops bearing the name Miles started up again under fresh management at roughly the same time. Large general and antiquarian stock. Open Sat, cl M.

The **Vintage Motorshop,** 500 Bradford Road, Batley, W Yorks, WF17 5JY (0924 470773), which opened in 1977, sells only books on motoring. However, within the speciality the shop offers a large stock, including car handbooks and workshop manuals. Fringe material covers motorcycle, railway, aviation and model railway books. Open from 11am on Th, F and Sat.

Graham Scott Phipps opened **The Mint Bookshop** in August 1980 at 32a Byram Arcade, Westgate, Huddersfield, W Yorks naming it after T. E. Lawrence's book. As a Lawrence enthusiast he also has a large portrait in pride of place in the shop — an attractive Victorian building decorated with wrought iron-work and hanging flower baskets. Needless to say, T. E. Lawrence is also the only speciality in a medium-size, very general, stock.

Holmfirth, south of Huddersfield, a little town set in spectacular country, was 'discovered' by tourists in the 1970s following the success of the TV series *The Last of the Summer Wine*, which was filmed there. Beardsell Books which started with two small shops in a conservation area, moved in 1981 to larger premises, **The Toll House Bookshop,** Huddersfield Road, Holmfirth, W Yorks (048 489 6541). Elaine Beardsell offers a small but diverse selection of s/h and antiquarian books. Cl M and T.

Alan Hill Books, 130 Whitham Road, Broomhill, Sheffield, S Yorks, 10 (0742 665768), 1½ miles from the city centre, opened in April 1980 in premises occupied for the previous three years by K. Books, the postal booksellers. A corner shop, it has approx 10,000 vols displayed in two ground-floor rooms and an office. The main speciality is local topography and history, and owner Alan Hill tries to ensure that this section always has a selection of 3—400 different titles on show. He specialises in railway books and ephemera, cricket and old Penguins. Although the bulk of the stock is general (ranging in price from 10p to £500) the needs of the university are inevitably an influence, eg its large music department ensures that the shop also has a good stock of sheet music and scores. Mr Hill came straight to bookselling from industry, but compensates for his lack of experience with an abundance of energy and a willingness to put himself out for customers. Six days.

Richard and Jane Williams*, 17 North Street, Winterton, Scunthorpe, South Humberside (0724 733788), are postal booksellers but allow their stock of several thousand Penguins to be inspected *by appointment*. They also sell general s/h books from a stall, **Browsabout**, in Scunthorpe market on F and Sat.

K. Books of Hull, 15 & 17 Hepworth's Arcade, Silver Street, Hull, Humberside, HU1 1JU (0482 26457), is housed in an old Victorian arcade with the characteristic glass arched roof, site of the original Marks & Spencer penny bazaar. Apart from an interesting display of s/h books the shop, which has been trading here since 1947, is widely known for its fine collection of facsimile antiquarian maps and prints covering all parts of Britain. Since the last edition the business has been taken over by Kaye (Books) Ltd, the well established Kaye family of postal booksellers. The shop is run by John Mendley, an authority on local history. About 12,000 books on show. Six days.

For bibliophiles with a sweet tooth there could not be a more delightful shop than **Honeyfields Books**, 31 Highgate, Beverley, Humberside, HU17 0DN (0482 885953), where they sell honey alongside books. The proprietor, Sally Davies, began dealing in books on beekeeping nearly 20 years ago, opening the present bright and cheerful shop in 1978. She also keeps bees at Honeyfields Apiary at Hutton (Driffield), but the stock of approx 17,000 vols is kept general. Highlights include a large section of local history, natural history, King Penguins and also a large stock of local postcards. As well as honey, the shop sells beekeeping equipment. Cl M and T.

The village of Haworth in W Yorks has a small, two room bookshop geared to its 'cottage industry' — the Brontës. **The Airedale Bookshop**, 100 Main Street, Haworth, in the small square at the top of the hill, is run by Avril and Freddie Maclean and also sells books on Yorkshire. Open every day except Friday because at weekends (ie Sat in winter plus Sun in summer) the Macleans open their other **Airedale Bookshop**, 3 Keighley Road, Streeton, Keighley, W Yorks (0535 54635) on the main A629 road between Keighley and Skipton. The stock of some 3,000 s/h vols here is fairly general.

Skipton has a population of around 13,000 but attracts five times that number of shoppers from the surrounding Dales — which means that **Craven Books**, 23 Newmarket Street,

Skipton, N Yorks (0756 2677), although a small shop, is very busy. Established in 1961 by Katherine Farey and Megan Fluck, both collectors but with no previous trade experience, the business occupies two rooms on the ground floor of a 17th-century house in the town centre. The s/h and antiquarian stock of approx 6,000 vols in the front showroom is general, although there is a strong section on Yorkshire and northern topography, with the few new titles also restricted to this area. The back room has a display of maps and prints. The owners have made no attempt to enlarge the business because they wish to retain the personal touch which obviously draws so many of their customers. Cl T and first M of month.

In the next road is **The Box of Delights**, 25 Otley Street, Skipton, N Yorks (0756 60111), opened in July 1979 by Sheila Coe, a librarian, former market stallholder and postal bookseller. The name comes from the title of one of her favourite children's books. She offers a 'pot pourri' of attractions in a stock of some 4,000 s/h vols complemented by such ephemera as Victorian greetings cards, old advertising material and sheet music. The stock is general, with an emphasis on juvenalia, from run-of-the-mill fiction to collectors' items. Cl T and Th.

Harrogate bookshops are all relative newcomers. Right in the centre, opposite the station, is **Sea Books**, 1 Cambridge Street, Harrogate, North Yorks, which was opened by John Courtney in the spring of 1980. Mr Courtney's background includes a spell in publishing and postal bookselling and he has a strong personal interest in maritime affairs; hence the shop's name and the fact that about 25% of his small stock (2–3,000 vols) is concerned with shipping and travel. Cl M and T.

The Harrogate Bookshop, 16 Cheltenham Parade, Harrogate, N Yorks (0423 56333), is on the first floor of a Victorian terraced building above a barber's. But browsers will certainly find it worth going upstairs as approx 15,000 s/h vols, very reasonably priced, are displayed in three large, well lit rooms and on the landing. The business was launched in 1978 by former TV director Jack Duncan and David Chilton, an ex-scientist. They specialise in such areas as lit and poetry, theatre, the Far East, mountaineering and natural history. Early in 1980 they were joined by music specialist Ian Linford and today the shop can offer some 4,000 music items, ie books, sheet music, scores etc. Six days.

The Barbican Bookshop, 1 Franklin Road, Harrogate, N Yorks a branch of the giant York operation, was opened in November 1976 to specialise in Christian literature, but has one room full of general s/h items, and a few antiquarian.

If you have an interest in geology, mountaineering or caving, there is a double reason for paying a visit to Giggleswick. Nearby is the Giggleswick Scar where a geological fault divides the limestone from the gritstone, and at the bottom of the fault is the Ebbing and Flowing Well. Its other attraction is **Post Horn Books**, Giggleswick, Settle, North Yorks, BD24 0BA (072 92 3438), actually just outside the village on the main road to the Lakes. The small shop carries a stock of approx 7,000 vols, with a specialist section on mountaineering and caving, on which owner Mary Hanson Moore is an authority and for which catalogues are issued regularly. However, as a qualified librarian the owner's knowledge is extensive and the bulk of her stock is of general interest. Visitors should have no trouble recognising the shop — there is a large Victorian rocking horse in the window. Cl M and for lunch F.

The bookselling career of Jack and Edna Ellis goes back to 1948 but it is with the **St Margaret's Bookshop**, 10–11 Kirkgate, Ripon, N Yorks, HG4 1PA (0765 2877), started nine years later, that they have really become identified. The shop was originally an early 16th-century jettied structure. It was constructed as a shop and later converted into separate private dwellings, but Mr and Mrs Ellis had them reconnected into one large and fascinating premises. The contrast between exterior and interior results from an 1800 road widening scheme, when the jettied front of the building was lopped off and replaced with plain brickwork. Inside, the huge oak beams, archways, nooks and crannies belong to an earlier period. Since the last edition a new roof has been installed and the premises redecorated. Books on the ground and first floors are new and the s/h stock (5–8,000 vols) is restricted to two rooms and a landing on the top floor. There is a cottage at the back with a reserve stock. The shop, incidentally, is named after the patron saint of learning. Early cl W.

At **Hambleton Books**, 43 Market Place, Thirsk, North Yorks, YO7 1PQ (0845 22343), geology, palaeontology and natural history are well represented in an otherwise small stock of some 3–4,000 books. The shop (which also stocks new books) was opened in 1980 by Anne Turner, just off the market square. Her husband is a geologist. The other speciality is books on the North Country. James Herriot fans might care to note that his surgery is a few minutes' walk away. Summer six days, although sometimes open Sun afternoon; winter ½ day W and cl at 4.30pm.

Fred Bettley Bookshop, Zetland Cinema, Richmond, North Yorks is not located in the cinema (surely fondly remembered by many thousands of ex-servicemen who have been stationed at Catterick) but in a small lock-up shop which is an integral part of the building. Mr Bettley took over what had been a snack bar in 1976 but until Easter 1980 he only opened on Saturdays. The shop carries a general stock of some 4,000 books with a tendency towards history, biography and English lit (including poetry and drama). It also sells prints and original paintings of local interest. Cl M and ½ day W.

After several years of dealing from Headington (Oxon), **Richard Dalby*** moved his bookroom at the end of 1980 to 4 Westbourne Park, Scarborough, N Yorks, YO12 4AT (0723 77049). His specialities are general lit, fantasy fiction and cinema. Business hours, but *by appointment* only.

In terms of stock size and quality, **A. R. Hattersley*** is one of the most important booksellers in the North but regrettably his largest selection at Hollins House, Grosmont, nr Whitby, North Yorks, YO22 5PU (094 785 329), can only be seen *by appointment*. Over 80,000 s/h vols, many rare and fine books, are laid out in a large house in its own grounds, a short walk from the village and railway station. With a collection of this importance one hesitates to talk about specialities (I have obtained a very wide selection of books from Mr Hattersley over the years), but probably his largest single category is shipping and voyages. The house was built around 1815 by the sister of Captain William Scoresby, the navigator and whaling captain, and inventor of the modern compass and other navigational instruments.

However, Mr Hattersley does have a shop only a few miles away, also with a strong maritime link. **Scoresby House Bookshop, Antiques & Restaurant** is located at Flowergate, Whitby, N Yorks (0947 5116), and the large ground floor is devoted to books (some 20,000 s/h and antiquarian) covering most subjects, but strong in travel, fine bindings and quality books. The house was built (c1840) in the town's main street as a mansion HQ for Whitby ship owners, and the association is preserved today with a collection of nautical objects. The rest of the four floor building is taken up with antiques, although there is a restaurant on the first floor.

Hanover Books bought the stock of Abbey Books from friends in 1972, and is now located in two premises in Whitby. A former antiques shop at 8 Hunter Street (0947 3587) has the bulk of the stock in three rooms filled to capacity; and a large Victorian house in Hanover Terrace is used for storing and sorting. Stronger subjects are local topography, marine, theology, textbooks and travel; old postcards also stocked. In summer ½ day W and cl lunch; winter cl M and ½ day W.

Great Ayton's main claim to fame is that the explorer Captain Cook went to school here. Today's youngsters are privileged to have **The Great Ayton Bookshop**, 47 High Street, Great Ayton, N Yorks (064 945 3358), to fire their imaginations. Opened in May 1979 by Hazel O'Sullivan, who is concerned with new children's books, and Madalyn Jones whose responsibility is a small stock of between 2–3,000 s/h vols, plus a few antiquarian items. Cl M, ½ day W, and open Sun pm.

After 17 years as an accountant, Victor Collinge opened his first bookshop in March 1980; because of its geographical position he called it **The Border Book Shop**, 61a Halifax Road, Todmorden, W Yorks, OL14 5BB (070 681 4721). The double fronted shop carries some 8,000 s/h vols plus new books in its main front showroom; their interest is very general. Cl T, and Sat pm; open Sun pm.

CHESHIRE, LANCS AND MERSEYSIDE

The only city walls in England still standing in their entirety
are those at Chester, and actually situated on the walls is **The
Lantern**, 11 City Walls, Chester, Cheshire, CH1 1LD (0244
26486), a building dating from 1768 and run now by Howard
Cooper and Kathleen Williams as a combined antiques
business and bookshop. The stock is divided between about
2,000 antiquarian and collectors' books and perhaps twice as
many s/h. On every day except W (when hours are 1–5) the
shop opens at 11.

In January 1979, **Books 'n' Things** opened at 16 Bewsey
Street, Warrington, Cheshire, WA1 1RQ (0925 572687), near
the bus and railway stations. The location might be
considered relevant since the proprietors Carol and Ray
Bailey specialise in transport, with a leaning towards
railways. However, the fact that the premises used to be a
betting shop has no relevance and the stock of over 7,000 vols
is general in appeal, with the only other speciality being local
history. W–Sat, plus Sun pm.

The Bookshop, 64a Park Road, Hale, Altrincham, Gtr
Manchester, WA15 9LR, opened by Peter Bell in 1977, was
taken over by Robin and Carol Booth three years later when
Mr Bell moved to Edinburgh (see 'Scotland'). The shop is
small and has a matching stock of 'good' s/h material, with a
strong emphasis on history and lit. Open Sat only.

Eric J. Morten, 50–52 Chestergate, Macclesfield,
Cheshire, is a 17th-century house originally converted into
two shops but which Mr Morten turned back into one big
display area with books occupying two rooms. The stock is
general, but with a large section of fine bindings and books
on collecting, as well as local topography (see also entry for
Manchester shop).

K.L. Books, launched in April 1980 by former university
lecturer Lewis Mather and his wife Kathleen, is in fact above
their children's shop 'Kids Stuff' at 176 Hurdsfield Road,
Macclesfield, Cheshire, SK10 2PX (0625 22714). The shop
sells toys etc, although for the sake of convenience children's
books are housed with them on the ground floor. The rest of
the stock, approx 10,000 s/h and antiquarian items, is

displayed in three rooms upstairs, and apart from a leaning towards non-fiction there is no speciality. Cl M and W.

The Garrick Bookshop, at 8–10 Wellington Road South, Stockport, Gtr Manchester, SK4 1AD (061 480 4346), has a s/h stock of well over 100,000 as well as new books. The shop, part of an old mill in the centre of the town and with a private car park at the rear, has been in existence for 46 years and for the past 10 has been run by Peter Aird, who worked for the previous owner for six years before that. The front shop area has a display of new books from which a long passage leads to two huge rooms devoted to s/h material. Specialities of the shop — from rare to new — are Cheshire local history, natural history, children's and illustrated books; also fine bindings. Six days.

Grenville Street Bookshop, 105 Grenville Street, Edgeley, Stockport, Gtr Manchester, SK3 9ET (061 477 1909), is what I would describe as a good 'old-fashioned' shop, and the proprietor Joseph Heacock strives to keep it that way. His stock of some 25,000 books ranges from paperbacks to scarce antiquarian items. Like all collections of this size, the interest is wide, though particularly strong on travel (Mr Heacock being keen on Arctic exploration) and topography. Juvenalia is also well represented, but then this applies to most subjects. The shop, which opened in May 1978, has a warm, friendly atmosphere. Cl M.

Stanley Du Feu has been buying and selling books since he was 13, in the 1920s. One of his maxims is to sell cheaply for a rapid turnover and this certainly applies to **The Bookroom**, 43 Market Street, Stalybridge, Gtr Manchester (061 303 1477), which opened in July 1980 opposite the bus station. After running a bookshop at Sudbury, Suffolk since 1969, Mr and Mrs Du Feu decided to move north to be nearer their family. They found a house with storeroom at Hyde, but almost immediately opened the retail outlet. The bookroom does not have its own frontage, being located at the back of their daughter's kitchenware shop. The stock is limited to 2,500 vols, but it is always worth a visit because most of it is changed every three weeks, if indeed the whole lot has not been bought by a passing dealer. Cl T (Mr Du Feu is usually only available on Sat).

Gibb's Bookshop, 83a Mosley Street, Manchester, M2 3LG (061 236 7179), has a stock of over 100,000 s/h and antiquarian books in one exceptionally large ground-floor showroom, with a warehouse next door not open to the public. Although the emphasis is on scholarly works in the humanities, literature, etc, there are a large number of cheaper items, eg world classics. The shop, established in 1926 by Robert Francis Gibb, was passed on to his two sons Robert and Anthony, who joined the firm after World War II. On the main artery between Piccadilly and St Peter's Square and next door to an art gallery, the shop is open six days.

Eric J. Morten, Booksellers & Publishers, Warburton Street, Didsbury, Manchester 20 (061 445 7629), has been referred to as the Morten Trust, for people who like wandering over properties that are part of our national heritage! The shop(s) must merit a visit, whatever one's taste in books. Eric Morten's background is traditional enough; his parents ran a bookstall in Manchester from 1918 and in 1960 he set up his own shop in the tiny, cobbled Warburton Street, a relic of early 19th-century North Country architecture. Established at no 4, he started expanding and took over numbers 6, 9, 10 and 2. The lower even numbers are converted, with minimum structural change, into one large, rambling area bulging at the seams with books. (Tethering rings remain from when the cottage at no 2 was used as an adjunct to the village slaughter-house.) With the acquisition of no 8, Mr Morten had every shop in the street, books extending over 17 rooms. It is without doubt the biggest 'village' bookshop in the North. On the opposite side of the road is a modern paperback department and small car park, in what used to be a coal yard. In fact, the whole area is dominated by books and the isolated shop providing culture of a different kind is the local bookmaker's — the only commercial enterprise that can compete with the Didsbury boom in books!

An ex-committee member of the ABA, Eric Morten adopts a very positive approach to selling. In the winter, he lectures to schools and evening classes on books and publishing three times a week. After an exhibition at a local school three years ago he was approached by a woman bookseller who was contemplating the sale of her shop in Macclesfield (which he bought next day). It is not unusual for customers to have a cup of tea or coffee thrust into their hands, although if you stop for refreshments, you'll never finish looking. Incidentally, the shop has most unusual and attractive letterheads with 10 or 11 period illustrations featuring aspects of bookselling.

Back in the centre is **Geoffrey Clifton's Theatre Bookshop**, Piccadilly Plaza, York Street, Manchester, M1 4AH (061 236 2537), housed in the attractive shopping arcade beneath the Piccadilly Hotel. The shop specialises in new, s/h and antiquarian books on all aspects of the performing arts, including puppetry. Mr Clifton, who came here in February 1979 and who numbers many 'show biz' celebrities among his customers, also sells vintage theatre and cinema magazines, posters, playbills, programmes and cards. Cl M.

Liverpool is a disappointing area now that Henry Young & Son and Parry Books no longer deal in old books, but fortunately Merseyside adequately compensates for the shortfall in the centre. The Liverpool Book Company has three s/h and antiquarian bookshops — two at Bootle and one at Waterloo. Peter Lovering, who runs the parent company, opened the first **Bootle Bookshop** with his brother at 374 Stanley Road, Bootle, Merseyside, L20 (051 922 8995), in 1972. Six years later the second **Bootle Bookshop** was opened in the same road at no 350 (051 933 4787) in equally large premises with stock housed on three floors. The shops now vie with each other to offer the most attractive selections, each having 30–40,000 vols in the areas of local history, travel, illustrated books, bound Victorian periodicals etc. Six days.

The Crosby Bookshop, 39 Crosby Road North, Waterloo, Merseyside, L22 4QB (051 920 7738), was opened in 1976, and is very similar in character to the others, with a very large general stock on three floors. Six days.

In 1979, this considerable wealth of books was enriched by the arrival of another good shop. **J. D. Roles** had been a postal bookseller for well over 20 years when he opened this shop at 55 Mount Pleasant, Waterloo, Merseyside, L22 5PL. The premises, a converted launderette four minutes' walk from Waterloo station, are shelved from floor to ceiling, to accommodate 25,000–30,000 carefully classified s/h and antiquarian items. Although there is no speciality, Mr Role's tendencies are towards 19th-century lit and children's books, early fantasy and SF; and he is a long-standing collector of Rider Haggard. Because Mr Roles is on his own and has to go out buying, hours are inclined to be unpredictable, although visitors should not be inconvenienced if they combine this with a trip to the Crosby Bookshop.

Back in the heart of the city there is just one 'shop' which must not be missed. **Alan Wilson**, 37 Bluecoat Chambers, School Lane, Liverpool, Merseyside, L1 3BX (051 708 0204), is not a conventional shop but a showroom, comprising three studios on the top floor of what was once the Bluecoat School for underprivileged children and is now functioning as an arts centre. The building itself has tremendous character, and the individual rooms are let out to artists and people involved in the arts. Mr and Mrs Wilson, booksellers for most of their lives, came here in 1975 to occupy one room and gradually expanded. Today they have approx 10,000 s/h vols displayed, mostly general but with the biggest section on aviation, followed by local history and military books. The stock is supported by further material which can be seen by appointment at their home. Cl M, rest of the week noon–5pm (4pm Sat).

Although catalogues give no indication of the atmosphere and service in any given bookshop, they do at least provide a measure of the quality of stock and one has only to see those of **C. K. Broadhurst & Co Ltd,** 5 Market Street, Southport, Merseyside (0704 32064), to recognise the hallmark of a leading bookseller. Proprietors of the business, established in 1926, are Edna and Charles Broadhurst — the latter a past president of the ABA. Broadhurst's offers a good selection of new books in a separate shop but the extensive stock of antiquarian and s/h books is displayed in 10 showrooms; strong in rare books, first edns, natural history and colour-plate works. The shop was appointed bookseller to the late King Peter II of Yugoslavia. Early cl T.

The speciality of **Clifton Books**, 5a Dicconson Street, Wigan, Gtr Manchester (0942 36716), is antique maps and prints, although it does have a stock of some 5,000 general s/h vols. Opened by Mr D. M. Shaw in 1969, the shop is situated two minutes from the central bus station. Cl M at 4pm, and W.

Willow House Books* operates from a bookroom opened by former librarian Mrs J. A. Whittle in December 1980 at her home, 21 Weldbank Lane, Chorley, Lancs, PR7 3NG (025 72 77884). The stock, which can be seen *by appointment*, consists of approx 3,000 vols broadly fitting into specific categories such as 19th-century lit, modern firsts, antiquarian, 19th and 20th-century illustrated works, naval history and seafaring. Catalogues issued.

The **Bolton Book Centre**, 12 Bark Street, off Bridge Street, Bolton, Gtr Manchester (061 764 3406), is only open on Sat because the proprietor Geoffrey Hall works in an office during the week, having been a postal bookseller for several years. The 'centre' is a converted two roomed office on the ground floor of a modern block, housing over 15,000 s/h vols with a broad interest; the only speciality being books on Lancs and Cheshire. If you happen to be in the town during the week, it may be possible to inspect the stock *by appointment*.

The **Crompton Bookshop**, 519 Tonge Moor Road, Bolton, Gtr Manchester (0204 50953), is a conventional shop on the outskirts of the town, on the main road to Blackburn. Opened in 1975, this double fronted shop has a stock of some 25,000 vols on two floors, with about 25% of it theology displayed in a room upstairs. The rest of the stock is of general interest. A prior phone call is advisable because, during the week, the owner, John Olive, is a social worker and although the shop is staffed five days closing times may be irregular.

The village of Littleborough, Gtr Manchester, is close to the Hollingworth Lake Country Park and only a couple of miles from the Pennine Way. So while the family is exploring you can find sanctuary at **George Kelsall: The Bookshop**, 22 Church Street, Littleborough, OL15 9AA (0706 70244), which replaced the bank in the village square in 1979. George Kelsall, formerly an architect, has some 7,000 s/h and antiquarian vols on display, covering most subjects but with strong sections on local topography and dialect, the North of England, the 'outdoors', and transport. Cl T, open all day F and Sat, and from 1pm M, W and Th, although he will see customers at other times *by appointment.*

The longest tradition in the North belongs to **Halewood & Sons**, 37 Friargate, Preston, Lancs, PR1 2AT (0772 52603), established in 1867 and now represented by the fifth generation of Halewoods. The business is managed by Horace Halewood, great-grandson of the founder, and his chief aide is now his own son. Different members of the family opened their own shops elsewhere — including one in Australia before 1914, although this was closed when the owner was killed in the war. This might account for the shop's strength in travel — it specialises in Australasia, America and Africa as part of its impressive stock of 100,000 s/h and antiquarian items, divided approx 50:50 between out-of-print and rare. Books in the main shop are displayed in 12 rooms from basement to second floor, while a second shop nearby has a smaller selection in several rooms, including new books. Collectors come from all over the world to Halewood's because of the exceptional stock; rarer books are not on show to casual browsers. With such a large collection, ranging from 25p to over £1,000, the average visitor is likely to find something of interest. Early cl Th and cl Sat.

The Carnforth Bookshop, 38 Market Street, Carnforth, Lancs (052 473 4588), has a longer association with the bookworld than first appears, being housed in a 19th-century building used until recently as a book bindery. Opened in 1977 by Peter Horrobin, managing director of a publishing house, the shop has new books on the ground floor and over 40,000 s/h and antiquarian vols in 10 rooms on the first and second. The only speciality is the Lake District and railways, but many of the sections are large enough to be regarded as specialities. The interest in railway books is geared to the presence of Steam Town, where such famous engines as The Flying Scotsman are kept. Cl Th.

CUMBRIA, DURHAM AND TYNE & WEAR

The Little Bookshop, 1 Cheapside, Ambleside, Cumbria (096 63 2094), in the heart of the Lake District, is a pretty Georgian corner shop, with three rooms devoted to a mixture of antiquarian and s/h material, strong in natural history, topography and travel. Opened in 1959 by Marion Hebden as an antiques and book business, she decided five years later to concentrate on the book side. A well established business which does not depend on the influx of tourists. Cl W.

Michael Moon's Bookshop, Beckermet, Cumbria (094 684 428), largest antiquarian bookseller in the county, is located off the A595 along the coast in a village which consistently wins annual awards for the prettiest village, 8 miles north of the Ravenglass & Eskdale miniature railway. Over 50,000 vols are housed in four large rooms of what was formerly the local Co-op store. Although the stock is general, Cumbria is an obvious speciality, and Mr and Mrs Moon are well known authors (eg *Bygone Whitehaven*) and publishers of books on local topography. In addition to a healthy shop trade, they issue regular catalogues and supply libraries, universities and collectors in 16 countries. Six days.

In 1978, Michael and Sylvia Moon found that, despite conversions, they could no longer control the numbers of books at Beckermet so they opened a second shop, **Michael Moon,** at 41–42 Roper Street, Whitehaven, Cumbria (0946 62936), a lovely Georgian town on the coast. The site they chose is full of character — they converted what was the local newspaper's printing works. The shop has a 50ft frontage and, to give some idea of the scale of the two operations, Mr Moon estimates that books fill over a mile of shelving. Whitehaven has approx 50,000 s/h and antiquarian vols on display, similar to those at Beckermet although, in the main, the older items are at the first shop. Cl W.

David Winkworth had been dealing in antiquarian books for about 12 years when, in 1979, he moved farther along the road to **D. R. Winkworth Antiquarian Books,** 102 Main Street, Cockermouth, Cumbria, CA13 9LQ (0900 822062), next to Wordsworth House, birthplace of the poet. At the new premises, which date back to Elizabethan times, the sale of books is combined with that of artists' materials. The books, several thousand laid out on the ground floor, mainly deal with local history, mountaineering, Wordsworth and the Lake poets. Upstairs is a gallery exhibition area and at the rear Mr and Mrs Winkworth plan a museum of bookbinding and printing. Th ½ day.

Brook Cottage Books, Braithwaite, Keswick, Cumbria, CA12 5SY (059 682 275), is situated in a 17th-century stone barn at the side of the road going west up Whinatter Pass, with the hills towering above. The business was opened on a part-time basis by Timothy Walsh in 1972, but six years later he was able to run it full-time, and because he and his wife live next door this can include evenings and weekends. The stock consists of some 6,000 s/h books of a very general nature, but there is a large fiction section and another on history (European and American). Mr Walsh shares the premises with his sister who runs a cafe and the books are reached through the cafe (which does not open as regularly as the bookshop).

The Bookcase, run by Mrs Gwenda Matthews, moved to 28 Castle Street, Carlisle, Cumbria, CA7 0NG (0228 44560), from another part of the town in June 1980. Housed on the ground floor of a Georgian building 200 yards from the cathedral, the shop has a general stock of approx 12,000 books displayed in two rooms; one of the larger sections is works of Cumbrian interest. Six days.

Past & Present, 44 Bondgate, Darlington, Durham (0325 59790), which opened in 1973, was taken over six years later by former army chaplain Alan Vokes and his wife Dorothy. About five minutes' walk from the centre of town, the shop has a stock of approx 8,000 s/h books covering a wide range of subjects, housed in a double ground-floor showroom and converted cellar. In fact there are books everywhere on desks, chairs and even the floor — which, as many browsers would insist, is just how it should be! The only speciality is local and county interest, including North Yorks. ½ day W.

Robert James Scott is one of the grand old men of bookselling. At one time his business had a stock in excess of 250,000 books and when he had to move in 1979 from the shop and warehouse he had occupied for 43 years he sold off

25 lorry-loads of books. The move was to the other side of the town, at 91 High North Gate, Darlington, Durham (0325 53767), where he has a shop and six rooms full of good material, including natural history, topography and such novel items as extra illustrated books; he also has a big stock of prints and engravings. Hours may be unreliable so a phone call is advisable.

The **North Gate Bookshop**, 50 Saddler Street, Durham, DH1 3NU (0385 63309), specialises in oriental studies, capitalising on the presence of the university's School of Oriental Studies and the Gulbenkian Museum of Oriental Art. Opened in 1974, having established its reputation in three years of postal trading, the shop is run by Geoffrey Roper, graduate in Middle Eastern studies at Durham University and former Fellow of the American University, Cairo. The range of out-of-print material covers all aspects of Middle Eastern and Oriental art and music, general history, travel and scholarly texts in all relevant languages. While obviously a 'must' for collectors and students, the shop is worth a visit from all book-hunters: the other half of the stock is reasonably general, with an emphasis on local topography and architecture and its only new books are on beer and brewing. The location is interesting, on the site of the medieval North Gate of the castle bailey — one of its bastions survives in the courtyard behind the shop, and the dungeon lies beneath it. Six days, other times by appointment.

The **SPCK** shop, 55–57 Saddler Street, Durham (0385 42095), is the group's largest in this country, being the university bookseller and having a s/h stock of 30,000 vols, with a reserve. Their coverage is obviously comprehensive. Six days.

Newcastle-upon-Tyne has two shops very different in character but collectively offering a good selection of interesting material. **Robert D. Steedman**, 9 Grey Street, Newcastle, Tyne & Wear, NE1 6EE (0632 26561), the more impressive, is an attractive shop in what is recognised as the best architectural street in the city. The business, in existence for over 70 years with a third generation of the Steedman family as one of the partners, concentrates on the better-quality book, old and modern, although a fairly extensive stock in four rooms on the ground floor does have a selection of cheaper items. Early cl Sat.

At the end of 1979 Brian Mills, former art teacher and postal bookseller from Derby, opened the **Newcastle Bookshop**, 1–3 Side (0632 615380), near the river Tyne in an area known as Quayside. The double fronted shop with its preserved 19th-century frontage consists of one large room housing approx 10,000 vols mainly of general appeal, but with Mr Mills' speciality, art and design. Since he lives on the premises, his reserve stock can be inspected by arrangement. Catalogues are still issued in this subject. Six days.

SCOTLAND

If one wanted to spend a book hunting holiday in Scotland, it would scarcely be necessary to move out of Edinburgh — where there are probably more good bookshops than in any city in the United Kingdom outside London. The rest of the country is less fortunate. Travelling north over the border from Newcastle, for example, one crosses a desert so far as bookshops are concerned, although there is an oasis known as **Barrow Books Ltd***, Leitholm, Berwicks (089 084 277). Cyril Barrow, who came here in 1966 from Edinburgh where he was already established as a bookseller, does not have a shop and he specialises in the social sciences, social and educational reform. Since Mr Barrow buys extensively in this specialist area he picks up other books, so people can often find something of interest in the attic of his office-showroom in the cottage adjacent to his house. In any case, the subject speciality is reasonably broad, and Mr Barrow is a man of considerable warmth — although he attributes his reputation for friendliness to the 'spirit' of the place, ie the magical border atmosphere. *Appointment only.*

Entering Scotland from the western side, bookshops are equally thin on the ground. **The Explorer's Bookshop**, at 24 River Street, Ayr, Strathclyde (0292 84505), is right opposite the cobblestone bridge, oldest in the town, known as 'Auld Brig' because of its association with Robbie Burns. Owned by Bruce Marshall, the double fronted shop has approx 12,000 s/h and antiquarian vols, and is strong on travel and children's books, with a large stock of maps and prints. Cl W and ½ hr for lunch. Mr Marshall*, a bookseller for over 10 years, keeps his 'better' material in a bookroom at home from where he issues catalogues. Some 5,000 mainly antiquarian vols, natural history travel and colour-plate books, can be seen *by appointment only* (056 386 274).

The major bookseller in Glasgow — in fact the oldest

surviving bookshop in Scotland, established in 1751 — is **John Smith & Son (Glasgow) Ltd**, 57 Vincent Street, G2 5TB (041 221 7472). John Smith, second son of the Laird of Craigend, was wounded while serving under Marlborough, and, although it was decidedly unfashionable for a man of military background, young Mr Smith was determined to try his luck as a bookseller. He was successful enough to pass on a thriving business to his son John, although it was John Smith III who was to prove himself a bookseller of rather special talents. Mr Smith received an honorary doctorate from Glasgow University following his editorship of the *Maitland Papers*, and also published Chalmers' popular sermons. The shop is near the centre of Glasgow and within five minutes' walk of both main-line stations. The interior has been completely rebuilt and refurbished, providing books — new and s/h — on six floors, with a high-speed lift. In 1980 a special exhibition room was opened on the third floor, where topical exhibitions are matched by special book displays. The stock is large and covers everything from out-of-print to rare, although the speciality is high-class works relating to all things Scottish. Early cl Sat.

The Bookshop, 138 Renfield Street, Glasgow G2 (041 332 7791), has been in existence for five years and is owned by Abdul Majid, who ran a smaller bookshop in the vicinity for several years, having originally come to the UK from Pakistan. The stock of approximately 20,000 books is general, although strong in books on Scotland, art and sport. Centrally situated, close to Buchanan Street bus terminal. Six days.

Largest bookseller in Scotland is **James Thin Ltd**, 53–59 South Bridge, Edinburgh, EH1 1YS (031 556 6743), started in 1848 by the great-grandfather of the present directors in one tiny shop now part of a huge complex of old buildings. Annual turnover is over £2 million, of which antiquarian and s/h sales account for only a small proportion, although even this is large enough to encompass three large rooms in one of the basement areas. The only s/h specialities are Scotland, Americana and illustrated (hand-coloured) works — although there is a wide range of better-quality books in most subjects. Early cl Sat.

On first appearances **The Edinburgh Bookshop**, 57 George Street, Edinburgh, EH2 2JQ (031 225 4495), looks like most other major bookstores but the antiquarian department is pleasantly different. The shop results from an amalgamation of two well known businesses, Robert Grant & Sons Ltd and William Brown (Bookseller) Ltd — which was the antiquarian part of the company, established in 1877. Catalogues are still issued in the name of William Brown, ABA. The front of the shop has a display of new books and paperbacks, but the antiquarian department at the rear carries a good selection of Scottish, family history, natural history, bindings and other fine books, set out in display cabinets arranged in the style of a living room in a superior house, complete with marble fireplace and Victorian fire. Above the fireplace is the original oil painting 'The Bibliophilist's Haunt', by Sir William Fetters Douglas — depicting an old bookshop. The whole area is elegantly decorated with chandeliers and has a fine Adam ceiling discovered during renovations a few years ago. Catalogues are issued infrequently on specialist subjects, eg *A Bi-Centenary List 1771–1971* produced for the Sir Walter Scott conference held in the city. Another unusual feature is a coffee room on the first floor, opened in 1947 and serving light refreshments. Early cl Sat.

McNaughtan's Bookshop, 3a Haddington Place, Edinburgh, EH7 4AE (031 556 5897), was started in 1954 by Major John McNaughtan when he left the army and carried on after his death nearly 20 years later by his widow Marjorie, who had always worked in the shop. It was taken over in 1979 by Elizabeth Strong, who had been her assistant for seven years. The shop, in a scheduled building, is a semi-basement of three rooms converted into one long and attractive show-room containing 30–40,000 books (including a cellar store not open to the public). The stock has a general appeal, although Ms Strong does specialise in early children's books, fine art and illustrated books, travel and topography. The address might be slightly confusing as it is really part of Leith Walk (broken up into several names), only a few minutes' walk from Princes Street. Cl M.

Another company operating from private premises, but

with a stock larger than many shops, is **R. & J. Balding Books Ltd***, on the second floor of corner premises at 25 St Stephen Street, Edinburgh, EH3 5AN (031 225 6895), also only five minutes' walk from Princes Street. Antiquarian and scholarly books occupy five showrooms with specialities in 18th-century English lit, social and economic history, travel and topography, 19th-century poetry and lit. Surprisingly for a firm which only started in 1972 but has gained an admirable reputation, none of the four executives had any previous retail trade experience. Two had been lecturers at the university, a third was a student and the fourth had worked with an English publisher in India. Normal hours *but appointment only*.

John Grant, 9 & 13c Dundas Street, Edinburgh, EH3 6QG (031 556 9698), one of the most distinguished names in Scottish bookselling, is run by Ian R. Grant, who was president of the ABA in 1954 and 1974, and his wife Senga who is a member of the committee of the ABA. The business was founded in 1874 by the first John Grant, widely known as one of the pioneers of remainder selling. His son was an academic man who, it was said, loved books more than selling them, and he was concerned not only with s/h books but prints, music and maps. The third generation Grant inherits many of the qualities of both, and is respected as a good 'all-rounder'. The present shop premises — divided by offices of the Marriage Guidance Council — carry a large and wide ranging stock, with additional accommodation at no 15a now used as a store. The antiquarian material is housed in two rooms at 13c and general s/h books with strong leanings towards the humanities, and prints, can be found in one large display area at no 9. Cl M.

Second Edition, 6 Howard Street (031 552 1850 evenings), is run by Maureen and Bill Smith. The Smiths lack trade experience but provide a good service encouraging and helping people to whom buying books is an unfamiliar experience. The policy seems to have worked, because, having opened in July 1979, their business has grown when the recession has made many s/h booksellers feel the pinch. A small shop, one room plus store, with a large window area, Second Edition is adjacent to Robert Louis Stevenson's birthplace in Howard Place, and Tanfield Hall, where the Scottish disruption (leading to the establishment of the Free Church of Scotland) took place. The stock of approx 20,000 vols, very general, is reasonably priced to ensure they don't stay on the shelves too long. Six days, incl Sun noon–5.30pm, and Sat all day.

The name of **Jerome Books**, 64 Cumberland Street, Edinburgh, EH3 6RE (031 556 2147), is a tribute by the owner John Hems to Saint Jerome, 4th-century translator of the Vulgate. Mr Hems, who was a professor of philosophy in Canada where he lived for 14 years, opened the shop (his first) in 1979, using part of his own collection as a nucleus. A tiny shop (one room plus store) in a street with historic associations just off Dundas Street, Jerome Books carries a necessarily small stock, mainly general but with a leaning towards scholarly books. Six days.

The **Broughton Bookshop**, 49a Broughton Street, Edinburgh, EH1 3RJ, has changed hands several times since the last edition but the character of the shop is much the same — informal and relaxed, with prices generally at the lower end of the spectrum. The present proprietor, Peter Galinsky, took over in March 1980, having worked for the previous owner for over a year. As an artlover one of his first actions was to convert the back room, hitherto used as a reserve stockroom, into a gallery to exhibit the work of local artists, although books remain his first priority. The stock, approx 8,000 vols, is general and ranges from paperbacks to antiquarian items. Cl M, hours 11.45–6pm.

In 1980, Peter Bell moved from Cheshire to open **The Bookshop**, 54 Candlemaker Row, Edinburgh 1, small premises about fifty yards from Greyfriars Bobby in the old part of the city. A former university librarian and writer, Mr Bell has about 4,000 vols with a strong academic bias on display in the shop, formerly part of the Harrow Inn. Catalogues of academic history and English lit issued. Six days.

West Port Books, 151 West Port, Edinburgh (031 229 4431), near the castle, was established in 1977 and taken over three years later by Bert Barratt, a forestry expert. He came to West Port via a spell in South Wales and another at the

Broughton Bookshop. A small shop with a stock of approx 8,000 s/h and antiquarian vols, general, but strong in fine arts. With the business Mr Barratt took over the well known shop's cat, one of the country's few four legged bibliophiles. Six days.

The **Grange Bookshop**, 186 Causewayside, Edinburgh, EH9 1PN (031 667 2759), in the southern part of the city, has a general s/h stock of some 15,000 books in two main rooms and corridors adjoining. The shop has been owned by William Blair, a former engineer, since 1958.

John Updike*, 7 St Bernard's Row, Edinburgh 4 (031 332 1650), five to ten minutes' walk from Princes Street, was launched in 1962 by John Watson and Gerard Nairn to specialise in better-quality 19th and 20th-century first edns, mainly in literature, illustrated, private press and fine bindings. There are 10,000 books housed in three rooms on the top floor of office premises. *Appointment only.*

Science and natural history are the twin specialities of **Jay Books***, run by June and David Brayford from their home, 1 Roull Grove, Edinburgh, EH12 7JP (031 334 1844), where they have approx 2,500 books on these subjects. The emphasis is on histories and biographies of scientists, and illustrated bird and flower books. *By appointment only.*

Margaret Jameson was following in her bookseller father's footsteps when she opened **Bookends,** 83 Portobello High Street, Edinburgh 15, on the road to Musselburgh, in May 1980. The stock of some 2,000 vols and 1,000 s/h paperbacks is general, although there is a fairly large section on Scotland. Cl M. Open 12.30–5pm in week, and from 11am on Sat.

The Bookshop, 30 Spittal Street, Stirling (0786 61771), on the approach to the castle, is attractively offbeat in style and atmosphere. The shop was opened by Robert McCutcheon in 1977, in premises designed as an auction hall in 1915. As such, it has a relatively small display window although the frontage is actually 25 feet long. An entrance hall leads to two short flights of stairs, one up into the main shop, the other down into a basement display area. The shop area is very large and includes a self-contained antiquarian room 18ft × 13ft. Mr McCutcheon, who has been in the trade for the past 16 years, is able to display some 20,000 hardbacks, plus

10,000 paperbacks. The range is very general; all fiction is kept in the basement and non-fiction above. Six days.

Gordon McNeill is another part-time bookseller working towards his first shop. Meanwhile **Dunollie Fine Arts*** operates from his home, 12 Townsend Place, Kirkcaldy, Fife, KY1 1HB, where he has approx 5,000 s/h and antiquarian vols and 1,000 paperbacks (mainly Penguins) available for inspection *by appointment only*. A lecturer in business studies at the local College of Technology, Mr McNeill's main expertise is in arts and antiques and so this section of an otherwise general stock is quite strong.

A group of young housewives had to battle with the Scottish banks to open and run the **Quarto Bookshop**, in St Andrews, Fife. However, one battle they could not win was against the developers and eventually they had to leave their good site near the university. Their new premises are at 8 Golf Place, St Andrews (0334 74616), less than 100 yards from the famous Old Course. Adapting to their new environment, books on golf have become something of a speciality, but the character of the business has not changed and the shop is still strong on Scottish subjects and used university texts. It is now run by Margaret Squires, who has a degree in PPE from Oxford, and Jennifer Green. Six days.

Bookranger* is the name of a business run by James W. B. Laing from his home at 'Cairnbank', 14 Hepburn Gardens, St Andrews (0334 75066), with its novel 'browserie' (ie converted garage) in which he has about 20,000 books, a general stock of items under £1. Better books are kept in the house and Mr Laing issues two catalogues a year. A former teacher before starting the Bookranger operation in 1969, Mr Laing is open on W and Sat, while the browserie can be viewed almost any day. However, *appointment advisable*.

Mair Wilkes Books, 3 St Mary's Lane, Newport-on-Tay, Fife, DD6 8AH (0382 542352 and 542167) is housed on the upper floors of an early 19th-century greystone house a few yards from the river. The business was started in 1969 from the homes of the two partners, James Mair and Alan Wilkes, who moved to their present premises eight years later. A stock of some 8,000 vols displayed in four rooms and a hallway is mainly general, but includes specialities in books on Scotland and psychology. Open Sat only, but other times *by appointment*.

Considering the sparseness of bookshops north of Edinburgh, it is rewarding to find three in Perth, Tayside — all very different. **The Perth Bookshop**, 3a Abbot Street (0738 33970), housed in tiny premises near the bus and railway stations, was established by former newspaper reporter Leslie Fraser in 1977 after a couple of years selling by post. Mr Fraser's stock of some 5,000 s/h vols is very general, but basically non-fiction and with a Scottish bias. However, what he has on display here is backed up by a good reserve stock kept at home. Cl M.

Melvens Bookshop, 176 High Street, Perth, Tayside (0738 35222), a subsidiary of Thin's of Edinburgh, is a delightfully big, modern store, but unfortunately the stock of s/h and antiquarian books is very small, being limited to a corner of the first floor. Six days.

Fairdeals, 17 Skinnergate, Perth, Tayside, in the oldest part of this attractive market town, has been run by J. P. M'Garrigle since 1978, although he has been a bookseller for many years. The father of Margaret Jameson of Edinburgh's Bookends, Mr M'Garrigle's small but select stock is general in appeal, apart from specialities in books on Scotland and fishing. Open from 11am, six days.

Largest s/h stock among the three retail outlets in Aberdeen is carried by **Winram's Antiquarian Bookshop**, 32 Rosemount Place, Aberdeen, Grampian (0224 630673), slightly off the beaten track but worth the effort to find it. The stock, in one very large room, is less than 10,000 vols but an interesting mixed bag from antiquarian to modern out-of-print. The main speciality is books on north-east Scotland, followed by good sections on natural history, shooting and fishing. Margaret and Ronnie Winram, who opened the shop in 1976, also keep a reserve stock at home so that their coverage in certain areas is quite comprehensive. ½ day W.

J. G. Bissett is one of the big names in Scottish bookselling with four retail outlets in Aberdeen, but unfortunately s/h and antiquarian stock represents less than 1% of its turnover these days. The department is housed on part of the first floor in Upper Kirkgate, Aberdeen, Grampian (0224 53528), and there are not more than 2,000 vols on display. John Milne, who looks after this part of the company's trading, has to be selective in what he buys because of the limited amount of space but this does at least mean that the stock is generally a cut above the usual run-of-the-mill shop stock. Six days, cl 4.30pm Sat.

The **647 Gallery** at 647 King Street, Aberdeen, Grampian, is an art gallery opened in 1974 to display the works of artist Bill Baxter, to which books were added a year later by his wife Rosemary. Books — the speciality is poetry and plays — started almost by accident with the nucleus of new selections written by Rosemary's Canadian cousin Earle Birney, who was in Britain at the time on a poetry reading tour. Today there are several hundred volumes (including new titles) in the speciality subject, as well as a few odds and ends. Six days, hours 2–8pm.

Mrs G. L. Sallows, Salix House, Banavie, Fort William, Inverness (0397 7544), has a small (under 1,000 books) stock specialising in mountaineering, fishing and local topography. The business was started by Geraldine Sallows' husband as a picture gallery occupying the drawing room of a Thomas Telford house built in 1806, from which there is a good view of Ben Nevis. An upper room overlooks the lock gates known as Neptune's Staircase, where the Caledonian Canal rises 200 feet. Six days.

Intrepid book-hunters prepared to undertake a two-hour crossing to get to Britain's most northerly s/h bookshop, run by **Gordon Hughes** at 2 Dundas Street, Stromness, Orkney, could be doubly welcome if they also take along some books for sale! The problem of having a shop in such a unique spot is that Mr Hughes doesn't get many opportunities for buying expeditions, so he is always on the look-out for stock. The shop is less than five minutes' walk from the pierhead of this ferry port, home of the writer and poet George Mackay Brown. The town, with a population of 2,000, is basically a long, narrow street by the shore, houses on the seaward side often having their own stone built piers. Mr Hughes does not have many more than 3,000 vols, mainly of local interest, but there can be few more picturesque settings for any bookshop. Six days summer; ½ day Th and cl lunch winter.

INDEX

251